Praise for *The Po*

"A deep well of both timeless and practica................ ...poches
new book helps us uncover the relaxed awareness and freedom that is our
very essence."

—Tara Brach, author of *Trusting the Gold*

"Knowing that nothing about mind is ordinary, Tibetan Buddhism
abounds with surprisingly simple, down-to-earth techniques for harness-
ing the innate magic of our mind, allowing it to transform adversity into
advantage. For many centuries, Tibetans have relied upon the easy-to-
apply slogans found in the Seven Points of Mind Training to serve as the
very heart of their spiritual path. Here, with crystal clear insight into the
complexities of modern life, the exceptionally learned Khentrul Lodrö
T'hayé Rinpoche inspires his readers to take up those same ancient tools
of lojong to infuse their lives with more compassion, equanimity, understanding, patience, and loving kindness for others."

—Chokyi Nyima Rinpoche, author of *Sadness, Love, Openness:*
   The Buddhist Path of Joy

"If you train the mind, you can live a happy and fulfilled life. *The Power of
Mind* is a practical manual sharing seven key points that form a complete
training. Anyone can apply them to their lives—you don't need to have
any particular belief system to embrace the benefits. Khentrul Rinpoche
shares his deep understanding of these teachings so that the subject is
most relevant for these times."

—Sharon Salzberg, author of *Lovingkindness* and *Real Change*

"This book is a user's guide for something that all of us possess: mind. It is
written in such clear, simple, and plain terms, yet contains deep meaning
and complexity. The wisdom that Rinpoche imparts in *The Power of
Mind* can benefit us all; from the absolute beginner to the most seasoned
dharma practitioner."

—Michael Imperioli, actor, director, and writer

THE
POWER OF
MIND

A Tibetan Monk's Guide to
Finding Freedom in Every Challenge

KHENTRUL LODRÖ T'HAYÉ

TRANSLATED BY
Paloma Lopez Landry

EDITED BY
Paloma Lopez Landry, Ibby Caputo,
and Paul Gustafson

SHAMBHALA

Shambhala Publications, Inc.
2129 13th Street
Boulder, Colorado 80302
www.shambhala.com

Cover photo: Eric Swanson
Interior design: Greta D. Sibley

9 8 7 6 5 4 3 2

Printed in the United States of America

Shambhala Publications makes every effort to print on acid-free, recycled paper.

Shambhala Publications is distributed worldwide by
Penguin Random House, Inc., and its subsidiaries.

Library of Congress Cataloging-in-Publication Data

Names: Khentrul Lodrö Thayé Rinpoche, author. | Lopez Landry, Paloma, editor. |
Caputo, Ibby, editor. | Gustafson, Paul (scholar on Buddhism), editor.
Title: The power of mind: a Tibetan monk's guide to finding freedom in
every challenge / Khentrul Lodrö T'hayé; translated by Paloma Lopez Landry;
edited by Paloma Lopez Landry, Ibby Caputo, Paul Gustafson.
Description: Boulder: Shambhala, 2022. | Includes index.
Identifiers: LCCN 2021052383 | ISBN 9781645470878 (trade paperback)
Subjects: LCSH: Blo-sbyong. | Atīśa, 982–1054.
Classification: LCC BQ7805 .K54 2022 | DDC 294.3/444—dc23/eng/20220110
LC record available at https://lccn.loc.gov/2021052383

When we look, what is it that binds mind?

Mind Binds Mind.

What is it that frees mind?

Mind Frees Mind.

CONTENTS

FOREWORD

Mind training, as taught by the Mahayana school of Buddhism, is a method for finding freedom from suffering that does not depend on seeking protection from gods or demons. Rather, by viewing every condition that causes suffering in our lives through wisdom and compassion, we can transform that suffering into positive experiences, a powerful force for personal growth, and deeper recognition of the reality of existence. This is a remarkable path of skillful means, in which the way to train the mind is directly pointed out. Just as we need to train our body, we also need to train our mind. Just as exercising the body brings greater physical well-being, exercising the mind brings greater mental well-being.

If you thoroughly train your mind, no matter your circumstances or environment, how busy you are, or the pressure you are under, you can live a happy and meaningful life. This is not just a platitude. Each and every one of us is capable of directly experiencing this for ourselves. "The Seven Key Points of Mind Training," for which this book is a commentary, is the finest of all mind trainings from Tibet. It includes both mind training through profound wisdom and through compassion. It explains how to take on the suffering of this life and how to face the suffering of dying. It shows how to accomplish our own happiness and how to accomplish the welfare of others.

With mind training, people of different ethnic backgrounds, different levels of education, and different kinds of beliefs can achieve exceptional benefit, as we Buddhists have directly experienced over the course of many generations and through myriad circumstances. I put these words into writing in order to provide a concise recommendation for this new mind-training book by my dharma sibling Khenpo Lodrö T'hayé. For all of you who read this, I offer aspiration prayers that it may be of benefit.

—Khenchen Tsultrim Lodrö Rinpoche, Sertang Larung

TRANSLATOR'S GUIDE FOR
HOW TO READ THIS BOOK

This book is a practice manual—a handbook of wisdom and practical advice for how to transform our lives, and in particular, how to transform all of the adversity that we encounter. Although mind training is a Buddhist teaching for cultivating mental well-being, it is applicable to everyone, regardless of whether we have a particular system of faith or not. These teachings have the power to bring a deeper sense of value to our lives and to motivate us to make the changes that will bring the happiness for which we yearn.

Khentrul Lodrö T'hayé Rinpoche received instructions on the "The Seven Key Points of Mind Training" from his teachers on numerous occasions while growing up in Tibet. These teachers were living examples who embodied the mind-training advice in their every action and their entire way of life. Rinpoche was so inspired by them that, despite being a consummate scholar of Buddhist philosophy, he saw that mind training is what we most need in these modern times. Since coming to the United States in 2002, he has taught on this text more than any other to audiences across North America.

The idea for this book started in 2006 and 2007, when Rinpoche gave a three-weekend series of mind-training teachings at a retreat center in Madison, Connecticut. Following the retreat, a group of his students were so moved by these instructions that they transcribed the teachings for personal study. While it began with the wish to create a useful transcription, as we organized and edited the text, we realized the profound gift we were given. Rinpoche had imparted personal advice for practicing each point. In total, he'd offered us seventy-six different techniques for taming the mind.

The Power of Mind follows the Tibetan Buddhist tradition of a teacher providing a commentary based on a root text, in this case, "The Seven Key Points of Mind Training." The root text consists of a sequence of pithy statements, called "slogans" in other translations, that are often condensed and difficult to understand without guidance. In this book, each statement from "The Seven Key Points of Mind Training" is presented one at a time, followed by the explanation of its meaning and the instructions on how to apply it to your life. The entire root text can be found in appendix 2.

In the Buddhist tradition, a qualified teacher's explanation of the root text is called a commentary. In fact, receiving oral instructions from such a teacher on how to practice the material is essential for applying it effectively. The commentary that you hold in your hands is like a key that will open up the meaning of the root text and help make it accessible to you.

This book is divided into seven parts, corresponding with each of the seven key points. Each point in the root text is then elucidated via numbered subpoints. The points and subpoints that are part of the root text are highlighted in bold and italics. The other headings throughout the book, which are not bolded, italicized, or numbered, are part of the commentary. A glossary and endnotes are available for additional support. Key terms are defined in unique ways in this tradition, and the glossary helps clarify them. The notes offer cultural context and flesh out concepts, since some foundational Buddhist ideas or aspects of Tibetan culture may be foreign to some readers.

What makes this commentary unique is Rinpoche's presentation, which is based on the oral tradition of pith instructions. This style of teaching provides less extensive information on a topic and instead emphasizes how to practice. Rinpoche explains how to apply each statement from the root text to our life circumstances based on his vast knowledge of Buddhist scripture, the instructions he received from his teachers, and his own personal experience. By taking knowledge and techniques and implementing them in our own experience, disturbing emotions will decrease while positive qualities such as wisdom, love, and compassion will increase—this is what it means to practice. In Rinpoche's words, practice is "to immerse your mind in positive qualities." This is what it means to be a practitioner.

I have had the incredibly good fortune of serving as Khentrul Rinpoche's translator since he came to the United States in 2002, and I interpreted every teaching he has given on "The Seven Key Points of Mind Training." I have witnessed the transformative effect that these teachings have had on my own life and on the lives of others who have studied and practiced them.

These mind trainings are a treasure trove of practical tools that I use all the time, especially when facing adversity. Whenever I encounter a tough situation, or even a minor annoyance, I find myself repeating the statements from this text, recollecting their meaning, and implementing them in that moment. And if I'm still struggling, I "throw the book at it"—I start at the beginning and apply each method, one by one, until my negative emotions subside. Mind training has shaped who I am today, and for this I will always be eternally grateful to Khentrul Lodrö T'hayé Rinpoche and to the lineage of teachers who have kept these teachings alive.

May this mind training be as powerful and beneficial to you as it has been for me.

—Paloma Lopez Landry

THE POWER OF MIND

INTRODUCTION

WHY TAME THE MIND?

Peace and happiness can be attained, but not by searching for something in the outside world. They start within us and extend out to the entire globe. *Peace and happiness are found within ourselves.* If our minds are disturbed, we can never find lasting peace and happiness. This is why the Buddha said, "Completely tame your mind." Taming the mind is the process of cultivating positive thoughts and emotions while learning how to reduce negative thoughts and emotions. It's truly the most important endeavor we can undertake in this life because until we tame our disturbing emotions, we'll never experience real peace of mind. Peace and happiness only come about when the causes and conditions for them are present. When that happens, they are inevitable, but when the causes and conditions are absent, peace and happiness are impossible to attain.

Every action that's ever been taken can be distilled down to the pursuit of happiness, even when it's disguised as a different motivation. History is essentially the story of our pursuit of happiness. So what have we accomplished in all this time? Not happiness. Not yet, at least. We've primarily focused on developing the external world in order to make our human experience better, but what exactly are we developing, and will it produce the results that we seek?

THREEFOLD DEVELOPMENT

If we want to change our experience, we need threefold development—of our external world, our actions, and our mind. These three sources are the keys to peace and happiness.

Developing Our External World

Let's first look at the world around us and what it has the potential to produce. Throughout history, we have spent most of our energy developing the external world, and, for the most part, we have succeeded in improving our quality of life. But there's a limit to the happiness the outer world can bring, and once we've reached that limit, we don't actually get *more* happiness. The potential to gain happiness from the outer world has to do with our basic needs being met, for example: enough food to eat, comfortable shelter, appropriate clothes for the weather, safe transportation, and medicine. When we don't have these things, we suffer, and so the happiness we get from the outer world is essentially basic physical comfort and the elimination of the discomfort that comes from not having enough. When we go past that point and try to squeeze more happiness out of the outer world—for instance, when we overdo something—what was once a cause of happiness can turn into a source of suffering. And even when we do get a sense of well-being from external objects, it is temporary and often unfulfilling.

For example, once you have a pillow that you like, having one hundred of them won't improve your physical comfort because more isn't always better. Not only does overeating make us feel uncomfortably stuffed but it's also bad for our health. The same goes for wealth—it can lead to physical well-being, but that doesn't mean it leads to more happiness. If it did, then the richest person in the world would be the most joyful, living in a constant state of peace, unburdened by disturbing emotions. Yet studies show that once a person surpasses a certain income, they don't gain in happiness and can even feel worse about their life. There is a Tibetan saying, "If you have a horse, you have a horse's worth of problems. If you have two horses, you have two horses' worth of problems."

As a species, it could be said that we have overdeveloped our world to the point of destruction. Innovations meant to make our lives better have led to many problems that threaten our very existence. The more we examine and reflect on this, the more we will see that of the three sources of happiness, the outer world has the least to offer.

Developing Our Actions

The second source of happiness is development of our actions, in other words, how we speak and behave. It takes little effort to offer a kind word to someone, and yet that action can have a significant positive impact on their life and ours. Tremendous harm can also come from speech. Lying, speaking harshly, gossiping about others' faults—these are some of the myriad ways we can express ourselves that increase unhappiness. And speech isn't limited to talking anymore. It includes all the ways we use words to communicate, such as on social media. Today, a single sentence can harm millions of people. We live in the age of weaponized words, and what we say directly affects our well-being and the well-being of others.

Because of this, we can easily hurt ourselves with our actions, as well as other humans, animals, or the earth. Even behavior that seems passive can cause harm. For example, it's important to examine the impact of our actions on the environment. The planet is our home, and our lives and the lives of future generations depend on it. We can be mindful of how every action we take will affect the natural balance of the environment, and we can work to preserve the earth, just as we make our bed and keep our home clean. Every action contributes to the formation of the future. That is our legacy, and our children and grandchildren will inherit the results.

The way we behave directly contributes to how we feel about ourselves. When we act in positive ways, we feel good and have a clear conscience. Even if we don't get exactly what we want, if we make every effort to refrain from harming others, in the end we will have the peace of mind that comes from knowing we did the best we could. When we act in negative ways, even if we succeed in getting what we want, our mind will be disturbed and we'll have a sense of discomfort. Gaining something at the cost of another's well-being never results in happiness. So if we want to improve our experience and the experience of those around us, we need to increase positive actions and decrease negative ones. This is how we develop our actions—the second key to peace and happiness.

Developing Our Mind

The third and final key to happiness is to develop the mind. While improving the outer world and our behavior can help, since everything begins with the mind, it is our primary source of happiness. That's why developing the mind is so important. I would say that approximately 95 percent of happiness comes from the mind, while only about 5 percent comes from external things. That's also why a person with a developed mind but a very low income can live a joyful life, while a person with an undeveloped mind who's very rich can be miserable. Peace and happiness are states of mind, and we need our mind to develop both our actions and our world. When our mind is undisturbed and we operate from a place of love, compassion, and knowledge, our actions improve, which in turn improves our world.

Unfortunately, throughout history most of our energy has been spent on material improvement rather than on developing the mind. Science and modern education place great emphasis on how the outer world operates and very little emphasis on how the mind works. If the science of the mind were universally studied—integrated into all curricula—we would have far less mental illness and suffering. Imagine if everyone studied how the mind works as much as we prepared for our careers. Imagine if we developed our minds to the same degree that we developed our outer world. We would have less war and more peace, happiness, and well-being everywhere!

It makes little difference how tall our skyscrapers are, how fast our technology is, or how much we develop our outer world if we fail to simultaneously develop our mind. By taming negative thoughts and emotions, we have the potential for not only temporary happiness but also ultimate happiness, and the personal benefit we will gain from developing our mind far exceeds the margin of happiness we might achieve from any other pursuit. When the mind is freed from afflictive thoughts and full of positive qualities, it is a state of joy, a state of peace.

And this is the purpose of mind training.

"The Seven Key Points of Mind Training" is the condensed essence of all of the practices taught by the Buddha for taming the mind. These pieces of pith advice have been passed from the Buddha to his students and from them to their students, in the form of an uninterrupted oral transmission from teacher to disciple, spanning from the time of the Buddha (over 2,500 years ago) until the present day.

THE POWER OF WORKING WITH THE MIND

What exactly is mind training, called *lojong* in Tibetan? *Lo* is a term for the "intelligent, thinking mind." *Jong* is a rich and complex term that could be translated as "to train," "to refine," or "to purify." Mind training is therefore what tames the mind.

Mind is defined as being conscious and aware. It is the knower of all objects and of itself, and every living being has mind, or sentience. Hence, we are called sentient beings. Because we have mind, we experience sensations such as pleasure and pain, and those sensations are why we want to have happiness and to be free of suffering. While all actions are based on this single pursuit, what we think and do often contradicts what we want. Only by taming the mind will we truly get what we want.

Taming the mind is the process of refining away mental afflictions until we aren't ruled by our circumstances and the negative thoughts and emotions they elicit. We gain control over our mind and hence our experience. This state of mental well-being doesn't depend on external conditions. When we engage in mind training, we set ourselves on a path—a series of steps that lead to a result—and that result is happiness. If favorable things happen, we use those circumstances to cultivate further causes for happiness. If unfavorable things happen, we don't become disturbed. Instead, we continue to engage in the causes for happiness. With mind training, no matter what occurs, good or bad, we transform whatever is happening into a source of happiness. All conditions become positive.

When we feel pleasure or pain, we may experience them physically or mentally, but both sensations are actually mind. They're not something else. An object without mind, such as a rock, is merely inanimate matter and has no sensations. Without mind, there would be no sensation of pain in the first place. A corpse feels no pain because a corpse no longer has mind. Similarly, if someone asks you, "Where is happiness?" where would you point? Nowhere, because happiness doesn't exist in some place or in an object. It isn't material. It is the mind itself. Happiness is primarily dependent upon the mind and not predetermined by other factors.

How much we suffer over something is based on how the mind perceives and relates to the problem. This is the reason people have different pain thresholds. If we categorically perceive an illness as being bad, for example, we will definitely suffer over it. But if, by using mind-training methods, our mind isn't disturbed by the illness, then all of the mental suffering associated with being sick will be absent, and even our physical suffering can be substantially reduced. It's even possible to be joyful in the face of illness. This is because it's not the illness that predetermines how much we suffer; it's the mind. This is not to ignore or deny the discomfort of illness but rather to change our relationship to it and to find constructive ways of taking action in response to the challenges it poses.

The seven key points are a complete set of trainings, and any one of us can apply them to our lives. That's the beauty of them. They're simple to understand and easy to practice. Once we know just these seven principles, we will possess an entire set of methods to thoroughly tame our mind, transform our experience, and change the world from the inside out. That is why it is said that *mind frees mind*. Everything we need is contained in this teaching. If we integrate these seven principles into our lives, all the happiness we wish for can be attained.

Setting Intentions

The outcome of every action begins with a thought. That thought is our motivation, the springboard for all action. So before we go further, let's start by expanding our mind.

As you begin, please cultivate an open attitude and a relaxed perspective, one that isn't easily disturbed. To do this, look to see if you have any afflictive thoughts motivating you to read this book, such as selfishness, desire, aversion, or jealousy. If you find these thoughts present, let them go by purposefully focusing your attention on a positive thought such as is described in the next paragraph. This is important because even when we do something seemingly positive, such as exploring methods for developing our mind, if our motivation isn't positive, even reading a book like this won't bring much benefit. If the container into which we pour this information is tainted, the results from practicing it would be tainted as well. This applies to everything we do.

Now choose the thought that you wish to motivate you. Since each and every action starts with a thought, it's essential to generate a positive motivation before engaging in any action. This means purposefully developing the thoughts that will produce a positive outcome. The best of all good intentions is *bodhichitta*, the commitment to tame our mind in order to free all beings from suffering and bring them to ultimate happiness. This is true love and compassion.

In addition to checking your motivation, whenever you sit down to study these instructions, please try to let go of whatever else is going on in your life. Our lives are filled with endless activities. There is, quite literally, no end of things to do, and that won't end until we put those things down or until we die. None of your plans will be ruined by laying aside thoughts of them while you read this book and reflect on its meaning. By letting go of your worldly concerns for this short time, your mind will gain the space to consider what is ultimately meaningful and what is actually a source of happiness. It will allow your mind to relax, opening it up to new perspectives and enabling you to make the most of this advice. What follows are the seven key points.

1. **First Key Point:** *Preliminaries, the Support for Practice*—These contemplations are what inspire us to practice. Reflecting on them gives us the reason for mind training.

2. **Second Key Point:** *The Actual Practice, Training in Bodhichitta*— Once we decide to tame our mind, we are ready for the main practice. The second key point is the practice itself. The primary focus is training our mind through compassion and wisdom, called relative and ultimate bodhichitta.

3. **Third Key Point:** *Transforming Adverse Conditions into the Path to Awakening*—Once we have a practice, we need to learn how to integrate it into all situations, especially when we experience adversity. So the third key point is learning how to transform adversity into positive qualities, the source of happiness.

4. **Fourth Key Point:** *Integrating Practice into Your Whole Life*— Once we have an established practice and methods for transforming adversity, we need to learn how to blend it into every aspect of our life. These instructions leave nothing out; they include how to practice during this life and also how to practice as we die. The fourth key point comprises the methods that completely integrate the practice into our life.

5. **Fifth Key Point:** *The Measure of Mind Training*—We need a goal to be motivated. Knowing the extent to which this practice will grow, as well as how to gauge progress on this path, provides us with a supportive framework, so the fifth key point is the measure of proficiency gained in mind training.

6. **Sixth Key Point:** *The Commitments of Mind Training*—To master mind training, we need to know what actions will contradict our practice, because the only way to evolve is to commit to refrain from actions that are contradictory to the trainings. So the sixth key point is composed of a series of commitments.

7. **Seventh Key Point:** *Advice for Mind Training*—Finally, for complete mastery, we need to know what actions will reinforce and strengthen our practice by following advice that enriches the trainings and brings progress. So the seventh key point is advice.

With these seven points, a practitioner has everything they need to tame the mind. Anyone who chooses to implement these trainings is a practitioner, be they Buddhist or otherwise. The practices belong to whomever applies them. Originating from the Buddha Shakyamuni's[1] teachings on love, compassion, and wisdom, these trainings were passed on from generation to generation and finally landed upon the great Indian scholar and realized master Jowo Je Palden Atisha, who distilled them down to seven key points in order to make the dharma available to all. You will find an extensive oral history of Atisha in appendix 1.

This distillation of key points has been preserved in an uninterrupted stream of teaching and practice from the time of Atisha in the eleventh century up until the present day. Now, almost a thousand years later, these teachings are more relevant than ever. I personally have been profoundly moved by mind training in my own life and having witnessed its impact on others, especially as I grew up hearing stories about the Tibetan lamas who endured innumerable hardships during the Cultural Revolution. The lamas who had knowledge of the mind-training teachings were able to embrace the suffering inflicted upon them and use it as a means to cultivate positive qualities and gain realization. They were like alchemists, transforming pain into something good. The majority of the mind-training instructions found within the Nyingma lineage, the oldest tradition of practice originating in Tibet,[2] is the specific tradition of teaching I received. It came through the great master Jamyang Khyentse Wangpo, who gave them to Kongtrul Yonten Gyamtso, who then compiled them into a transmission that forms one section of a vast body of teachings called the Treasury of Oral Instructions. I received the entire Treasury of Oral Instructions from His Holiness Katok Moksa Tulku, along with many other mind-training instructions from my root guru, His Holiness Jigme Phuntsok Rinpoche. This extremely brief account verifies the source of these teachings and how they have been passed on in an unbroken lineage of transmission from teacher to disciple up to the present day. It is this that I shall now pass on to you.

PART ONE

BUILDING A FOUNDATION FOR FREEDOM: THE PRELIMINARIES

THE FIRST KEY POINT
The Preliminaries, the Support for Practice[1]

Just as we cannot build a house in the air but instead need a solid base, finding freedom also begins with building a foundation. The preliminaries are the necessary preparation for effective meditation. Using these contemplations, our priorities will change—we'll learn to let go of the causes of suffering and begin to adopt thoughts and actions that lead to genuine happiness. We must want freedom to find freedom. This motivation is the foundation for all spiritual practice.

First, train in the preliminaries.

This contemplative training in the preliminaries, called the four thoughts that change the mind, consists of reflecting upon the following, each of which has its own chapter in part 1: this precious human life; impermanence; karma, cause, and result; and the dissatisfactory nature of existence, or suffering. Each of these four thoughts can be applied in a formal meditation setting or simply be related to any aspect of our daily life. They give us a unique perspective on our life and on specific situations, which then enables us to apply the other trainings and leads us to a growing sense of certainty as to the nature of existence and the wish to be free;

in other words—renunciation.[2] They are called the preliminaries because the more we develop an awareness of these four basic attributes, the more we will yearn to find freedom from suffering and the more we will want to practice to arrive at that goal.

1

This Precious Human Life: The Power of Being Human

For the first of the four preliminaries, *this precious human life*, reflect on the freedoms and advantages of human life and consider the value of being human. Compare your situation with other species in order to understand the opportunity humans possess. Of all living beings in the universe, how many are human? And of those, how many practice a genuine spiritual path? Even more so, how many spend their lives trying to help others? These kinds of questions put the preciousness of our lives into perspective.

It's important to take into account a much broader perspective than just this present life. This life is not our first, nor will it be our last.[3] For innumerable lifetimes, our fundamental consciousness, the mind, has been propelled uninterruptedly from one life to the next through the force of habitual imprints. What reincarnates is not the physical body. It is the mind.

We can see how our mental habits affect us when we consider how we move between waking and sleeping states. As you read this, you are experiencing the waking state, but when you sleep, a whole different set of experiences manifest as a dream state. Where did the consciousness come from in that dream? From the previous waking state. A stream of uninterrupted moments of consciousness continues from waking into sleeping without ceasing. When we wake in the morning, where did that consciousness come from? From the previous moments of sleep.

In the same way, from the Buddhist perspective, when we die and the body and mind separate—consciousness simply shifts into another moment of experience. The transition from one lifetime to another is based upon an uninterrupted stream of consciousness, which is similar to transitioning from waking to sleeping. So in the Buddhist view, what we see and perceive in a new life are determined by the habitual imprints within an individual's mindstream—in other words, what we see, think, and experience has an impact on both our current life and beyond. This view of the continuity of consciousness is vital to fully comprehend what it means to have the freedoms and advantages of a precious human birth.

To have freedom means that we have not been born into a state of existence in which there is no opportunity to practice. States where there are no such freedoms include being born into the animal or hungry ghost realms.[4] Many of these states of existence are characterized by so much suffering or such intense ignorance that beings cannot even consider searching for a spiritual path, let alone practicing one. If we were born into one of those states, we would not have the freedom to understand a teaching that explains the causes for happiness or how to find an end to suffering. We would be unable to practice such teachings. We need a proper physical support to understand the teachings and to apply them in practice. To be born human and to have the leisure to practice means we possess certain freedoms.

To have advantages means that we have circumstances in our lives that enable us to search for an authentic path and then to accomplish it. These advantages include where we are born, our mental faculties, and the general conditions of our lives. When we have the necessary circumstances in our lives, we have the advantage of being able to practice. If you are reading this book, for example, you already have certain freedoms and advantages.

The majority of us don't think about what it means to be human, nor do we consider the true potential of human life. If we don't appreciate the freedoms and advantages that we have, we won't use them fully. It is important to think carefully about the choices that we make.

Another way to develop appreciation for the rarity and value of our human birth is to reflect on some comparisons. Think big. As previously mentioned, consider all living beings on earth. Among them, how many are human? Among humans, how many have freedoms and advantages? As mentioned, humans are a small proportion of the living beings on earth. In fact, a single glass of pond water may contain millions of microorganisms. This means a relatively small amount of water could have more beings than the entire human population. Now consider the number of beings inhabiting the ocean and earth and compare that to the number of human beings. It's almost unfathomable. These kinds of comparisons show us how rare it is to be born human. What this means is that far fewer beings engage in the causes and conditions[5] necessary to produce a human experience compared with those producing other states of existence. It's not as rare to be born as an animal or another type of being. When we look at the numbers, we can see that a human life is truly a miraculous feat.

In Buddhist scriptures it is said that beings born into nonhuman states are as numerous as nighttime stars, whereas beings born as humans are exceptionally rare, as rare as stars visible in daylight. Look at the stars in the sky and reflect on how rare it is to be born as a human!

Human life is rare to attain because it is not easy to create the combination of causes and conditions that produce human birth. It is not as if we suddenly appeared here for no reason. We did not burst out of the ground, nor did we fall out of the sky or magically appear. Our body, mind, and each of our many positive circumstances were created by a complex network of causes and conditions. At some point in a previous life, we engaged in the positive actions that produced the specific result of a human birth. We don't know when that might have been, but it is the reason we have been born as a human being in this life.

In Tibet, there was a famous spiritual teacher named Chey-ngawa, who is known far and wide as being a paramount example of someone who truly realized the value of human life. He didn't want to lose a single moment of this precious opportunity to engage in positive actions, so he hardly slept. One day, one of his students, Tönpa, expressed concern that if Chey-ngawa did not sleep he would get sick, and he encouraged his teacher to sleep more. To that suggestion Chey-ngawa replied that while it was wonderful to have good health, when he thought about how hard it was to find the freedoms and advantages of human birth, he knew he didn't have time to squander a moment. It is said that Chey-ngawa accumulated more than nine billion mantras over the course of his life. Although most of us won't become as diligent as this great master—nor are we being asked to—we will find that as our awareness of the value of this life increases, what is important to us and how we choose to use each moment will change.

Once we become cognizant of the fact that human life is rare and difficult to obtain, the next question to ask is: How can we make this life ultimately meaningful? If we spend our whole life fulfilling basic needs and short-term material goals, we are not fulfilling our human potential. And if we strive to accomplish only worldly aims, such as seeking riches, power, or fame, we won't find true happiness. Should we throw away the potential for ultimate happiness in order to merely fill our stomachs with fine delicacies, quench our thirst with a variety of drinks, or buy a bigger house or nicer car? Is that truly how we want to use this rare opportunity of being human?

Let's aim higher by thinking about what will make this life truly meaningful. We have the opportunity to create the causes for both temporary and ultimate happiness, which will benefit ourselves and others. This human body and intelligent mind are the essential supports for attaining these goals.

Temporary happiness means finding true joy in this life by working on our mind so that happiness is not dependent upon external circumstances. Ultimate happiness is achieved by fully entering a path that leads to freedom, a path based on purifying ourselves of obscurations and flaws while realizing our true nature, replete with all positive qualities.[6] By pursuing both temporary and ultimate happiness, we will not only realize our capacity to benefit ourselves but also to benefit others. This is the power of being human. We don't want to take this opportunity for granted. We now have something precious, something rare and hard to find that is a source of temporary and ultimate benefit. If we maximize the potential of being human, the short- and long-term results will be positive. So look closely at your goals and actions and see if you are fulfilling your potential.

HOW TO PRACTICE

This practice offers instructions on basic seated meditation, which you will use as the framework for all the "How to Practice" sections throughout the book. The length of time you spend is entirely up to you, but being consistent, and even designating a specific time in the day to practice, is very helpful. Aim for twenty to thirty minutes a day to start. You can begin with less too, but don't overcommit yourself. It is better to start with shorter sessions and then slowly lengthen them, than to start out too long and not be able to sustain them. Some of the concepts here will be elaborated on as you continue to read and develop your practice, so don't worry about perfectly understanding everything right away—it is called practice for a reason!

The format for sitting meditation is always the same whether we are meditating on the four thoughts, love and compassion, wisdom, or any other practice. Every session should have three parts: the excellent beginning consisting of cultivating the aspiration of bodhichitta; the excellent main part, practicing non-referential wisdom; and the excellent conclusion, dedicating the merit and making aspirations. These are called the three excellent principles of practice.

The Excellent Beginning

First, cultivate the key points of body, speech, and mind. The *key point of body* is to sit in proper meditation posture. Find a quiet environment conducive to meditation and prepare a comfortable seat. A good meditation seat is one that enables you to maintain the key points of sitting meditation posture without holding the muscles tightly. For example, if you are able to sit on the floor cross-legged, it is helpful to use a cushion just under the sitting bones to lift and tilt the pelvis forward. This allows the spine to straighten and the muscles to relax. Relaxed muscles are a good indicator of a comfortable seated position. If you are not able to sit cross-legged, sit in a chair instead, allowing your feet to be flat on the floor and your spine straight (you may use a cushion under the sitting bones as previously described).[7] Proper meditation posture, also called the seven key points of posture, will support the mind in both settling itself and focusing clearly.

The first key point of posture is to sit cross-legged (or on a chair as needed). Second, rest the hands in the gesture of meditative equipoise, which means either resting face down on your knees or folded one atop of the other in your lap. Third, keep the spine straight. That means the vertebrae are aligned like a stack of coins so that your muscles are not tensing. Fourth, leave the shoulders wide open. Fifth, tuck in the chin just enough so that the neck and spine align. Sixth, leave the tongue resting at the front of the hard palate just behind the front teeth. And the seventh key point of posture is to leave the eyes open and the gaze lowered, resting on the empty space just in front of you, below the nose. Allow the breath to flow naturally.

When we sit in this way, the alignment of the body straightens and opens our nervous system, vascular system, and other systems of channels, which are the conduits for energy movement throughout our body. This movement affects what kinds of thoughts arise. That's why certain positions make the mind more agitated, while others cause it to be sleepy and dull. When the body is properly aligned, the channels are straight. When the channels are straight, the mind becomes more easily focused, which contributes to the development of positive mental states such as love and compassion.

The *key point of speech* is to clear the breath. For more elaborate meditations, and in other contexts, this may involve clearing stale air from the lungs by expelling the breath through specific breathing techniques. For the purposes here, simply allowing your breath to slow into its own natural rhythm when at rest is sufficient. Take a moment to notice the breath and allow it to gently settle.

The *key point of mind* is to set your intention. Begin by examining your motivation with the thought, "Why am I doing this meditation?" We may have positive, negative, or neutral thoughts motivating us to practice. As much as possible we want to have a positive frame of mind. The most positive thought is the altruistic intention of bodhichitta, or great compassion for sentient beings, which we will discuss in more detail in chapter 6. Reflect for a moment on your motivation until you generate this thought: "In order to free all beings from suffering, and in order to bring them all to true and complete happiness, I will do this practice."

Once you've established the key points of body, speech, and mind, it can be helpful to pray to the buddhas and bodhisattvas—awakened beings who have actualized bodhichitta. Imagine that a realized being you feel connected to appears before you. Pray to that being and to all enlightened beings for the support of their presence and realization. Request their help to overcome ordinary mind (see page 129) and to cultivate the qualities of bodhichitta. Pray that you can accomplish the practice you are about to do, then allow your mind to merge with their enlightened mind. Rest there for a few moments. This concludes the excellent beginning.

The Excellent Main Part

This is the main meditation session. Ideally, no matter what practice we are doing, we incorporate the wisdom of true nature.[8] Since the purpose of practice is to overcome ignorance—the nonrecognition of true nature (see page 54)—it makes sense that the main practice incorporates the wisdom that realizes true nature. For newer practitioners, it is sufficient for the main part to simply consist of one-pointed focus on the key points of whatever practice we are doing. In other words, we should apply ourselves wholeheartedly to the meditation. For this chapter that means the contemplation of this precious human birth.

The concepts introduced in this book are cultivated in formal contemplative meditation, which means you alternate between examining and resting. Contemplating this precious human birth involves bringing to mind every aspect of your life, the world, and all beings contained within it and reflecting on the value of being human.

This thought process means thinking about and analyzing the way things are using a specific topic, for example, thinking about and analyzing what it means to be human. Apply the concepts introduced in this chapter to your life and discover what being human means to you. At a certain point in this analytical process, when the mind grows tired of contemplating or when you have an insight, let go of the thought process and allow the mind to rest. The past has already ceased; the future is yet to be. Don't think about the past, don't imagine the future, don't get caught up in the present. Meditate with the mind of right now. This is not the time to rehash everything that has ever happened in life, nor is it the time to make plans. Resting enhances the insight because the mind is worn out through the contemplative process. Just relax and drop all deliberation, allowing the mind to naturally settle for a few moments. When thoughts start moving again, pick up the contemplation where you left off and continue thinking about this precious human life.

Review the following list of concepts introduced in this chapter by reading one point at a time and then reflecting upon each point individually (summarized below). Alternate between contemplative and resting meditation throughout the session.

Key Points to Contemplate

- What does it mean to have freedoms?
- What does it mean to have advantages?
- How can you make this life ultimately meaningful?

The Excellent Conclusion

This is the dedication of the merit and making aspirations. When we dedicate the practice, we give away the merit we have generated for the welfare of others. For example, we might think, "I dedicate the merit of this practice on precious human birth to all beings that they may be freed from suffering and attain both temporary and ultimate happiness." Then we make aspirations in which we wish for the welfare and happiness of others. For example, we might think, "May all beings be happy and may all beings be free." It is also powerful to recite dedication and aspiration prayers from the buddhas and bodhisattvas, which are prayers universally recited by Buddhist practitioners and qualified spiritual teachers. The compassionate wishes expressed in these prayers are vast and will broaden and enrich our practice. See appendix 5 for dedication and aspiration prayers.

When we dedicate the merit and make aspirations the idea is to recall the original intention of the practice and to share its benefits with all beings. In addition, by properly dedicating the merit and making aspirations, we seal the practice so that what we generate does not become depleted but continues to grow and expand. You can think of it like a merit bank and investing your merit instead of depleting the principal by living off it. When you don't dedicate the merit, those positive actions are causes that produces one result and then are finished, similar to the principal, or the original amount of money committed to an investment. But when you dedicate the merit to the welfare of all beings, you connect to numberless objects, expanding its scope and power. Further, when you dedicate it for the purpose of ultimate happiness, it continues to bear fruit until the goal is attained, like a good investment that perpetually grows until you are done investing.

Off the Cushion

You can use this practice to change your perspective and manage your emotions in response to any situation in life. For example, if people, events, or even an email or text begins to upset you—pause. Refresh your perspective. Think about the vast extent of existence and reflect on how you have such a rare opportunity to be human. Ask yourself whether getting upset and reacting in a defensive or angry way makes this human life meaningful. Is it worth it? At the time of death, how will you feel about your behavior? Will these actions produce future positive experiences? Consider this human life to be a short moment in time, during which you have the potential to gain ultimate freedom from suffering. Do you want to waste it being angry or justifying your negative thoughts and actions? Resolve to act in a way you won't regret at the end of your life.

2

Impermanence:
No One Lives Forever

Even though we have this extraordinary human life, it is impermanent. Nothing lasts forever, yet we don't relate to things in terms of impermanence. Instead, we have a strong tendency to fixate on things as lasting. Each day, we think our bodies and possessions are the same as they were the day before, and that even the earth is the same. This underlying belief in permanence is the feeling that phenomena have a duration, that moment to moment they remain the same. To see the world in this way is to perceive things as if they are permanent.

It's important to understand what *permanent* and *impermanent* mean. *Permanent* means never changing, that something or someone by its very nature is constant and stays the same. If something or someone is permanent, there can be no moment-to-moment change and no end. *Impermanent* means constantly changing or never the same. Change happens every single moment. So, while we may have the freedoms and advantages of being human, we won't have them forever. In all ways, this human life and the opportunities it provides are impermanent.

There is only one certainty in life: we will die. The time of death is unknown and the circumstances that will cause us to die are uncertain.

We know that we will die but we don't know when. This is not a story about someone else. Simply look around you. Some people die as children, some as adults, and others in old age. But there is no guarantee that life will extend to old age. The time of our death is completely unknown.

There are few conditions that sustain life compared with the many conditions that can end it, and even supportive conditions can become a cause of death. For example, food, which is considered life-sustaining, can become a cause of death through food poisoning or allergies. Our life is as fragile as a candle in the wind; if you place a candle outside, there are more conditions that will put the flame out than will sustain it.

We need to cultivate certainty about death. It is certain that we will die, although we don't know when or how. We have no guarantee that we won't die this afternoon or that we won't die tomorrow. In fact, each day chips away at how much longer we have to live. To illustrate this, imagine you have fallen off a cliff and are hanging on by the tufts of grass at the cliff's edge. In the daytime, a white prairie dog comes by and chews off a piece of grass. In the nighttime, a black prairie dog comes by and chews off a piece of grass. As each blade of grass is consumed, you are closer to losing your handhold and falling off the precipice. In this story, the white prairie dog is daytime, the black prairie dog is nighttime, and the abyss beyond the cliff is death. With the passing of each day, we are closer to our death.

In considering impermanence, it's important to also reflect on other kinds of perceptible change, such as the shift from season to season. Or think of change caused by the elements, such as natural disasters. Consider how everything we own eventually gets old, breaks, or simply ceases to be a part of our life. Think about how all situations inevitably change. This first contemplation, based on the obvious changes that occur in all aspects of our lives, is called reflecting on perceptible impermanence.

Continue to develop awareness of impermanence by contemplating subtle, imperceptible impermanence. In other words, contemplate ever-constant change. The moment when we notice something has changed or is broken is not the moment it suddenly became impermanent. Imperceptible impermanence can be understood in terms of increments of time. Time is actually a measurement of change. One day is a day's worth of change. A day can further be divided into sections such as daytime and nighttime, and further broken up into hours, making twenty-four hours of change. Each hour can then be divided into minutes, which can be divided into seconds, and those into nanoseconds, and so on. Each is a measurement of change. The time it takes to snap our fingers is a finger snap's worth of change.

Imagine you have one hundred leaves of a plant stacked on top of each other. The leaves are thin and fragile. It would take less time to pierce through them with a stake than it would for you to snap your fingers. You might think that you pierced through them all at once, but the reality is that there was a moment, albeit imperceptible, when each leaf was pierced. Countless imperceptible moments of change make up the swift action of piercing a stack of leaves. This is the constant impermanence that every aspect of our life is undergoing. It's not that things are the same from one moment to the next, in other words, *permanent*, and then something happens and suddenly they become impermanent. Nor is it that things are impermanent only because of the obvious changes that we see. There isn't a single moment when we're not changing. Nothing and no one is ever the same moment to moment.

IMPERMANENCE AS INSPIRATION

We may ask, "Why should I think about impermanence? How does it benefit me?" Contemplating impermanence brings our perception into harmony with the way things are, which refines and tames the mind. The closer our perception is to how things actually are, the less we suffer because we no longer have the expectation that things should be lasting. We stop relating to things and people as being opposite their actual nature. In particular, it becomes evident to us that everything here in the universe, all of what we call cyclic existence, will fail us, because all things by their very nature are impermanent. This is one of the fundamental pitfalls of existence. What is the benefit of knowing this? When we clearly determine that there is nothing lasting to be found in this life, we are inspired to search for what is ultimately true and reliable. We search for what won't fail us. Understanding impermanence ignites a desire within us to practice a path that will lead to truth.

The more aware we are of impermanence, the more motivated and inspired we become to use this human life. When someone understands life's transitory essence, they are motivated to make use of the opportunity at hand before it's gone. Arriving at the thought "Not only must I make this life ultimately meaningful, I must act to use it quickly" enables us to overcome the habit of procrastination.

For the person who has ongoing and deep awareness of impermanence, there are many benefits, both temporary and ultimate. Temporary benefits occur in this and future lives, but especially in the present moment. For example, if we relate to something or someone as if they are unchanging, we are shocked and devastated when one day we see perceptible change. We can't believe it. We think, "I never expected this to happen!" Our minds fill with fear, anger, anxiety, and worry. This is because we had false expectations. We subconsciously related to and believed that this person or thing was permanent, that they should have remained the same. If, however, from the very beginning we clearly and consciously knew that eventually this person or thing would change, we wouldn't freak out about it. We'd think, "Oh yeah, I knew this could eventually happen because it was always impermanent." Operating with a healthy expectation of change prepares our mind for the inevitable changes that will come, and it helps us to cope with those changes. A practitioner who knows impermanence has a much greater capacity for carrying adversity onto the path.

In addition, knowing impermanence improves our relationships with family, friends, and romantic partners. When two people appreciate how impermanent life is, they inevitably have a better relationship. Why is this? Because they know that each moment with this person could be their last. We know that life's circumstances could change at any time, and we don't take each other for granted. This awareness helps us to be more present and to appreciate whoever we are with. This is especially true when it comes to romantic relationships, such as marriage. If we relate to one other as permanent, we can take each other for granted and fail to appreciate the preciousness of the time we have together, causing the quality of connection to decline. It may seem counterintuitive, but knowledge of impermanence deepens and strengthens the relationships that we already have.

Think about how old you are right now. Think about all of the material possessions you've acquired and all of the experiences you've had from the day you were born until this very moment. How lasting has any of it been? How much actual happiness, without worry or suffering, have you gained from those things? At any moment in time, no matter how much we've obtained or achieved, we have a similar extent of desire for more or different things and circumstances in the future. Why should the results of all that we acquire in the future be any different from the results of the past? Everyone has this problem. Even though everything in the past didn't last or didn't work out because it was impermanent, we still somehow keep thinking that in the future the situation will be different. We imagine that we are going to find or create a circumstance in which we have permanent happiness. It's like trying to grasp empty space. Do you think space can be grasped? Do you think that if you put in enough effort you can find the perfect, everlasting situation? Do you think that you can accomplish what you are seeking?

No matter how much we try or how much we hope, there will never be anything to hold on to. Nothing can stay the same forever, which means that all our efforts to make it remain so are futile. Remember this when making your plans, hoping for the happiness that will come from the illusion of a perfect or permanent situation. If history gives us any indication, it's unlikely, if not impossible, to achieve such happiness from life. And if we continue to try, we will only experience more problems, more worries, and more fears. Because nothing that we achieve will ever last. There will never be a point when there is nothing left to do. When we lack the simple awareness of impermanence, our mind gets uptight about everything. We constantly struggle against change, trying to keep things the same or chasing after other circumstances. We think, "This time it will be different." We are filled with false expectations, and the mind gets agitated even about little things. But knowing impermanence brings us relief because finally we are seeing things as they actually are. For example, when we accept that nothing lasts, such as our home or job, then as things naturally change, we don't resist the change as much because we already knew it could happen. To understand this, bring to mind a situation you knew wasn't sustainable, but you couldn't accept its impermanent reality. Think about how much extra fear, anxiety, and suffering you endured until you finally let it go. Expecting unforeseen change relaxes our mind and we become more spacious and flexible, which is why knowing impermanence brings enormous benefit to our lives right now.

But how does knowing impermanence ultimately benefit us? We see that all living beings are in this constant struggle against impermanence, striving to make existence permanently happy but never accomplishing that goal. So, now what? We begin to realize that what we are looking for is not found outside of ourselves. It is within our own mind, within our own heart. Because nothing external lasts or is permanent, there is nothing to become attached to. There is no object or circumstance in conditioned existence that is permanent. This means the objects and circumstances we strive for are not ultimately reliable, and they will inevitably fail us. In this way, we see the essence-less nature of cyclic existence. There's no core; there's nothing to grab on to. Knowing this motivates us to be diligent. This keen awareness inspires us to pursue true and ultimate happiness, and to use the support of this human life—now, while we have it—to strive for that goal.

This is why the Buddha said, "Of the many perceptions cultivated in meditation, the best is that of impermanence." Not only does this inspire us to practice diligently, using the time that we have, but it also helps us to deal with everyday life and its constant transitions. This is especially the case when it comes to facing adversity. If we were aware of impermanence, relating to everything and everyone as temporary, we would not become overwhelmed when impermanence becomes obvious. The shock we normally experience simply wouldn't happen. This is because we would not have had expectations for that person or situation to stay the same in the first place. Truly understanding impermanent nature—that anything can occur at any moment—prepares us for change and expands our capacity for relating to every situation in a way that is less painful. This is essential for carrying adversity onto the path.

When reflecting on impermanent nature, whether while sitting in formal contemplative meditation or simply when thinking of the impermanence of whatever is happening throughout the day, there are some basic methods that are useful.[1] The primary contemplation is to purposely cultivate thoughts of gross impermanence (i.e., perceptible change) and the more subtle, imperceptible constant change explored earlier in this chapter. Spend some time reflecting on the impermanence of everything—the universe and all sentient beings within it—in terms of perceptible change and ongoing imperceptible change.

THE FOUR ENDINGS OF IMPERMANENCE

Another method for contemplation is to use "the four endings of impermanence" taught by the Buddha. The first of these is "all birth ends in death." Everything that is born will die. There is no other ending. When we consider the past, there is no being about whom we could say, "Well, out of everyone I've known, this one never died." Even among the renowned saints and accomplished masters throughout history, there isn't a single one left other than their name and legacy. If even these great saints and masters died, why not us? Everyone is subject to impermanence. We can't avoid or escape it. So death is the first ending of impermanence. "All birth ends in death" also means that everything made or produced ends in obliteration.

The second ending of impermanence is "what goes up ends up coming down." As an example, consider people who gain positions of power. No matter how high their position or elevated their status, it is never a permanent situation. Eventually they fall from power. Even if we achieve the highest status in a country and become king, queen, or president, eventually we will succumb to the loss of that exalted state. Another way of thinking about this is to consider material matter, such as a building. No matter how sturdy we build it, no matter how thick we reinforce it, it will eventually fall. Consider what happened to New York's World Trade Center on September 11, 2001. The buildings stood so high, a seemingly permanent fixture on the skyline, but in the end, they collapsed, in what became one of the most painful tragedies in the modern era for the United States of America. There is no such thing as a permanent structure, just as there is no such thing as lasting fame. In one place or time, a person may be a common household name, but in a different place or time, that person may not be known by anyone.

The third ending of impermanence is "all that is accumulated ends in exhaustion." Everything that we acquire—wealth and possessions—will eventually be used up, lost, or even stolen. As much as we accumulate, one day these things will no longer be ours. Yet we suffer so much in the process of gathering and maintaining our wealth and possessions. In the beginning, we undergo all kinds of hardship in order to acquire wealth; in the middle, we suffer over trying to increase that wealth and safeguard it; and in the end, we suffer when we are separated from it. We should always consider these realities, especially when we are willing to forsake the welfare of others in our pursuits. All wealth and possessions amassed will, at some point or another, be gone.

The fourth and last ending of impermanence is "all gathering ends in separation." For instance, no relationship lasts forever, and every gathering of people eventually ends in farewell. Organizations and groups assemble, only to later disperse. It's this way even for our families. Maybe now we have a family that lives together, but that is temporary. Eventually our children move out. Even if we don't separate by choice, at some point we are separated by death. One day we are a tight family unit and then we are scattered across the earth or just a memory to one another. Even our body is a collection of parts that at some point will no longer be connected. We have this gathering of skin, muscle, bones, ligaments, organs, and so on, all joined together for the period of time we call "this life." But when this life ends, these parts will separate from each other. Our teeth are a great example, which we can see while alive. In our youth our adult teeth replace our baby teeth, but as we age they decay and fall out. If we are lucky enough to live to a ripe old age, we may eventually die with no teeth at all. All composite things that come together eventually end in separation.

The point of contemplating these four aspects of impermanence is to reflect deeply on cyclic existence. No matter how we think about it, there is nothing that is permanent. No particle of phenomena can be found that is permanent, not our circumstances, our bodies, our relationships, or our possessions.

We currently have a precious human birth, but there is not a lot of time to put its potential to use. We may appreciate it, but then we think, "I'll put it to use after I finish this project," or "I'll put it to use next week, next month, or next year." And that's how we procrastinate in making use of this opportunity, by thinking we'll get to it later. Each moment that goes by is one less moment we have, and we don't know how much time we have left. So start making use of these freedoms and advantages right now. Once we start this process, even if we die soon, we've already set out on the path to freedom. Practicing impermanence has the immediate benefits of bringing greater joy and appreciation to our lives. Even more beneficial than that, it spurs us on to liberation. The time to start using our human potential is now.

HOW TO PRACTICE

The Excellent Beginning

Find a comfortable, quiet spot. Sit in meditation posture to cultivate the key points of body and speech (see page 17 for a full explanation). Then, cultivate the key point of mind by setting your intention. Think, "In order to benefit all beings, I will realize the impermanent nature of everything—especially this life—and make each moment meaningful."

The Excellent Main Part

Review the concepts introduced in this chapter by reading one point at a time and pausing to contemplate each one. The points are summarized below. Reflect on its significance, apply it to specific objects or situations in your life, and discover what it means for you. Occasionally, when you arrive at an insight or if you tire of thinking, let go entirely. Don't think about the past, don't imagine the future, don't get caught up in the present. Just relax and drop all deliberation to allow the mind to settle naturally without contrivance for a few moments. When thoughts start moving again, pick up the contemplation where you left off and continue thinking about impermanence.

Key Points to Contemplate

- What is the definition of *impermanence* and what is the only certainty in life?
- What are perceptible forms of impermanence?
- What are imperceptible forms of impermanence?
- What are the benefits of having a keen awareness of impermanence?
- What are the four endings of impermanence?

The Excellent Conclusion

Dedicate the merit generated by this practice and make aspirations. Think, "I dedicate the merit of this practice on impermanence to all beings that they may be freed from suffering and attain temporary and ultimate happiness." Then, make aspirations for the welfare and happiness of others. Think, "May all beings be happy and may all beings be free." (You can also use the dedication and aspiration prayers in appendix 5.)

Off the Cushion

You can use this practice to change your perspective and manage your emotions in response to any situation in life. To do so, build a habit of remembering impermanence, called mindfulness. Set a goal to remember impermanence as many times in one day as you can, perhaps beginning with once an hour, by relating to everything and everyone with the recognition of their impermanent nature. Then set the goal to do that for one week. Continue to extend this practice over time, habitually bringing to mind the effects of impermanence. Whatever you are doing and whoever you are with, think that you, they, and the activity are impermanent. For example, when you meet someone, think, "This could be the last time I see them." Then, treat the person as you would wish to treat them if you knew it would be the last time you met.

When you become upset about something, pause. Give yourself a moment to gain perspective. Remember that everything is impermanent and nothing lasts, whether good or bad. To expect otherwise is a mistaken perception. Consider the entire universe and all that has come and gone, and ask yourself, "Will this matter to me when I die? Will I regret these thoughts or actions?" Whatever your current situation, it is brief and maybe even inconsequential in the larger scheme of existence. One day it will be a distant memory, likely forgotten. By giving ourselves perspective and remembering that everything is impermanent, we can more constructively and positively respond to the changes we inevitably encounter and to the situations we dislike.

3

Karma, Cause, and Result:
Actions Have Consequences

We speak of impermanence, the end of life, and death, but then what? When we die, what do we bring with us? Our actions, what we call karma, are the only things that accompany us. Positive actions and negative actions will be what pull us along, forming the basis of our future experiences. At the time of death—the greatest display of impermanence—we carry only our karma with us. We cannot bring our loved ones, power, fame, or beauty. All of our hard-earned possessions will be left behind. We can't even bring a needle's tip with us. Everything will be abandoned except for the results of the positive and negative actions we have accumulated. These come with us, and they are what we become.

When we use the Sanskrit term *karma*, which translates literally to "action," what do we mean? An action is a cause that produces a result. Karmic results are not the immediate effects of an action in the moment. Instead, they are results that ripen when the action's habitual imprint in our consciousness becomes our future experience. These actions are determined to be either positive or negative based on the future experience they produce. An action is called positive, or virtuous, when it creates a cause for future happiness. This means the action becomes a source of future happiness, joy, or pleasure. An action is called negative, or non-virtuous, when it results in future suffering—physical, verbal, or mental. There are no alternative results for harmful actions. Such actions never give happiness a chance to ripen. When we die, the habitual tendencies of these positive and negative actions are what form our future experience. The results of our actions are infallible.

So when we speak of cyclic existence—*samsara* in Sanskrit—we are speaking of a series of causes and effects that form habits and repeat themselves.[1] When we reflect on the various realms within cyclic existence and specifically contemplate the suffering that beings endure here, we may wonder, "Why is there so much suffering?" The answer is that beings suffer because they have the causes for suffering.

Each action is like planting a seed in the field of consciousness. The seeds become habitual tendencies, the latent causes in our consciousness that awaken through conditions and form our experiences and perceptions. We might have doubts about this. We might wonder, "If everything is produced by habitual tendencies imprinted upon my consciousness, why does the world feel so real? Why are rocks so hard? Why is the earth so stable and solid?" Remember that we have a long-standing habit of believing that phenomena are real and solid. This habit of solidifying appearances has been reinforced each moment since beginningless time. Up until now, we have assumed that everything we experience is real and that it inherently exists. We believe that phenomena exist "out there" and are independent from us. We give them an identity, which they lack, and believe them to be true. This is a deeply entrenched habit. For example, if in a dream someone hits us on the head with a rock, it hurts! Or if we can't find food during a dream, we get anxious and feel even hungrier. In reality, we don't even have a body in that dream state, let alone a stomach! Yet this doesn't stop the experience from seeming real, nor does it prevent it from happening in the dream. Our dreams and our waking states are formed through habits. All the realms of samsara and the individual experiences of each living being are created by the habitual imprints of previous actions.

Harmful and negative actions create less fortunate states of existence as well as unpleasant and unwanted circumstances. Positive and beneficial actions bring about more fortunate states of existence as well as pleasure and joy. There are two kinds of positive actions: those that merely produce good experiences and states within cyclic existence, and those that take us beyond this cycle and contribute to finding ultimate freedom and peace. The first of these are called ordinary positive actions because they produce ordinary states of existence, albeit pleasant ones. This type of virtue is based on ordinary perceptions, intentions, and ignorance. The vast majority of positive actions fall into this category. Then there are positive actions that—by virtue of our motivation, view, and other factors—contribute to transcending cyclic existence. Our actions become especially potent when we are motivated by the pure wish to benefit others (i.e., bodhichitta), and we recognize the wisdom of true nature.[2] This type of positive action becomes not only the cause for temporary happiness for as long as we continue to be born into samsara but also contributes to ultimate liberation.

If we understand every action to be a cause that produces a result, there is no action that is too small. Every act should be considered a decision, and we should be conscientious as we decide whether to engage in an action or refrain from it. Never underestimate an action or disregard it because it seems insignificant. No action goes unaccounted for.

If we think, "Oh, it's only a small beneficial action. It doesn't matter," we forget the power of accumulated actions and the possible positive impact it could have on others. Many drops of water will eventually fill a bucket. Each and every action brings about a result, and together, cumulatively, they determine our experience. It's the same with negative actions. We shouldn't think, "Oh, it's just one action," or "It's such a small thing. It's inconsequential. It really doesn't matter if someone else is harmed." No action is so small that it should be disregarded; even a small spark can start a forest fire. Every single action, without exception, will bring about a result—its positive or negative effect—and collectively those add up. They will appear as our future experiences.

What we want, our heart's desire, is happiness. Yet we engage in actions that result in unhappiness. What we don't want is to suffer, yet we're constantly accumulating the causes for suffering. So when we investigate our actions, we see that what we do and what we want are often in opposition. We would already be happy if we had the true causes for happiness and no causes for suffering. So again, consider every action to be like planting seeds in the ground of consciousness. When the conditions supporting the seeds' growth unfold, they will manifest as the flowers or weeds of our experience. If we sow a poisonous seed, it will grow into a toxic plant. If we sow a medicinal seed, it will grow into a nourishing plant.

This is the very reason why, despite the fact that all living beings are in the pursuit of happiness, they aren't finding it. Even a fish swimming in the ocean is moving toward pleasure and away from pain. The method of pursuit may vary in complexity and intelligence based on the species, but ultimately the actions of every living being boil down to this fundamental desire.

If everyone is pursuing the goal of happiness, we may wonder, "Why aren't more people achieving it?" The answer is simple: we are not creating the causes for happiness. This is an important point to consider when thinking about karma, cause, and result. We need to look at the nature of each action, but we also need to look at the endlessness of cyclic existence. All beings have been caught up in it since beginningless time. When we act out of selfishness, jealousy, desire, anger, or other afflictive emotions or when we harm others to get what we want, we are ignoring the fact that we are forging a future of suffering. These actions will produce negative results. Regardless of how a result may look in the immediate situation, the true result will always be similar to the cause.

When we reflect on cause and result, we gain the insight that cyclic existence is entirely the product of our actions. We will also be inspired to take great care with every action. A practitioner who has spent time reflecting on karma will engage in as many positive actions as possible while avoiding harmful ones. When we focus on generating positive intentions[3] and engaging in positive actions, our entire experience will be transformed as we sow the seeds of happiness.

To practice this contemplation, sit down to meditate for a designated period of time. It's good to designate a specific amount of time in which you are committed to do nothing else but practice. This could be ten or fifteen minutes, thirty minutes or an hour. It's better to start with shorter periods of time and gradually increase as your capacity grows. Think about positive and negative actions and what defines them. What kinds of actions might be considered positive and why? Likewise, reflect on negative actions. What are the results that they bring? Analyze how actions are causes that produce results until the mind becomes tired or until you come to some insight. Then allow yourself to rest, not thinking about the past, not thinking about the present, and not thinking about the future. Simply rest in that insight right there. In this way, lead the mind to an understanding of how all our experiences are produced through previous actions and how all actions produce the future.

HOW TO PRACTICE

The Excellent Beginning

Sit in meditation posture to cultivate the key points of body and speech (see page 17 for a full explanation). Then, cultivate the key points of mind by setting your intention. Think, "In order to benefit all beings, I will realize that my every action is a cause, which will produce a future result, and act accordingly."

The Excellent Main Part

The following list summarizes the main concepts introduced in this chapter. Take one point at a time and pause to contemplate each. Occasionally, when you arrive at an insight or you tire of thinking, let go entirely. Don't think about the past, present, or future. Simply allow your mind to rest naturally without contrivance. When thoughts start moving again, pick up the contemplation where you left off and continue thinking about how actions are causes that produce similar results.

Key Points to Contemplate

- What is karma?
- Does everything have a cause and is everything a result?

- If there is a cause, are results inevitable?
- Are the immediate effects of an action the same as a karmic result?
- What kinds of actions would most likely produce happiness versus ones that produce suffering?

The Excellent Conclusion

Dedicate the merit generated by this practice and make aspirations. Think, "I dedicate the merit of this practice on karma, cause, and result to all beings that they may be freed from suffering and attain temporary and ultimate happiness." Then, make aspirations for the welfare and happiness of others. Think, "May all beings be happy and may all beings be free." (You can also use the dedication and aspiration prayers in appendix 5.)

Off the Cushion

Use this practice to change your perspective and transform your experience. To do so, build a habit of being aware that everything that happens to you is a result of a cause and that every single action you do will produce a similar result. Set a goal to remember karma as many times as you can in one day, such as once every hour, by relating to every experience as being a result and everything you do as being a cause. Then set the goal to do that for one week. Continue to extend this practice over time, habitually bringing to mind the infallibility of causes and results. For example, when you talk to someone, think, "These words will produce a like result that I will experience. Would I want to have someone speak to me like this?" Then, treat this person as you would wish to be treated.

When something disturbs you, pause. Give yourself a moment for perspective. Remember, "Everything I am experiencing now is the result of unknown previous actions. It is not random or unfair, even if it is difficult. A result can only happen when its cause is in place. By experiencing this now, I am exhausting my storehouse of previous negative actions." Then, reflect on how to respond to this situation.

What actions will you choose to take? What causes will you create for your future experiences? Think deeply about your reactions because they will become your future. Always act and react as you envision your future experiences to be.

4

Suffering:
The Unsatisfying Nature of All Things

The contemplation of impermanence dispels the belief that phenomena remain the same and that there should be a permanent circumstance to work toward. The contemplation of suffering addresses the notion that it is possible to find or create true and lasting happiness in this world. We need to acknowledge this assumption and then investigate it. Is it possible to achieve complete happiness within cyclic existence? Most people function under the expectation that their efforts to achieve happiness, if done right, will be successful. As a result, the vast majority of our actions, and most of our time and energy, are invested in worldly pursuits.

But just because we dedicate most of our lives to finding happiness within samsara doesn't mean it is possible to do so. Unfortunately, so many of us avoid the most important questions in life. Because we don't investigate enough, we assume that things exist exactly the way we perceive them to be. We operate under false assumptions, believing that things stay the same each moment, that a permanent, desirable situation can be created, and that happiness will result from worldly pursuits. Without looking deeply into any of those underlying beliefs, we pursue them. Ask yourself, "Can true and ultimate happiness be found here?"

Cyclic existence—samsara—or what we could call "the universe," is vast, and the living beings that inhabit it are innumerable. It is important to take into account the full scope of the universe and to reflect upon the perceptions and experiences of all living beings. Then ask yourself, "What are samsara's defining characteristics?"

No matter where we are born within cyclic existence, there is no place without suffering and no place where true happiness can be found. Every realm has some form of suffering. Each state of existence, in fact, is categorized and labeled based upon how much suffering is experienced by beings there.

THE SIX CATEGORIES OF BEINGS

The hellish states of existence, called *naraka* in Sanskrit, are defined by the suffering of intense cold or heat. The hungry-ghost realms, called *pretas*, are defined by the suffering of hunger, thirst, and discomfort. The animal realms are defined by the suffering of mental dullness, a lack of intelligence, and bewilderment. The human, demigod, and god realms—what we call the higher or more fortunate states—do not transcend suffering either. When compared with the less fortunate states, they seem better, but they still have a great amount of suffering. Any happiness or pleasure found in these more fortunate realms is temporary and does not last. The happiness experienced is by no means ultimate. It is impermanent by nature and, at the very least, will bring suffering when it ends. That is why happiness is entwined with suffering, why it's fraught with it. From this perspective, the defining characteristic of samsara is suffering. See appendix 3 for further description of the six classes of beings.

These states of existence are merely appearances resulting from our individual habitual tendencies. They are karmic appearances and nothing more than habits playing themselves out as our experience. They do not exist somewhere else, outside, as set environments. Nor are they created by someone else. Nobody made a hot hellish place for beings to languish. Nobody made the frozen, desolate lands where someone might suffer in naraka. Our individual actions form these myriad experiences. They are like dreams, the mind's own projections, completely personal and manifesting as experience and individual perception. These different states are no more real than the worlds we experience at night. In a nightmare, we experience fear and suffering because we believe what is happening is true. But the reality is that it's merely an appearance resulting from our mind's confusion and habitual patterns. It is nothing more than that. In fact, it is because we believe in the truth of those appearances that we react and experience suffering while dreaming. We can think of the hell realms in a similar way. These realms are not some external place created by someone else. Rather, they are appearances that result from one's own actions. They aren't ultimately true or valid. They arise in our perception based on habitual imprints—in other words, our karma. These realms are our mind's own manifestations and nothing more than that.

THE THREE KINDS OF SUFFERING

Another way to contemplate the suffering of cyclic existence is to consider the three kinds of suffering: the suffering of suffering, the suffering of change, and the all-pervasive suffering of everything composite. No state of existence is entirely devoid of these three.

The suffering of suffering refers to any experience that is unpleasant, unwanted, or painful. Every unpleasant sensation falls under this category. This is the obvious suffering that all beings experience to varying degrees at any time—heat, cold, hunger, thirst, birth, aging, sickness, death, and transmigration.[1] This type of suffering includes not only physical pain but also mental unhappiness such as depression, sadness, and the full range of disturbing emotions. Though the less fortunate realms are states in which beings predominantly experience suffering, the fortunate realms also have their share of suffering. As humans, for example, we have the suffering of birth, sickness, aging, and death. We also suffer from not getting what we want and from getting what we don't want.

Contemplate the suffering of suffering in this way by bringing to mind the specific and obvious suffering that different kinds of beings experience. Take this to a deeper and more personal level by thinking of a regular day in your life. Count all the sensations, positive and negative, physical and mental, that happen during the course of a day. Be honest with yourself and ask the question: "Do I experience more pleasant sensations or more unpleasant sensations?" Think carefully. Most of what we consider pleasant is actually an alleviation of a previous discomfort. Only a few moments are truly pleasurable or joyful. Even so, as humans, we have it better than most beings. In other states of existence, beings experience much more suffering of suffering.

The suffering of change is predominantly experienced by those of us in the higher and more fortunate states. This category of suffering actually involves pleasant sensations. Although we feel happiness, it never lasts, and we experience a great deal of anguish when it ends. Even if we recognize that we haven't found true and lasting happiness, we believe that it can be found somewhere. We tell ourselves that it's just around the corner. It will arrive when this situation ends or when that circumstance begins. We imagine that there is some great happiness to achieve in our lives, yet all the while, our lives are constantly fraught with problems. Whatever happiness we do experience eventually turns to suffering. At the very least, it doesn't last. It changes, and then we suffer.

For example, we may believe that getting a promotion or being voted into a position of power will bring us happiness. And if we succeed, we may be elated and happy about it—at least at first. But not long after assuming the position, we begin to experience the stress of the job and all the problems that come with it. It is the same with happiness gained from becoming famous or acquiring wealth. We start off feeling good, but then those feelings change and, before we know it, we find ourselves suffering. For another example, consider eating. We may have just had lunch. When we were eating, it tasted delicious, and it felt so good to get food into our stomach. But perhaps we overate. No matter how much we enjoyed eating, just moments later we may feel bloated and uncomfortable. The previous pleasant feeling has now changed to an unpleasant one. Even if we ate the right amount, we only feel satisfied for so long before we're hungry again. Whatever pleasant feelings we have while eating are actually a false sense of happiness because in reality, we are only alleviating our previous hunger pangs. Such happiness isn't true or lasting.

Another way to illustrate the suffering of change is to consider how you feel when you're complimented or criticized. When someone says something complimentary, we feel a moment of elation. But if a few minutes later someone puts us down, then that previous positive feeling disappears. Short-lived, pleasurable moments feel good at the time, but they don't provide any lasting or true peace and joy in the mind. As we discovered before, they are often not even overtly pleasant but instead merely a relief from previous discomfort. So even though the human state is called "fortunate," we're not overwhelmingly happy. There's nothing in this state that we can fully place our trust in or rely upon. There is no genuine, lasting happiness found in ordinary existence.

The all-pervasive suffering of everything composite is inherent in all phenomena.[2] This is not a direct sensation of pleasure or pain but instead the ever-present causes and conditions of suffering within each appearance.[3] Either the way we relate to them causes us mental suffering or in relation to them we create the causes for suffering. These are prevalent in all states of existence, high or low, occurring in every moment and in relation to everything and everyone that we connect with.

To see how everything we relate to is intertwined with suffering, look at the thoughts and feelings you experience in relation to possessions. Bring to mind something specific that you own, and examine your experience with that possession from the beginning, in the middle, and at the end. We suffer if we don't have a car, but if we have one, we suffer as well. We suffer if we don't have wealth, but we suffer if we have it too. Consider how much hardship you're willing to endure to accumulate money and to protect it. Think about all the time and effort—and the afflictive emotions—involved in acquiring it. Then, in the middle, once you have accumulated wealth or acquired something of value, you feel anxious about how to keep it. You worry, "What if I lose it? How can I protect it?" This is the suffering of ownership. At the same time, there is the suffering of trying to increase wealth. Then, in the end, there is the suffering from the inevitable loss or decline of it. At the very least, there's the suffering that comes from having to leave it all behind when we die. Compounding all of this, we may have engaged in negative actions to acquire that wealth, which will produce suffering in the future as well.

Look at the dream of owning a house. How many hours do you have to work to purchase the house? Then, once you own it, how much time and energy goes into maintaining it? How many expenses are associated with maintaining and repairing it? But owning a house isn't the only issue—now you have to furnish it as well. You've spent all that money on a new couch, table, and chairs. You want them to stay nice for as long as possible. How much mental space is taken up by worrying about and caring for those items? As time goes by, the house gets older, things break, and the list goes on. In other words, if we own a house, we have a house's worth of problems. If we have three houses, we have three houses' worth of suffering. It is the same with all possessions.

Everything is somehow related to suffering. Even a pair of shoes. If you have a pair of shoes, you have two shoes' worth of suffering. If you have a car, you have a car's worth of suffering. This is the all-pervasive suffering of everything composite.

As we contemplate and meditate on the three kinds of suffering, it's important to remember that these experiences are our mind's projections. There isn't a thing called suffering that exists outside of ourselves. Rather, our way of relating to the objects we perceive causes us to suffer. For this reason, we have different degrees of suffering in relation to different objects, and it is entirely possible not to suffer over them. Suffering is relative. It only exists "in the eye of the beholder." The value of this contemplation is that it helps us to become aware of the extent to which we suffer. It also reminds us that although suffering does not exist "out there," we still experience it. This knowledge engenders in us the determination to find freedom. It is possible.

As with each of the previous three contemplations, this fourth and final thought that changes the mind is most thoroughly integrated into our experience when we meditate by alternating between contemplation and resting. Sit down and reflect on each of the six classes of beings.

Think of the different kinds of suffering that characterizes each of their realms. Imagine yourself experiencing each of them. How would it be? Make sure to imagine it so thoroughly that you become convinced that there is no utopia in cyclic existence, no place where total happiness is found. Whenever you come to an insight or the mind tires of the evaluation, let yourself rest without thinking about the past, present, or future. When thoughts begin to stir, continue contemplating where you left off. In this way alternate between contemplative meditation and resting meditation.

THE WISDOM OF THE FOUR THOUGHTS

The purpose of this investigation is to examine the basic characteristics of cyclic existence and to realize its inherent pitfalls. The four thoughts that change the mind—precious human birth; impermanence; karma, cause, and result; and suffering—are called that because they change the mind's attachment to not just the less fortunate states but to the whole of cyclic existence. We need to overcome this intense attachment because if our mind doesn't change, we will continue to fall into the problems of existence. We will remain bound to cycle through the different states of existence because of our pursuit of forms, sounds, tastes, scents, tactile sensations, and all our other worldly concerns. For example, when we see a beautiful form, we want it, just like a moth's fatal attraction to a flame. Or when we grasp for a tactile sensation, we are like a hot elephant stepping into a cool, muddy bog in which it becomes stuck and cannot escape. Or when we crave a delicious taste, we are like a fish caught on a hook when enticed with bait. Whenever we encounter any of the five desirable sense pleasures, our mind becomes overwhelmed with desire and we engage in the very actions that produce all of our problems and prevent us from finding freedom. These form intense and pervasive habits in the field of our mind that cause us to repeat these actions over and over and keep creating the interdependent causes and conditions for all future births.

No matter how much we do here, we just keep cycling. There is no ultimate fruition or end, and we constantly perpetuate suffering. Once we recognize this, we become aware that there is nothing here that will fulfill our ultimate wish. There is nothing to grasp onto or rely upon. Everything is fallible, false, and deceptive, and no ultimate meaning can be found.

The immediate effect of this knowledge is that it tames the mind, and we experience less suffering. Diligent investigation leads to a greater wish to be free, which becomes the impetus for practice. This understanding is also the basis for transforming adversity into the path. This is what inspires us to search for ultimate truth, to seek out what is infallible, unchanging, and absolute.

We might wonder, "Can we find ultimate truth?" Yes, we can. That's exactly why we examine our experience from the perspective of these four thoughts. It will enable us to discover what is ultimately meaningful, and it's the basis for our pursuit of the path. Each reflection helps us to see the world in accordance with the way things are, which in turn tames the mind and decreases our suffering. These thoughts also show us the necessity of finding liberation from suffering.

In other words, we will gain wisdom, and from that comes many positive qualities. For example, our compassion increases as we become aware of what beings undergo in cyclic existence. We can empathize and see the experiences, perceptions, and sensations of other beings. We come to realize that just as we don't want to suffer, no beings want to suffer. When we truly see that, we wish for all beings to be free from suffering. True compassion arises. That's why it is important to contemplate and reflect in a very personal and vivid way. It is true that we all suffer, even though none of us want to. We are powerless in that regard. We want to find happiness, but we aren't finding it. This reality is worthy of great compassion.

HOW TO PRACTICE

The Excellent Beginning

Sit in meditation posture to cultivate the key points of body and speech (see page 17 for a full explanation). Then, cultivate the key points of mind by setting your intention. Think, "In order to benefit all beings, I will realize the unfulfilling nature of existence."

The Excellent Main Part

Review the following list of the concepts introduced in this chapter by reading one point at a time, alternating between contemplative meditation and resting meditation.

Key Points to Contemplate

- Consider the characteristics of cyclic existence—can true and ultimate happiness be found here?
- What are the six categories of beings and what kinds of sufferings are experienced by each?
- What are three kinds of suffering?
- What are the benefits of understanding the suffering in cyclic existence?

The Excellent Conclusion

Dedicate the merit generated by this practice and make aspirations. Think, "I dedicate the merit of this practice on suffering to all beings that they may be freed from suffering and attain temporary and ultimate happiness." Then, make aspirations for the welfare and happiness of others. Think, "May all beings be happy and may all beings be free." (You can also use the dedication and aspiration prayers in appendix 5.)

Off the Cushion

Relate to everything from the perspective of the three kinds of suffering. If you are enjoying something, remember you can't keep it forever and make a point to appreciate it more. If you are disturbed about something, pause. Adjust your perspective. Reflect on these points: We suffer when our expectations of samsara are not met. We struggle when we expect samsara to be a source of joy when it is actually a source of suffering. If we didn't have unreasonable expectations of samsara, we wouldn't be so disappointed. Bring these reflections and an awareness of the three kinds of suffering to every challenging situation.

You can also increase your acceptance of suffering by comparing your suffering to that of other living beings. Considering the experiences of those in the less fortunate realms may not end suffering, but it can help put your situation into perspective. Compare the weight of all phenomena in the universe, beginningless and endless cycles of existence, to this one single moment. Ask yourself, "When I die, will my reaction to this situation have been worthwhile or will it have created more suffering in the present and the causes for future suffering?" Use whatever understanding of suffering you have to talk yourself out of a negative reaction in the moment.

PART TWO

MIND FREEING MIND: THE PRACTICE

THE SECOND KEY POINT
The Actual Practice, Training in Bodhichitta

Freedom doesn't come from external circumstances—it comes from within. Practice is the process of our mind freeing itself through great compassion and profound wisdom. To succeed, we must transcend theoretical concepts and make these teachings our direct experience.

5

Ultimate Bodhichitta: The True Nature of Reality

Finding freedom begins with the wish to be free from suffering. The main practices that lead to this are those that cultivate the awakened mind, or *bodhichitta* in Sanskrit. Buddhist teachings describe two aspects of bodhichitta: relative and ultimate. Although "The Seven Key Points of Mind Training" emphasizes training in relative bodhichitta, it also includes explanations of ultimate bodhichitta so that we learn to integrate the practices in wisdom right from the start. Relative bodhichitta is an attitude of great compassion for sentient beings. Ultimate bodhichitta is the wisdom that realizes the true nature of reality. These teachings contain instructions for cultivating each aspect of bodhichitta through both formal meditation and informal practice in day-to-day life.

Because the ultimate nature is so profound, we first need to refine and tame our mind in order to realize it. This is achieved by giving rise to relative bodhichitta. Once we have trained thoroughly in the relative bodhichitta practices of loving-kindness and compassion, we will see that to benefit others in the ultimate sense, we must realize the true nature of all things. This is the aim of mind training—ultimate bodhichitta. As the coarse layers of our obscurations are refined away, realization will gradually awaken within us.

Though the practice itself begins with relative bodhichitta, the root text for the seven key points starts with an explanation of how to practice ultimate bodhichitta. This concise presentation is extremely profound, so you are not expected to gain full comprehension from this explanation alone. Most practitioners are unable to realize ultimate truth without first having tamed their mind through the practices of relative bodhichitta. Ultimate bodhichitta is introduced here in order to inspire you to engage in the gradual stages that lead to the realization of wisdom. Later, it needs to be studied in much greater detail.

RELATIVE AND ULTIMATE TRUTH

To understand ultimate bodhichitta correctly, we need to understand the two truths: *relative truth* and *ultimate truth*. The way things appear—all appearances and perceptions—comprise relative truth. The way things are—the absolute nature of appearances and mind—is ultimate truth. Relative truth encompasses all the deluded, dualistic experiences of samsara, including concepts of perceiver and perceived, or subject and object.[1] Our experience of objects and our mind that perceives them is relative.

The Tibetan word *kun-dzob* is translated as "relative truth," but it literally means "all false truth." Our experience is false because it is based on a nonrecognition of true nature and is thus distorted, fabricated, not absolute, and not identical to others' experience. Our previous exploration of the four thoughts, which examine the nature of the way things appear, offers some illumination on this. Through continued reflection, we come to see more and more clearly that appearances and objects of mind are transitory, unreliable, and fallible. Moreover, the dualistic appearances of samsara are rooted in a nonrecognition of true nature, often translated as ignorance. Ignorance is also defined as the belief that things are opposite to what they actually are.

On a subtle and imperceptible level, and at more gross levels, we believe phenomena to be what they are not. Through the power of misapprehending phenomena, a belief in the identity of self and other is born. On that basis, all disturbing emotions form. And, when disturbing emotions are present, negative actions will inevitably follow. The results of these actions are infallible and manifest as the myriad appearances of cyclic existence. It all begins with a false perception, which produces a false sense of reality. Since the root cause of relative truth, the dualistic mind, is mistaken, then what comes from the dualistic mind is not true. That's why it's called relative or all-false truth. Also, because everything perceptible is composite, all phenomena appear to be born or produced, to have a duration and a cessation. But none of that can be ultimately relied upon. This is relative truth.

Ultimate truth, *don-dam*, translated as "ultimate" or "absolute," refers to the true nature of appearances, or the way things actually are. Because ultimate truth is the inherent nature of perceiver and perceived, it's always the case. It's not produced and does not cease. It's undeceiving, unchanging, and unfailing. It is the way things are, the absolute nature.

The intention of authentic meditation is to lead us to progressively deeper insights, beginning with what is relatively true and culminating in the wisdom that realizes what is ultimately true. The mind that realizes true nature is called supreme wisdom, or *prajna* in Sanskrit. Only knowing (supreme wisdom) can eliminate unknowing (ignorance). Being in opposition, these two ways of seeing things cannot coexist. Ignorance is the source of all suffering, and supreme wisdom is the source of freedom from suffering.

1. *Consider all phenomena to be like a dream.*

Our mental habit is to believe that whatever we perceive in the world is valid and true. Typically, we believe that everything we see is real and we relate to everything based on the seeming truth of the way things appear to us. These perceptions are what we call relative reality. We don't bother to question or investigate those perceptions. Whatever our consciousness experiences, whether images, sounds, tastes, smells, or tactile sensations, we feel that these objects truly exist outside of ourselves. When we examine them thoroughly, though, we will find that this is not the case. The entire universe and all beings are appearances that manifest through ingrained habits imprinted within our mind. These habits are projected onto our experiences. Our mind then becomes confused about the nature of these appearances and takes them to be real. As long as we don't question reality, as long as we persist in not investigating and examining everything, as long as we assume that phenomena are what we believe them to be—for that long, we will suffer.

It is the same when we dream. When dreaming, we experience joy and sorrow even though they are nothing more than our mind's projections. This occurs because our habitual tendencies are projected as the dream world. For as long as we don't realize we are dreaming, we won't question the appearances, and we will believe our dreams to be real. But the moment we wake up, we know the experience was false and no longer suffer over it or become attached to it. The main difference between dreams and waking life is that we have the habit of believing our waking experiences are true. But in terms of their actual nature, there is no difference at all.

When we investigate appearances from the perspective of what is ultimately true, we see that by their very nature, all appearances are empty of inherently existing. Dreams are a great illustration for relative reality. Another illustration is the reflection of the moon on water. These examples reveal to us how we can perceive something clearly and distinctly, even though it doesn't exist. The truth we invest in it doesn't equate with what is actually happening.

The phrase *all phenomena* in the root text describes the objects of perception, including the outer universe and every being within it. In this context, it means everything that is not mind.[2] All the objects we perceive arise from confusion. Since phenomena lack the existence we attribute to them, they are no more real than a dream.

WHEN IS A HOUSE A HOUSE?

What would it mean if something or someone had inherent or true existence? It would mean that the object—be it a sentient being, a tangible thing, or a situation—would have to be completely independent of everything else. It could not be dependent upon any other factor to exist.

It could neither be a product of causes or conditions, nor could it be defined in relation to something or someone else. To truly exist, its nature could not be relative.

When investigating this object, we would have to be able to establish clear proof that it ultimately exists as that thing, no matter what the situation or who is perceiving it. To truly exist, we would all have to perceive it as exactly the same. The object would not be relative to us but would exist independently. Typically, this is how we relate to everything and everyone. We believe things and people exist as being exactly how they appear to our perception, when in fact, they do not.

If we begin to investigate our experience from the ultimate perspective, we will see that our perceptions have nothing to do with how things actually are. Take, for example, the concept of a house. When we see a house, we automatically assume that it exists. "There is a house," we think. However, if we examine the house more closely, we will see that it is merely a conceptual label projected by the mind based upon a perceived object. We perceive a house, but we can't actually find a single object existing autonomously that can be called "house."

When looking carefully at this object called "house," we see a conglomeration of many parts and subparts. Which part is actually the house? Is the floor the house? Are the walls the house? Is the ceiling the house? Or perhaps the building materials are the house? Is the wood the house? Or the drywall or nails? Consider every part and ask yourself, "Which part is the house?" Examine closely, because if a house exists, we should be able to find it. But instead we find that each part has its own conceptual label and is not the house. So the house is not the parts that compose it. Still, when you cannot find the house in those parts, continue looking. Consider that for a house to exist, it must either be identical to the parts that compose it or something other than those parts. If it exists as something other than those parts, where is it? You might think that although each individual part is not the house, when all the parts are gathered together in a specific shape, to serve a specific function, then there is a house. If you've come to that conclusion, then you agree that there is no single thing called "house" that exists in and of itself.

We can also examine the parts that compose this so-called house. Take a wall, for example. Notice how the mind automatically assumes that a wall exists. Now look closer. Where is the wall? Is the wall the top section or the bottom section? Is it the outside surface or the components inside? If you look at the different aspects of the wall—the top, bottom, inside, and outside—you have four different labels. The concept of a wall has been replaced with four other concepts.

Continue to investigate the building materials and try to find the wall. Is the wood the wall? Is the drywall the wall? Is the insulation the wall? Obviously, none of these parts are the wall. So where is this wall? If it exists, we should be able to find it. Is the wall identical to its parts or is it distinct from them? If the wall and its parts are identical, then every piece of wood in the frame could be called "wall." But if the wall is separate from its parts, then where is it? All we can say is that when certain materials are gathered in a specific way, we call it a "wall," but other than that label, there is no wall that exists as a specific, independent, single object.

Keep going with this kind of analysis, breaking down each component of any phenomena into parts and subparts. Each label will disappear as it is replaced by new labels. No matter how hard we try, we will find that we never land upon a single object that exists in the way that we have labeled it. This insight is the first step to seeing the false nature of appearances. We assume that objects, such as houses and walls, are real and exist the way that we conceive them. But as we can see from our analysis of these objects, we are merely labeling the way things appear on the coarsest level. We are not seeing the way things actually are.

So, we will never find an actual thing that exists; rather, we will discover the object is merely appearing, dependent on many factors. This is called interdependent origination. Because things appear in relation to each other, they have no independent or autonomous existence. All we can say is that phenomena arise interdependently and therefore do not ultimately exist. The house is only perceived as a house if it has walls, windows, and a front door. The front door is only perceived as a front door if it is placed in a specific location. So the house arises interdependently with the walls, windows, and front door. There is no house that exists by virtue of its own nature, because if there were, it would have to be completely independent. It could not exist in relation to anything else.

The language we use to ascribe characteristics to phenomena are also mutually dependent designations, which is another reason they occur interdependently. "Beautiful" is a concept that exists only in relation to "ugly." "Tall" only exists in relation to "short." We understand these concepts only in relation to their opposites. Without "big," we could not have "small." None of these labels exist or are used independently; they are dependent upon something else.

Take, for example, an illusion. A magician will use space, substances, light, smoke, and whatever else is needed to create an illusion. When all the right conditions are gathered, we might see a horse or an elephant or a cow. Even though these images are an illusion and don't actually exist, we still experience them. They appear clearly to our senses because of interdependence. The mere appearance of phenomena and the fact that they can be experienced by our senses doesn't mean they must actually exist there.

Looking at the reflection of our face in a mirror is another example of interdependence. To create this reflection, we need a number of interdependent factors—the shiny and reflective surface of the mirror, our physical form before it, the light, and so forth. When interdependence is just right, we can see our face on the mirror although no actual face exists in the mirror. We know that what appears arises due to interdependence, that there is actually no object there. It is the same with all of our experiences. Since nothing in our experience can be found to exist in and of itself, we say that appearances are false or empty of inherent existence.

EVERYTHING IS EMPTY

The concept of emptiness, or *shunyata* in Sanskrit, takes some study to properly understand, but it is important to recognize that emptiness in this context does not mean nothingness.[3] It does not mean that something was destroyed and therefore no longer exists, nor does it imply empty space, voidness, or nonexistence. After all, you can only conceive of nonexistence in relation to existence and vice versa. So nonexistence cannot be the ultimate nature of the way things are, because it has a dependent relationship with another concept. This view is explained in the *Heart Sutra*, which reads, "Form is emptiness; emptiness is form. Emptiness is not other than form, and form is not other than emptiness." [4] All perceptions are empty by nature, yet they appear. Form and emptiness are not two separate things or two sides of a coin. They are one and the same.

The first time I heard about emptiness I was a young monk, and I was very naughty. One time, the older monks were called to a teaching while we younger ones were told to go play outside. But I wanted to know what the older monks were doing, so I spied on them through a crack in the door. I remember the lama saying, "Everything is empty." And then he gave meditation instructions for practicing this. I decided that I wanted to try it too. I went to a hilltop and followed his advice, allowing my gaze to rest on the empty space in front. I thought that space was the emptiness. It felt good, but the mountain on the horizon kept getting in the way. I thought, "If only that mountain weren't there, then I could meditate on the emptiness that's on the other side of the mountain too!" It wasn't until years later, after receiving many more detailed instructions, that I realized that the problem was not that the mountain was appearing but that the appearance itself was empty. That mountain was never actually in my way!

It is important to apply the view of emptiness toward the objects we feel the strongest attachment or aversion to, such as our body. Consider how much we cherish our body. We grasp it more tightly than any other object. We think, "This is my body!" We assume that our bodies exist in the way we perceive them, but if we investigate, we cannot find a body that is separate from the individual parts—from arms and fingers to heart and bones to individual blood cells, and so on. Each part has its own name. So, where is the body? Although we fixate on the body and think of it (and ourselves) as a singular existent thing, no single thing exists independent of all other body parts that we can identify as a body. Isn't it amazing that we spend so much time fussing over something that can never be found?

It's important to remember that this process is not intended to deny the fact that we experience these objects. We cannot refute—on a relative level—that we have a body; it appears to us due to interdependent causes and conditions. The question is whether the way we relate to our body or other objects accords with their true nature. Consider the following example. Imagine if someone, walking at dusk, stumbles across a thin striped rope in the grass and mistakes it for a snake. Their reaction might be to panic. (At least that's how a Tibetan would react. Those of us from the Himalayas are terrified of snakes!) If, after that initial freak out, they investigate the snake with a flashlight and discover there is only a rope in the grass, their previous concept of a snake, which was based on misperception, immediately vanishes. The suffering and fear the original thought produced disappears along with it. The idea of the snake is replaced with a new thought, "It is a rope," and with this new concept comes all of the corresponding mental states and experiences. The habit to grasp to things as real is so strong that as soon as the concept of a "real" snake ceases, another concept about a different "real" object immediately replaces it.

Now we turn the investigation to our new concept of a rope. We can see that the rope is actually made up of multiple strands of colored string braided together. As soon as we pull it apart, the previous concept of a rope is replaced with the concept of red, white, and blue strings. If the rope existed as a single object in and of itself, we would be able to find it, but instead we find strings. Now, look at the strings. Cutting them up, we find that they are actually strands of fiber. As soon as we arrive here, our idea of string is replaced with a new concept. If we keep investigating, dissecting all the way to atomic particles and beyond, we still won't ever arrive at a single, independently existing object. If we consider each concept carefully, from the snake down to the tiniest particle, we will see that nothing can be found. The value of taking the time to break down each level of misconception is that it leads us to deeper and deeper understanding of emptiness. This is necessary because each layer of mistaken assumptions about the nature of appearances is an underlying cause for our suffering, which will not end until we clear away this confusion.

If we begin to comprehend this view with thorough investigation, we will develop a basic understanding of the way things are, and we will arrive at the meaning of emptiness. But if we do not examine phenomena, we will continue to misapprehend reality. In addition, merely reading this teaching will not be enough to change our perceptions. To fully realize emptiness, seek out and study other teachings such as the *Heart Sutra* or other Buddhist texts on emptiness from the genre known as Madhyamika, or the Middle Way approach. These teachings investigate the nature of reality in an accurate and detailed manner. Studying them will benefit our training, because if we develop a deep knowledge of true nature, it will help us to tame our mind. In addition, for practitioners who are training in other Buddhist practices within the sutras and tantras, understanding this view correctly is critical. It is the underlying principle of all practice. For the purpose of this text, we can think of this concise teaching as a means to inspire us to develop more wisdom.

The search for ultimate truth begins by contemplating the nature of the outer world, the objects surrounding us. These contemplations on false labels and concepts are like a spark that will begin to ignite realization within us. Study teachings like this again and again and repeatedly apply these methods until you have determined that all phenomena are like a dream.

2. Examine the fundamental nature of unborn mind.

Once we discover that outer objects do not ultimately exist, we turn our attention to our mind. Does the perceiver of these objects exist? If we examine carefully, we will see that, like objects, the mind appears due to interdependent factors and has no independent existence of its own. It, too, is empty. We cannot find a mind that exists independently. When we don't realize this, we believe in what we think and we believe in our emotions, which are a main source of suffering.

Let's start by examining our emotional reactions. When an emotion occurs, our mind fixates on the perceived object that inspired the emotion. How we experience this object derives from our belief that the object actually exists, which we addressed in the previous contemplation.

We also have mental habits—beliefs, concepts, feelings—that arise in relation to what we perceive. So right from the outset we begin to see that our perceptions do not exist independently. They occur due to many causes and conditions.

Take anger, for example. Anger arises when we perceive an object, such as a person, place, or thing, that we don't like. Our previous habits and concepts about the object reinforce our dislike of it, and as these causes and conditions come together, we become angry. Therefore, anger only occurs in dependence upon and in relation to other factors. Does this anger have true existence? Is it actually somewhere? We assume the emotion is valid and real, and we attribute an identity to it. We think, "I'm so angry," and we continue to reinforce and solidify the emotion. But if anger possessed inherent existence, it would not arise in relation to anything else. It would be permanent and autonomous. It would exist in and of itself. Yet we know that anger only occurs when interdependent causes and conditions converge. When certain factors are present, we experience anger, but when they are absent, we don't. This shows us that anger is not an independently existent thing.

Continue searching for the nature of anger. The moment you experience anger, look directly at it and attempt to determine its characteristics. What is anger exactly? Does it have a shape or a color? Think about its source: Where was this anger before I experienced it? Is there a place where anger originates? Think about its residence: Where is this anger while I experience it? Does it have a specific location where it abides? Does it exist inside the body or outside of it? When the feeling of anger subsides, where does it go? Is there some *thing* that goes some *where*? Investigate! Search for it. Be thorough. Continue to look for anger until you conclude that you cannot find its origin, its residence, or the location of its cessation.

We can use this contemplation to work with any emotion, though it is particularly helpful when you feel strong emotions such as desire, anger, or jealousy. Whenever a disturbing emotion arises, stop focusing on the feeling and justifying a negative response. Instead, look at the emotion just as it is. See that it holds no truth. When you arrive at this insight, let the mind rest. According to the Mahayana,[5] when we rest the mind at the moment an insight is generated, we call this "profound insight meditation," or *vipashyana* in Sanskrit. The term can also be translated as "seeing more," which means that, as we meditate, we are seeing more than our ordinary perception; we are seeing the way things are. Do this every time you investigate your mind and arrive at some understanding. When you cannot prove that mind exists or when you have a glimpse of mind's empty nature, let the mind rest. Allow yourself to be absorbed in this understanding. In this way, join contemplative meditation with resting meditation and bring an intellectual understanding of emptiness into your experience.

You can also apply this search-and-discovery process to all mental states. No matter what aspect of mind we look into, be it positive, negative, or neutral thoughts or emotions, we will discover the same thing. So now we can see that disturbing emotions and our emotional responses come from our belief in the reality of what is perceived and in the inherent existence of the perceiver. As we develop deeper insight, the wisdom generated will counteract disturbing emotions.

For the practice to be effective in clearing away negative emotions, we need to develop stable insight. Applying the practice once or twice won't tame the mind. Profound insight deepens over time as we engage in repetitive training. Once we have developed certainty about the empty nature of mind, negative emotions will subside the moment they arise, and the mind will be released from their influence. Such emotions will be experienced as insubstantial and will no longer have power over us.

This insight is not something that can be produced or contrived. We discover it as we search for and gradually uncover the empty nature of mind. Once we recognize this nature, we can allow our mind to rest totally in the fundamental nature of unborn mind.

3. Even the remedy naturally subsides on its own.

Through each of these steps, we are slowly dismantling our concepts, beginning with the objects of perception and continuing on to the perceiving mind. Yet even as we deconstruct these notions, our mind tends to grasp for something that is real and true. We might now grasp at the wisdom that remedies our suffering and afflictions. We might think: "The perception of emptiness exists. This insight is true." But if we look carefully at the wisdom, we will see that it too, like everything else, merely occurs due to a gathering of interdependent causes and conditions. If mind cannot be found, then wisdom, which is a component of that mind, is equally impossible to find. Look at the remedy itself. Examine it until you resolve that it too is empty by nature. By allowing the mind to rest in that final insight, even the remedy naturally subsides on its own.

4. Rest in the true essence, the ongoing state of the ground of being.

Up until this point, we've been developing an understanding that the way we perceive things is not in accord with the way things actually are. To help put this into context, here's a summary of the steps. First, we investigate the nature of objective appearances to discover that they are like a dream. Second, we investigate the nature of both conceptual and nonconceptual mind to determine mind's unborn nature. Third, we investigate the nature of the investigator of that true nature—wisdom, the remedy to ignorance—to see that it too is empty. The final practice is to immerse ourselves in the wisdom that knows that nature by simply allowing the mind to settle within that insight.

The first three steps are called contemplative meditation because they involve study and analysis to discover the nature of objects, the mind that perceives them, and the wisdom that knows true nature itself. This generates the wisdom of study and contemplation. The last step does not involve investigation; it's what follows the investigations, when the mind can rest in that knowing of emptiness without analysis. It is simply being in the knowing and resting there uncontrived, like water merging into water, without the duality of perceiver and perceived.

Meditation is always preceded by knowledge. We study and contemplate something until we understand it, and then we blend it with our mind in order to directly experience that truth. The process of blending is meditation.

Some people say they don't want to engage in investigation and analysis because it's too conceptual. This is a huge mistake! How can you do wisdom practice without wisdom? Without first arriving at an insight about true nature through study and contemplation, what insight are we bringing into our experience through meditation? Without the correct view, we cannot have correct meditation. Without correct meditation, we won't have correct conduct.[6] In short, if our knowledge of true nature—what we call the view—is not clear, our entire practice of the path will be mistaken.

When we train our minds, our approach to the view evolves as we gain more experience and insight. Initially, we should spend most of our time focusing on contemplative meditation, engaging in longer periods of investigation and shorter periods of resting. As our understanding grows, we should spend about half of our time investigating and half of our time resting. Eventually, our study and practice will lead us to develop utter conviction about the nature of emptiness. Once total certainty is gained, we can simply recollect the view and then rest, immersed in this insight.

Until you are absolutely certain, question everything. Continue to study the meaning of emptiness and constantly apply the various lines of reasoning to every aspect of your life. If we don't investigate the nature of things, we won't gain true understanding and confidence. It is not enough to be told about the view or to simply believe in it. We can only cut through our doubts if we find the answers to our questions. Our mind will be liberated only if we come to realize the true nature for ourselves. That's why we have to go through the stages of investigation and meditation in order to bring an end to mistaken views and to remove disturbing emotions and suffering. Without developing absolute certainty in this view, meditation will not have power and it will not be effective. If our meditation is ineffective, how can it possibly free us from the powerful grasp of cyclic existence?

Finding freedom does not mean that we run away or escape to another country. We don't need to drive out of town or fly somewhere far away. True escape is found within the mind itself. It comes from ridding ourselves of our flaws, overcoming disturbing emotions, and ending harmful actions so that we no longer experience their results. This is what it means to end the cycle of existence. By engaging in study, contemplation, and meditation, we set in motion the process that achieves this result.

BUDDHA NATURE

If we engage thoroughly in the formal contemplative practice of ultimate bodhichitta, we will discover the nature of reality. Then, without the need to investigate further, we can simply rest in the ongoing awareness of ultimate truth. Eventually, our understanding will evolve into a direct experience of not only the empty nature of all phenomena but also of the absolute nature of mind. Once at this stage, the need to investigate will become less necessary. Recognizing buddha nature, the ultimate truth, is the final aim of mind training. True meditation is based on wisdom.

What is buddha nature? Its essence is *emptiness* and its nature is *clear luminosity.* These two qualities are not actually separate, so true nature is described as the unity of emptiness and clarity.[7] It is free from all ordinary conceptual frameworks and elaborations. It is the ultimate nature of mind, just as it is, uncontrived, resting in its own ground. Through practice, the conditions that obscure us from seeing and experiencing mind's true nature are gradually refined away. As we gain more subtle levels of experience, eventually we will see mind's essence.

In the Mantrayana teachings, also known as the path of secret mantra,[8] a teacher might directly point out the true nature of mind. The instructions for this are not given here, but it is important to understand how the two systems of practice relate to each other. A practitioner who is ready to enter Mantrayana receives the necessary transmissions and then practices what are called the development and completion stages.[9] These practices mature and refine the mind of the practitioner so that when the nature of mind is introduced by a qualified teacher, the student has a direct experience of it.[10] Typically, under the guidance of such a teacher, a practitioner would complete a series of preliminary practices, or *ngondro*, taught in this approach, which are particularly effective for preparing the mind to receive instructions on the ultimate nature of mind. These are more elaborate than those practiced here in the mind-training approach and are taught in other contexts.

The teachings are given in this way because we need to learn to work with the mind as it is now before receiving such profound instructions. We need to go through some degree of training to transform and refine our minds. When we practice lojong, we gather an immense amount of merit and purify many obscurations, which prepares us to see the nature of mind when it is pointed out. But if we don't train our minds, it's unlikely we'll be able to grasp the instructions.

All mind training leads us to an understanding of true nature, the sublime unity of emptiness and luminosity. In this realization, there is nothing to do and nothing to make, nothing to abandon and nothing to adopt. No ordinary mental processes apply to ultimate nature because it is timeless and uncontrived, and it has always been present. This final contemplations on ultimate bodhichitta, *Rest in true essence, the ongoing state of the ground of being*, pertains to a practitioner at this level, one who is able to rest uncontrived with an ongoing awareness of mind's true nature. Such a practitioner no longer needs to do analytical meditation.

In order to develop the capacity to recognize ultimate nature, we must work with our mind and begin to clear away obscurations and negativity. This process will allow our mind to become clearer and our understanding to deepen and grow.

5. *During post-meditation, see everything as an illusion.*

Formal meditation is when we sit down and focus solely on a practice, such as contemplative and resting meditation. Post-meditation, or what we call informal practice, refers to the rest of the day, anytime we are not sitting on a meditation cushion.

The wisdom we generate by formally meditating is not intended to be left on the cushion. The dedicated focus of formal meditation has great value, and it's absolutely necessary to progress, but so is daily integration. It's essential to bring wisdom to each and every moment and situation, to every aspect of our lives throughout the day. If we don't, even though we may undergo some transformation through formal training, it won't be enough to totally change our mind. A habit can only be overridden by a stronger habit. If our habit is to practice for just one hour out of every twenty-four, we will be like a rubber band that is stretched then released right back to how it was before. Our mind will revert to its ordinary perceptions in daily life. It's common for people to meditate a little, and even to see a small improvement, but then to become ensnared in negative thoughts during the rest of the day. They end up having a constant stream of disturbing emotions because they misperceive the nature of reality. We forget to practice, which means we don't turn our insights into our experience, and we forget the view. Then we may feel as if practice is futile because, although we meditate formally on the view again and again and have some understanding, we haven't developed further.

It is important not to mistake understanding for realization. We may understand emptiness, at least on an intellectual level, and we may develop that understanding through contemplation and resting meditation, but if we lose that when we engage in the rest of our life—the time when we most need wisdom—then we have not realized anything. In some ways, post-meditation is the most important part of the practice because it makes up the majority of our day. It's also when we encounter situations that really test our mind and reveal where we're at and what we need to work on.

When everything is going great in our lives and we sit down to meditate and it feels good, we might think that our wisdom is progressing. This good feeling is supported by removing all distractions and being quiet and comfortable. In those moments, we feel like our meditation is really good, but actually, that doesn't mean our practice has progressed at all. It's easy to practice when everything is just right. But a good feeling isn't how we measure progress. We measure it at other times, when we are really struggling and bombarded with a seemingly endless stream of unwanted circumstances. That's when we know how strong our practice is. It is during difficult times more than ever that we need to put great effort into remembering the wisdom insights and applying them with special care.

POST-MEDITATION PRACTICE

We need to bring whatever understanding we have of ultimate nature into our present experience. That is what it means to do post-meditation practice: to regard all phenomena as illusory. Like dreams, all of our experiences lack inherent existence on every level. We know that the objects that manifest in our dreams do not exist. Our waking experience is no different in terms of its true nature. If we were to wake from it, we would see just that.

When we investigate, we can see this truth. Appearances and perceptions arise and are experienced, but when we look, we see they do not have any inherent truth. They don't ultimately exist as they appear, yet still, they are experienced, like reflections in a mirror. There is no actual physical form in the mirror, yet there it appears. You could also compare the illusory nature of phenomena to an echo. Yell in a canyon and the sound of your voice will reverberate back. Investigate that echo. Where is it? Is it in the rocks or outside of them? Or maybe it's between the rocks? You can't find any place where the sound waves actually exist. To practice wisdom in post-meditation, recognize what appears to be like an illusion, a dream, the reflection in a mirror, or an echo.

To integrate insight into our lives, we need two tools: mindfulness and vigilant guard. To be mindful means to remember the methods for taming the mind and cultivating its positive potential in any situation.[11] Remember the techniques you have learned and apply them right at the moment you need them. Being mindful means to not forget the practice.

Vigilant guard is what we use to check on our mindfulness. It means to be aware of the state of our body, speech, and mind at any given moment. It's like a sentry walking around a castle. Every few minutes the sentry checks the gates to make sure all is secure. In the castle of our mind, the vigilant guard checks the gate of every situation and asks: "What is the state of my mind? What am I doing? Why am I doing this?" When we are vigilant in this way, we will see that either mindfulness is in place or that it has been forgotten. If mindfulness has slipped away, we should reinstate it immediately.

Practicing dharma depends upon mindfulness and vigilant guard. Since everything is contingent on presence of mind, self-evaluation is critical. How many times a day do you remember the practice with mindfulness? How many times a day do you check the state of your thoughts and actions through vigilant guard? Between the time you wake in the morning and the time you fall asleep at night, you have countless thoughts and emotions. How many of them are positive? How often do you cultivate the practice? It's worthwhile to take notice. Sometimes you might notice that an entire day has passed and you haven't practiced for a single moment. The goal is to have mindfulness continually, no matter what we are doing. If we can achieve this level of mindfulness, our lives and practice will become one.

At first, it's really hard to practice all the time because our minds are so untamed. We haven't yet developed a habit for practice, and we're not used to working with the mind in this way. We may find that we have mindfulness and vigilance just once a day, maybe when we wake up or before we go to sleep at night. It's also possible that days or weeks go by without even once recalling the practice.

Practice is a habit. To form it, begin with the intention to be mindful and vigilant. Think, "I am going to cultivate mindfulness and vigilant guard." Then try to reaffirm that commitment as much as possible. When you wake in the morning, make the commitment for the day. As you remember more and more to check and cultivate mindfulness, the habit will slowly grow. Eventually, there won't be any situations in which you forget to practice. Your experience will become an uninterrupted stream of mindfulness. Practice will always be a component of whatever is going on.

HOW TO PRACTICE

The Excellent Beginning

Sit in meditation posture to cultivate the key points of body and speech (see page 17 for a full explanation). Then, cultivate the key points of mind by setting your intention. Think, "In order to benefit all beings, I will realize the ultimate nature of all things."

The Excellent Main Part

In the following list, review the concepts introduced in this chapter by reading one point at a time, alternating between contemplative meditation and resting meditation.

A brief summary of this section: Training in ultimate bodhichitta consists of five statements, which provide a guideline for the process of generating ultimate bodhichitta. The statements 1, 2, and 3 pertain to formal contemplative meditation on ultimate nature; statement 4 is the meditative absorption based on that wisdom; and statement 5 refers to informal practice during daily life.

Key Points to Contemplate

- What are the two truths and how do they relate to your life?
- Investigate statement 1: *Consider all phenomena to be like a dream.* Follow it with resting meditation (resting meditation in this section corresponds to the fourth statement on page 65).
- Investigate statement 2: *Examine the fundamental nature of unborn mind.* Follow it with resting meditation.
- Investigate statement 3: *Even the remedy naturally subsides on its own.* Conclude with resting meditation.

The Excellent Conclusion

Dedicate the merit generated by this practice and make aspirations. Think, "I dedicate the merit of this practice on the ultimate nature of reality to all beings that they may be freed from suffering and attain temporary and ultimate happiness." Then, make aspirations for the welfare and happiness of others. Think, "May all beings be happy and may all beings be free. May everyone realize the true nature of mind." (You can also use the dedication and aspiration prayers in appendix 5.)

Off the Cushion

This practice corresponds to the final statement, *During post-meditation, see everything as an illusion*. If you are enjoying something, enjoy it as a magical illusion. The moment you recognize its illusory nature, let your mind rest for a moment right there in the midst of whatever you are doing. If you are disturbed about something, pause. Adjust your perspective and recognize the illusory nature of the situation. Then allow your mind to rest for a moment right there.

If that isn't sufficient, consider that the reason you are upset is that you believe that whatever you are experiencing exists exactly as you perceive it to be. Think about how different people or even different species can perceive the same person, place, or situation completely differently. This is because the object doesn't inherently exist according to our perceptions. It is not what determines our experience. Rather, how the mind perceives objects determines our experience. Once you are able to acknowledge this, use any of the methods of examination presented in this chapter and analyze the true nature of the experience. When you reach an insight about its empty, illusory nature, allow the mind to rest right there, immersed in wisdom insight. This is vipashyana practice off the cushion.

6

Relative Bodhichitta:
The Awakened Heart

The source of all genuine happiness, both temporary and ultimate, is the wish that others find happiness. In *The Thirty-Seven Practices of a Bodhisattva*, Ngulchu Togme says, "All suffering, without exception, comes from wanting to find happiness for oneself. Perfect enlightenment comes from wanting to find happiness for others."[1] The root of all suffering is our intense clinging to the idea of our identity—what we call the self—and the extreme attachment to that self—what we call selfishness—which leads to afflictive thoughts and emotions. The root of all happiness is the wish to benefit others. This motivation, which is focused on the welfare of others and the pursuit of ultimate freedom, is what we call bodhichitta.

We all have the potential to attain ultimate happiness, the state of total realization, *enlightenment*. Why? Because enlightenment is already the nature of our mind. We call it the ground buddha nature. To awaken to it, we need the support of this precious human body, the condition of a qualified spiritual teacher, and the skillful methods of a teacher's advice and guidance on the path. Because we innately possess the ground for awakening, once we have the support, the conditions, and the methods, the results—temporary and ultimate happiness—are ensured.

PROFOUND COMPASSION AND WISDOM

Bodhichitta is the consummate kind heart. It is the ground from which all positive qualities and insights grow, the springboard for our spiritual journey. If we are motivated by the great intention to benefit others, calm abiding, also known as *shamatha*, and other forms of meditation will be easily accomplished, and profound insight meditation, vipashyana, which is the recognition of true nature, will progress. The entire path of realization depends upon developing bodhichitta. If we aspire to reach a state of total perfection—enlightenment itself—we need to arouse this awakened intention. Bodhichitta has two qualities that arise simultaneously as our motivation: the compassionate wish to benefit others and the wisdom to pursue ultimate perfection. These qualities are what motivate a bodhisattva practitioner.

The compassionate wish to benefit others is focused on all living beings without exception. It embraces humans and nonhumans, those with a physical form and those without one. Ordinary motivation is biased and judgmental and favors some beings over others, but this motivation is based on the recognition that all beings yearn for happiness and seek freedom from suffering, even as they engage in the causes of suffering and disregard the causes of happiness. That's why bodhichitta motivation extends compassion to every living being, all of whom experience pleasure and pain. A practitioner with this motivation often thinks, "Wouldn't it be wonderful if all beings were free from suffering and its causes?" And, "May all beings be free." And, "I will free each and every being from suffering."

The second aspect of bodhichitta is wisdom. In addition to profound compassion, we recognize that it isn't enough to merely reach a temporary end of suffering in one situation or to just find circumstantial happiness. All happiness in this world is conditional and short-term. We are often left feeling unfulfilled, and we even suffer over those moments of so-called happiness. We want beings to find temporary happiness such as nutritious food, comfortable homes, and other positive worldly circumstances, but the final goal is to attain ultimate happiness that is free from suffering. To bring beings to that state, we must purify our obscurations and realize our true nature.[2] The more wisdom we cultivate, the more we see the need to pursue this ultimate goal and to bring all beings to that state.

WHAT'S YOUR MOTIVATION?

In Sanskrit, *bodhi* means "enlightenment" or "the state of total purification and realization," and *chitta* means "the heart mind of that." Without the intention of bodhichitta, we cannot attain bodhi. If we meditate without the motivation of bodhichitta, it might be virtuous, but it won't be a cause for enlightenment. This is why Patrul Rinpoche, a renowned saint of Tibet, said, "If you have bodhichitta, bodhi will be attained. If you don't have bodhichitta, bodhi is far away. May the unmistaken seed of enlightenment, bodhichitta, be born in my being." When we look at the path followed by the buddhas and bodhisattvas of the past, present, and future, and when we think of the qualities cultivated by realized beings, we see that the heart of their practice and the primary cause of all of their qualities was bodhichitta. Their path was to give rise to bodhichitta. All of their conduct and meditation complemented that practice. Bodhichitta is what motivates all realized beings.

How many of our thoughts are genuinely motivated by the compassionate wish to benefit others or the wisdom to pursue the ultimate goal of enlightenment? All day, thoughts surface like waves on the ocean. They are relentless and endless. Among all of these numberless thoughts, happening day in and day out throughout all our lives, how many are of bodhichitta? How many are so vast in scope as to be concerned with the welfare and ultimate benefit of all beings? This thought is extremely rare. The great Indian master Atisha, the revered teacher of these mind-training techniques, saw the value of this kind heart. The main way he benefited beings in Tibet was by spreading these teachings and encouraging people to generate a kind heart. This perspective was exemplified in all of his actions. He would even greet people by asking, "Have you cultivated a kind heart?" And when they later parted, he would remind them, "Cultivate a kind heart."

This motivation is the opposite of our ordinary motivation. We work for our own happiness and seek to avoid suffering because we believe our happiness and suffering are the most important things. That is what sparks everything we say and do. But that motivation—thinking only of benefiting ourselves—is one of the greatest hindrances to spiritual practice because it prevents us from making progress on the path. Even in worldly affairs, selfishness causes great harm. We can see this play out in every aspect of our lives in ways large and small. When someone is a ruler of a region, for example, and that person is only concerned with their own wants and needs, it results in great harm for the ruler and for the people who live in their country. On an individual level, our thoughts are dominated by "what I want" and consistently centering our own desires above the needs of others, but we aren't able to accomplish what we really truly want. Even when we're healthy and all of our material needs are met, our mind still isn't happy. We might get depressed or angry or jealous. The more we are concerned with ourselves, the more disturbing emotions we have. And as our disturbing emotions increase, so too does our suffering.

All disturbing emotions are rooted in self-clinging.[3] Our desires and attachments, our anger and aversion, our jealousy and pride all come from a belief in self. Of course we need to find happiness, but we should think carefully about how we go about doing that, about what works and what doesn't. Seeing oneself as more important than others and thinking primarily of personal concerns definitely does not work. It has not worked in the past, and it is not working in the present. In fact, it's an attitude that only causes more problems. The only way to achieve true happiness is by thinking of others, by developing an altruistic intention and benevolent mind, and by acting upon that basis.

Sentient beings are as limitless as space itself. They live in the sky, on and under the earth, and in the water, and each and every being is seeking happiness and is motivated by the need to find it. A well-known Buddhist proverb says, "Even the eyeless ants march toward happiness. Even the legless worms wiggle toward happiness. Each one is trying to be faster than the other. It's as if the entire world is in a great competition, a race toward happiness." Each of us struggles to achieve happiness however we can, and while in this sole pursuit, we continue to suffer.

THE MINDSET FOR MIND TRAINING

From beginningless time until now, beings have pursued their self-interest. Yet we cannot find an example of anyone who, motivated by selfishness, achieved everything they wished for. Throughout all of history, there is no example of a person who focused on themselves and found complete freedom from suffering. We do have examples of buddhas and bodhisattvas who are motivated by the wish to benefit others and who have achieved a state of total perfection and freedom from suffering. But in our own lives, we have all kinds of problems and are unable to get what we want, which is a sign that we're going about it all wrong. We need to change our intention and the way we go about achieving happiness. We need to change our minds and our motivation at the very core, which is the point of these mind-training teachings. We need to practice bodhichitta and integrate that view into our experience so that it becomes the basis of everything we do.

It's like we need to take the shirt we're wearing and turn it inside out. Before we begin mind training we think, "I want happiness. I don't want to suffer." Once we begin mind training, we think, "I want others to find happiness and I want others not to suffer." We've turned our perspective inside out. We start right there.

Bodhichitta is the supreme practice for taming the mind. Everything hinges on whether we have it or we don't. To develop bodhichitta to the fullest extent, we have to train our minds through formal meditation practice. Taming the mind and the process of changing our experience does not happen outside of ourselves. It's not about manipulating outer phenomena. It's a process of changing ourselves from the inside. At first the training can seem like a contrived process. But if we meditate again and again, and we train in the practice over and over, it eventually becomes our ongoing experience and completely natural. Until that point, we need mind training.

THE THREE BASIC STAGES

In mind training, there are three basic stages for developing love and compassion: equalizing ourselves with others, exchanging ourselves with others, and cherishing others more than ourselves. These stages correlate with the way love and compassion grow in us. First, we need to recognize that all beings are equally important when it comes to finding happiness and alleviating suffering. This is the foundational viewpoint upon which we begin practicing *tonglen* (see appendix 4), exchanging our welfare for the suffering of others, which deepens our wish to benefit others and increases our capacity to put that intention into action. Eventually, the practice of tonglen will lead us to feel that others are more important than ourselves. It won't be a forced or artificial feeling. As we gradually train, it will increasingly become our natural response. Although we haven't reached that stage, we should make the aspiration that one day, we too can be like the buddhas and bodhisattvas. The aspiration that our love, compassion, realization, and positive qualities become identical to theirs creates an interdependent connection with these realized beings, which helps us to become like them. As we continue to train our minds, understanding will blossom into realization, and eventually we will be able to benefit others far beyond our current capabilities.

There's a simple example used to illustrate the progression from equalizing oneself with others to exchanging oneself with others. Imagine two people walking together on a road. One person is wearing shoes and the other person is barefoot. The person with shoes feels bad for her companion's suffering, so she offers him one of her shoes. Now, each has one foot with a shoe, which is pain-free, and one foot that is bare, which is painful. So their happiness and suffering are equal. If the traveler with the shoes was a practitioner who trained in exchanging her happiness for the suffering of others, she would give both of her shoes to the other person and endure the difficulty of walking barefoot by herself.

This practice can sound daunting. We might think it sounds too difficult to see others as equally important as ourselves, let alone to hold them as even more important. And it's true, it would be difficult to act like that right now. But that's because it isn't realistic right now. We always train within our capacity. Sometimes, when we're doing our best, we may stretch to the limit, but we shouldn't step beyond that point. This practice is meant to be done within our comfort zone and then, with training, our capacity grows.

Bodhisattvas are not ordinary beings; they are beings who have fully realized both ultimate and relative bodhichitta, and so they are totally selfless and only have concern for others. Because they have fully realized the nature of reality, they have no attachment to or belief in a self. So when a bodhisattva puts others before themself, it's painless. Even if a bodhisattva were to be cut with a knife, they wouldn't experience suffering in the same way as we do.

One of the special features of the Buddhist path is to abandon extremes. We abandon the intense desire for sense pleasures and the pursuit of great wealth and many possessions and strive to be content with what we have. But we also abandon the extreme of asceticism, where one undergoes physical pain and suffering as part of spiritual practice. The Buddha said severe self-discipline isn't necessary to achieve realization. Instead, we engage in formal and informal training in bodhichitta, and slowly but surely we will achieve our ultimate goal.

EQUALIZING OURSELVES WITH OTHERS

Equalizing ourselves with others means to see others as equally important as ourselves. All sentient beings—each and every one of us—wants happiness. No one wants to suffer. From this perspective we're all the same. As we train in equalizing ourselves with others, we recognize what we have in common with other beings, and we develop the perception that everyone has an equal need to find happiness and freedom from suffering.

Right now, we're biased toward our own feelings and concerns, and we're partial toward our loved ones and close friends. We get angry and feel aversion when we think someone has obstructed our happiness or the happiness of our friends and relatives.

Then there are the people we don't feel that connected to. They are neither friends nor adversaries, and we tend to have a bland, neutral feeling toward them. It's important to understand that our disinterest is not the same thing as seeing other beings as equal to ourselves. We want to work through this neutrality until we can view everyone as equally important. If we don't view others as equally important, we won't be able to progress to exchanging ourselves with others.

How can we hold everyone's welfare in mind without bias? Start by recognizing that everyone wants the same thing. We want happiness for ourselves. That's our first thought in every situation. Then, we engage in physical and verbal actions motivated by our desire for happiness. We need to recognize that just as this is the case for us, it is the case for all living beings. With training, we will eventually see there is no difference between our own happiness and the happiness of everyone else. As much as we work for our own happiness, we will work to bring happiness to others. One effective way to train in equalizing ourselves with others is to meditate on the four immeasurables. These are immeasurable love, immeasurable compassion, immeasurable rejoicing, and immeasurable equalness.

We all have love and compassion to some extent. It is the innate potential of every living being. Even ferocious beasts that kill many animals can show concern and care for their mates and offspring. As humans, we are concerned for our loved ones, and we want them to be happy and to not suffer. But we have a narrow focus. If we only care for and protect a few individuals or if our aim is only for their temporary happiness, then we do not have what we call immeasurable love.

Immeasurable love is immeasurable because it embraces the welfare of all sentient beings, whose numbers are uncountable. It is immeasurable because its aim is not limited to one situation, such as wanting happiness for someone in their relationship or in their job, but wanting them to have complete happiness—temporary and ultimate. And it is immeasurable because the results of having it—both the immediate effects in our lives and the final result of complete awakening—are infinite. The results cannot be measured because the qualities and realization that come from having these immeasurables are vast and boundless. This immeasurability applies to each of the four immeasurables.

The practice of immeasurable love leads to the wish that all living beings, without exception, find both temporary and ultimate happiness. The practice of immeasurable compassion considers the suffering of all sentient beings and leads to a sincere wish that they be free from suffering and the causes of suffering. The practice of immeasurable rejoicing leads to a rejoicing in the positive qualities and good fortune of others. The practice of immeasurable equalness leads to a relinquishing of feelings of attachment and aversion toward those we like and dislike. This view leads us to extend our love and compassion equally to all beings.

Immeasurable Equalness

In Buddhist texts, the four immeasurables are taught in the order they are listed above, but in practice, immeasurable equalness comes first. Focusing on immeasurable equalness enables us to transform our prejudiced minds, which are attached to some beings and averse to others. If we don't begin to view everyone equally, we won't be able to cultivate immeasurable compassion, love, or rejoicing for them.

To cultivate immeasurable equalness, imagine that all living beings are here with you right now. Then, think of how many you actually love and care about and imagine them standing on your right side. Notice your feelings of attachment. Continue by thinking of everyone you don't like, those who you despise or even hate, and imagine them standing on your left side. Notice your feelings of aversion. Now, think of the rest of the numberless beings throughout the universe and notice how you don't think about them much at all: your feelings toward them are neutral.

When we step back and look, there are very few beings on our right side and even fewer on the left. The vast majority of beings are not even within our scope of concern. Our feelings of attachment, aversion, or neutrality are the ordinary mind's habit, our usual mode of operating. Reflect on how this mind of attachment and aversion is the source of all disturbing thoughts and emotions. Consider how much suffering is caused by those mental states and the actions that result from them. Now think about how everyone, those to your right, left, and the rest, are all suffering because of their attachment and aversion. Make the aspiration that you and all beings be free from attachment and aversion. Say, "May all beings abide continuously in immeasurable equalness, free from the bias of attachment and aversion."

Another way to reduce attachment and aversion and to expand the view that all beings are equal is to contemplate the uncertain nature of all relationships. Start by thinking about your relationships with people who have harmed you or those whom you dislike. Someone who is now your adversary could have once been your childhood friend. Similarly, someone who you once disliked could now be a trusted business partner or even your spouse. And someone you currently consider to be a loved one could become an enemy.

We believe in the labels of *friend* and *enemy* and treat them as if they are unchanging. But these designations do not last forever. This perspective becomes even more clear when we think about our relationships in the context of past and future lives. Your current nemesis could have been your mother, child, or spouse in a previous life.[4] In a future life, the person you currently love could become your worst enemy. Everyone, at some point or another, has been or will be our loved one, our greatest supporter, and our hero.

When contemplating the uncertain nature of relationships, we don't want to conclude that nothing matters or to become indifferent toward others. Instead, we want to see that all sentient beings are equally deserving of our care. Throughout the day, notice attachment and aversion in your mind and also notice when you see it in others. Continuously generate this wish, "May all beings abide in immeasurable equalness, free from attachment and aversion." Or reflect with a simpler thought, "May all beings be free from attachment and aversion."

Immeasurable Love

To cultivate immeasurable love, consider how each and every being just wants to be happy. Since they don't know what the causes of happiness are (such as inner development and positive actions), their pursuit of happiness is often misguided, and so they engage in the causes for suffering. Start by thinking about the person whom you feel the closest to, whom you love the most, maybe your mother or child. Think about how they want happiness and aren't finding it or creating the causes for it. Make the wish, "May they find happiness and the causes of happiness." Gradually broaden the scope of your focus to other loved ones and then to different beings whom you know and don't know. Throughout the day, notice how everyone you encounter wants happiness and see how they are not engaging in the causes that produce it. Keep expanding your scope until all living beings are embraced with the wish, "May all beings have happiness and the causes of happiness."

Immeasurable Compassion

To cultivate immeasurable compassion, focus on the suffering and unhappiness of beings. See how no one wants to suffer and yet everyone is engaging in the causes of suffering. Start by thinking of someone you care about deeply, or someone you know who is in a lot of pain, or someone who is creating the causes for suffering. Think about their suffering and generate the wish, "May they be free from suffering and the causes of suffering." Gradually expand your focus to more and more beings until your contemplation embraces all living beings in the universe with the wish, "May all beings be free from suffering and the causes of suffering." When we want all beings to be free of suffering, that is immeasurable compassion. Throughout the day, remember this practice and wish that everyone you meet be free from suffering and its causes. Make the wish again and again, and do whatever you can to alleviate the suffering of others in your actions.

Immeasurable Rejoicing

To cultivate immeasurable rejoicing,[5] focus on the happiness, good fortune, prosperity, and success of others. Be sure to include the causes of happiness too, such as positive actions, virtue, and merit. Since by now we have already embraced the welfare of all beings, and since we already love them, it should be easy to celebrate their good fortune. Bring to mind someone you are close to who is happy or who is actively engaging in the causes of happiness and think, "May they never be separate from this happiness and its causes." Gradually extend this contemplation to more and more beings, making that wish for each and every one of them. Finally, make this aspiration for all living beings wherever they are in the universe. Throughout the day, whenever you encounter someone who has something nice, such as a desirable car or house, lots of love in their life, or positive actions that will produce future happiness, make this wish: "May they never be separate from such happiness and may they have even more of it!" This is the true meaning of rejoicing, and it is a source of great joy for ourselves too.

Often, when we see others' good fortune, we feel a twinge of jealousy or competitiveness. We may not be entirely happy that things are going well for them. This sort of thinking is a nasty habit that causes us pointless suffering. Break this habit by rejoicing in their good fortune and wishing that they always have such positive circumstances. Say, "May they never be separate from this and may they have even more of it." This contemplation, practiced over and over again, is an antidote for jealousy, and it's essential for developing immeasurable rejoicing.

HOW TO PRACTICE

The Excellent Beginning

Sit in meditation posture to cultivate the key points of body and speech (see page 17 for a full explanation). Then, cultivate the key points of mind by setting your intention. Think, "In order to benefit beings, I will cultivate love and compassion toward all beings equally."

The Excellent Main Part

Review the following list of key points introduced in this chapter by reading one point at a time. Alternate between contemplative meditation and resting meditation. You may wish to do separate sessions for each of the immeasurables in order to deeply immerse yourself in their individual qualities.

Key Points to Contemplate

- **Immeasurable equalness.** Follow the instructions in this section by imagining your loved ones to your right, enemies to
  your left, and all the rest of sentient beings who you don't
  know in front of you. Notice the attachment, aversion, and
  neutrality. Reflect on how attachment and aversion are the
  sources of all disturbing emotions and harmful actions, and
  think about the changeable nature of these relationship designations. Relate this to your own experiences and observations
  of everyone in the world around you. Each time you recognize
  attachment or aversion in your own or others' minds, make
  the aspiration, "May all beings abide in immeasurable equalness, free from attachment and aversion." Let go and rest for
  a moment before continuing. Then shift your focus to different
  people and classes of beings in order to embrace all beings
  with this intention, until it expands immeasurably in your mind.
- **Immeasurable loving-kindness.** Start with someone close to
  you, such as a parent or child, and contemplate how they want
  happiness yet often experience unhappiness. Notice what
  kinds of actions they are taking to produce future happiness.
  Then, when you see how they lack happiness or the causes
  for happiness, make the aspiration, "May they find happiness
  and the causes of happiness." Let go and rest for a moment.
  Then, expand your focus to any or all of your other loved ones
  and repeat the contemplation, aspiration, and resting meditation. Alternate between different groups of people or species of beings—consider those for whom you feel attachment,
  aversion, or neutrality. Repeat the contemplation, aspiration,
  and resting meditation for each group of beings, until finally
  you embrace all beings in the universe with the aspiration that
  each find happiness and the causes of happiness.
- **Immeasurable compassion.** Follow the same steps as above,
  but focus on how each being suffers and creates the causes of

suffering. At each step, contemplate until you feel compassion toward each being(s). Then make the aspiration, "May they be free from suffering and the causes of suffering," followed by resting meditation. Gradually expand your focus until you embrace everyone in the universe with the wish, "May all beings be free from suffering and the causes of suffering."

- **Immeasurable rejoicing.** Follow the same steps as above, but focus on the favorable circumstances that people experience— their positive qualities, good relationships, abundance of food, material wealth, good health, education, success, and opportunities. Don't forget to include their positive actions. Be creative and be specific—the sky is the limit when it comes to rejoicing in the good fortune of others. Shift your focus from specific individuals, then move to groups of people and other beings as with the prior practices. With each contemplation, make the aspiration, "May they never be separate from such happiness; may their happiness continually increase!" followed by resting meditation before continuing to the next source of rejoicing.

The Excellent Conclusion

Dedicate the merit generated by this practice and make aspirations. Think, "I dedicate the merit of this practice on the four immeasurables to all beings that they may be freed from suffering and attain both temporary and ultimate happiness." Then make the aspiration, "May all beings be happy and may all beings be free. May everyone abide in the four immeasurable qualities." Recite the aspiration prayer specific to the four immeasurables below. (You can also use the dedication and aspiration prayers in appendix 5.)

May all beings, equal in extent to space, have happiness and the causes of happiness. May they be free from suffering and the causes of suffering. May they never be separate from supreme happiness without suffering. May their minds abide continuously in the immeasurable equalness free from the bias of attachment and aversion.

Off the Cushion

For the informal practice of immeasurable equalness, throughout the day, focus on becoming aware of the attachment and aversion in yourself and in others. Notice how, when we are motivated by attachment or aversion, we are more likely to treat others unequally and to produce the causes of suffering for ourselves and others. Each time you notice attachment or aversion, make the aspiration, "May they and all beings be free from attachment and aversion." Make the practice more personal and relevant by changing the aspiration that you repeat to make it more specific for each situation you encounter.

For the informal practice of immeasurable loving-kindness, throughout the day, focus on how each being in every situation just wants happiness. Notice when they aren't happy or when they are not creating the causes that produce happiness. Each time, generate loving-kindness making the aspiration, "May they and all beings have happiness and the causes of happiness."

For the informal practice of immeasurable compassion, throughout the day, focus on the way in which each being suffers or is engaging in actions that will result in future suffering. Each time you notice this, generate compassion by making the aspiration, "May they and all beings be free from suffering and the causes of suffering."

For the informal practice of immeasurable rejoicing, throughout the day, focus on the good fortune that other people experience, especially the qualities and possessions you most admire and desire. When you notice someone else has something positive or is experiencing happiness, rejoice by making the aspiration, "May they never be separate from such happiness; may it always increase!"

EXCHANGING OURSELVES WITH OTHERS

The next stage of cultivating bodhichitta is to practice exchanging ourselves with others. One simple method for training our mind in this way is to imagine that we are another person. Think, "I am that person and that person is me." Imagine all of their circumstances and how it would feel to be them. If we were them, we obviously wouldn't want to suffer, and we would want happiness. This is how it is with all beings.

The most direct method for exchanging ourselves with others is tonglen, a meditation practice of giving (*tong-* in Tibetan) and receiving (*-len*). In the root text it says, "Train in giving and receiving alternately. Do so by riding the breath." But what is it that we give, and whom do we give it to? We give our happiness and its causes to all sentient beings. And what is it that we receive and from whom? We receive or take on the suffering and the causes of suffering of all sentient beings. When we give our happiness and its causes because we are motivated by the wish that others find happiness, we are practicing loving-kindness. When we take on others' suffering and its causes because we are motivated by the wish to lessen suffering, we are practicing compassion.

Tonglen is a transformative meditation practice. It is one of the most profound methods for taming the mind because it engages our deeply ingrained habitual tendencies and cultivates the opposite. Even though Atisha was highly realized, he still practiced tonglen. In fact, it was his main practice. The practice of tonglen is also taught in many famous texts on bodhichitta. In *The Way of a Bodhisattva* by Shantideva, the most well-known treatise on the practice of bodhichitta, tonglen is the primary method taught for developing love and compassion.[6] Tonglen is also the main practice in Ngulchu Togme Zangpo's *Thirty-Seven Practices of a Bodhisattva*.[7] All of the life stories of the buddhas and bodhisattvas of the past begin with love and compassion. For many, their realization ripened through the practice of tonglen.

CHERISHING OTHERS MORE THAN OURSELVES

Until we become a bodhisattva, we will not be able to truly cherish others as more important than ourselves. The whole path aspires to this outcome, and while on the path, we cultivate the qualities that take us from here to there. So while right now we would not actually give our life or limbs on behalf of another being, to train our mind we can imagine ourselves as a bodhisattva who is able to do this and make aspirations to become one. This practice increases our capacity. If we can't imagine ourselves as a bodhisattva or set the intention in practice to become one, our capacity won't grow.

To practice cherishing others more than ourselves, sit in meditation. Then, imagine that you have no self-clinging at all. Envision your mind—oriented solely toward other beings without the self-centered mechanism that it ordinarily operates from.[8] Now your mind is other-centered, just like the buddhas and bodhisattvas who dive into any of the states of suffering with great enthusiasm in order to benefit others. Then, imagine that your body emanates in as many numbers as there are beings in the universe and appears before each and every being throughout the six realms. Imagine that you serve each and every being in any way they need and in doing so, completely eliminate their suffering. Think that they are free of all suffering and its causes, that they have full and complete happiness.

Another way to meditate on cherishing others more than ourselves, which makes this practice even more personal, is to imagine that you personally go to each and every being and take their place, thereby completely freeing them from suffering and ensuring their happiness. You imagine this with specific beings that you know, or whose circumstances you are aware of, or you can imagine yourself with the different classes of beings. In each realm, recall the primary sufferings of the beings there and imagine their sufferings ripen upon you while those beings are healed and freed. Pray not only that their present sufferings immediately ripen upon you but also that the entire storehouse of their accumulated negative actions ripen upon you, thereby freeing them entirely from suffering, its causes, and its results. You might also try imagining any situation and then envisioning not being concerned for yourself at all and only being motivated by the wish to help others.

In each of these meditations, by imagining that we have a bodhisattva's capacity, our mind's way of thinking changes, and the depth of our love and compassion increases. While this more expansive way of thinking is practiced in formal mind-training sessions, in terms of actual actions, start with the small things; there's no need to stretch beyond your current capacity.

6. *Train in giving and receiving alternately. Do so by riding the breath.*

Now we are ready to practice the main training of tonglen. Start by cultivating the excellent beginning, then allow the breath to flow naturally through the nose. Although Atisha's tradition emphasizes breathing through the nose, you can also breathe through the mouth if that is more comfortable for you. It's important to do what is natural and not to get hung up on the breath.

GIVING AND RECEIVING: TONGLEN

Bring to mind the object of tonglen—whomever you are focusing on—using the sequence of contemplations explained in the following pages. At each step in the process, it's important to feel that the being you're imagining is right in front of you. Look closely at their experience until you feel empathy for them. Remind yourself that, just like you, they want happiness and don't want to suffer. It is essential that we bring their specific sufferings to mind and focus on them. We can't feel compassion for another unless we know their suffering. Contemplate their circumstances from every angle until you feel moved by genuine love and compassion. You can use any number of reflections on the suffering of beings and their causes, such as was described in the preliminaries, in order to elicit deeper love and compassion.

The easiest way to train in tonglen is to use the breath, which provides a focus for the mind. You can also do tonglen without the breath, especially during post-meditation. But for formal meditation, using the breath is helpful because it focuses the mind and prevents distraction.

Once you have generated the object of tonglen, imagine that the accumulated suffering and the causes of suffering for those beings rides the breath in the form of black light, which you breathe in. This black light dissolves into the self-cherishing that abides in the heart.[9] As the black light disappears think, "They are freed from all suffering and the causes of suffering."

Then, imagine that all of the happiness and the causes of happiness in your life take the form of white light. Your wealth and possessions, your health, your positive circumstances, everything that is good in your life gathers like warm sunlight. As you breathe out, imagine that this light rides on the breath and dissolves into the beings before you. Visualize this light, with all of its positive and healing qualities, permeating these beings. Think, "They now have complete happiness, temporary and ultimate, and the causes of happiness."

During the in-breath, focus on compassion, the wish that others not suffer; and during the out-breath, focus on loving-kindness, the wish that others find happiness. You may find that it feels rushed to complete the thought of compassion for each in-breath and then the thought of loving-kindness for each out-breath without any breaths in between. If so, it's okay to do an in-breath with the visualization and thought of compassion and then breathe in and out until the full meditation on compassion is complete. Then, at the next out-breath, do the visualization and thought of loving-kindness and breathe naturally for however long it takes to complete the meditation of loving-kindness. Continue to alternate in that way. The key point of the meditation is not the breath or the visualization of light; it's the generation of compassion and love. This is why it is so important to thoroughly reflect on the situation of each being before starting the tonglen visualization. Merely focusing on your breath or visualizing black and white light is not going to make you more compassionate or loving! The breath and the visualization are tools to help the mind focus and deepen love and compassion.

This practice is done in gradual stages by shifting the focus to different types of sentient beings through the course of the meditation. The first object of tonglen should be someone for whom we feel immense gratitude and love. Start with your mother or father, or anyone whom you love dearly and who has been kind to you in this life. Begin with this person because you already have love and compassion for them and an emotional connection that makes it easier to generate even greater love and compassion without much contemplation. Imagine this person in front of you and bring to mind their suffering. Once you feel moved by a deep wish to free them from suffering and to establish them in both temporary and ultimate happiness, do the tonglen visualization.

The second object of tonglen is our loved ones, family, and friends. This can be another person or a group of people, but the focus is on beings we already care about. Once again, this connection makes it easier to generate deeper love and compassion. Start with one relative or friend, and then slowly include more and more people until you are doing tonglen for all of those you care about. Imagine them before you. Contemplate their joys and sorrows until you feel a deep yearning for them to find true happiness and to no longer suffer. Then, engage in tonglen practice.

The third focus of tonglen is beings who suffer more than most, specifically those in the less fortunate realms, such as hellish states of existence, hungry-ghost realms, and the animal kingdom (see appendix 3). Think about each of the unfortunate realms sequentially. Start by bringing to mind the suffering that a being in a hellish state endures, such as intense heat or cold. Imagine that these beings appear in front of you and consider that at some point in time, each one of them has been your mother, father, sibling, or child. Try to develop a sense of closeness and warmth for them. Reflect on how self-clinging and disturbing emotions led them to unwittingly create the causes for the intense suffering of the hellish states. Reflect on their situation until you are moved by overwhelming love and compassion. Then do the tonglen visualization.

Next, focus your attention on hungry ghosts and bring to mind the torment of unceasing hunger and thirst, the agony that these beings experience. Contemplate as you have before until you feel moved by love and compassion. Then do tonglen. Next, turn your attention to animals and the suffering they endure. This contemplation may come more easily than the others because you have likely observed animals' suffering before. There are so many aspects we can reflect upon, such as how some animals are preyed upon and in constant danger, while others kill to survive and create the causes for an even less fortunate rebirth. Focus on these and other aspects of animal suffering that you are familiar with until you feel moved out of love and compassion to do tonglen.

The fourth object of tonglen is humans who are destitute and suffer more than most and those whom we know engage in harmful and negative actions. Bring to mind people who experience intense physical or mental pain. Imagine those who are dying in hospitals; people who are living in fear because of violence and war; those who are homeless, starving, or suffering from mental illness; and people who have been devastated by natural and manmade disasters. Reflect on the circumstances of these people, and when you feel genuine care and compassion for them, do tonglen.

Also bring to mind people for whom you feel little or no connection. We have met countless people like that in this life, those toward whom we feel neither attachment nor aversion. We don't see them as adversaries or as friends, and we know little to nothing about them. Beyond that, this world is filled with innumerable people whom we have never met and who are completely outside of our awareness. Bring to mind people you have seen but ignored as well as all of the people with whom you have never had contact. Imagine ways in which these people suffer and seek happiness. Then, practice tonglen.

The fifth object of tonglen is our adversaries. It is most challenging to generate love and compassion for those who cause us or our loved ones harm, the people we consider to be our enemies. These are people we don't like, people we feel jealous of or anger toward. That's why for true

change to take place, this stage is crucial. We usually feel the exact opposite of love and compassion toward our enemies. We feel aversion, anger,
or hostility, emotions that are the true enemies of love and compassion.
For as long as we hold on to these disturbing emotions, they will continue to cause us suffering and will be an obstacle to spiritual growth. So
bring your adversary clearly to mind. Imagine they are right in front of
you. Contemplate their suffering until you feel love and compassion for
this person. It may take longer, but make the effort. Use all of the tools of
contemplation to change your perception. Work to see this person in the
same way you see a loved one. They want happiness and don't want to suffer, yet they still engage in actions that cause suffering. Reflect on your
enemy's situation until you feel genuine compassion for them. Once you
feel that they deserve happiness and should be free from suffering, practice tonglen.

The sixth and last object of tonglen practice is all sentient beings.
Consider how every single being wants happiness and doesn't want to
suffer, yet their actions often run contrary to their wishes. Also, consider
how, since everyone has at some point been a mother or father, son or
daughter to you, they have been kind to you. Contemplate this until you
feel genuine love and compassion, and then do tonglen practice for all beings simultaneously.

The most effective way to practice tonglen is to alternate from one object to another, gradually moving through these six stages. Take your time
with this. The value comes when we actually generate feelings of love and
compassion. We don't want to simply go through the motions. You can alternate through all six objects in a meditation session, or you can simplify
the practice by focusing on just one or two of the objects.

There is a good reason for this progression. We could simply bring to
mind all beings and do tonglen for everyone at once. But this can be im-
personal. It may elicit a feeling of love and compassion in meditation, but
it also may feel distant or vague, creating a sense of all beings that is more
hypothetical than when we imagine a person we love standing before
us. The value of reflecting on the suffering and experience of individual

beings and realms of beings is that we generate empathy and care for each and every one that is personal and intimate. This enables us to relate to others from a loving and compassionate perspective in our daily lives. So in this way, alternate through the practice, changing the object of meditation until at the end of the session, all beings are held as the object of tonglen. This is the most effective method for changing our hearts toward others under all circumstances.

It can be helpful to pause slightly between the inhalation and exhalation to ensure that your visualization and intention are clear. For example, when you imagine the suffering of another being entering your heart, pause and think: "They are now free of suffering and its causes forever." Then, when you breathe out with the visualization of white light, imagine that this light fills the bodies of sentient beings, giving them whatever they need, and bringing them temporary and ultimate happiness. At the end of the exhalation, pause for a moment and think, "They now have temporary and ultimate happiness." These slight pauses complete the visualization and reinforce the loving and compassionate thought. Remember, the focal point is love and compassion! The breath is just the means to support that aim.

Practicing tonglen even once or twice can change the mind, because it's opposite to the way we usually think. We usually seek everything good for ourselves and push everything we don't want toward others, which is the very attitude that prevents us from finding happiness and effectively helping others. The radical shift in perspective that comes from tonglen can make our self-centered focus become other-centered.

START WITH INTENTION

Some people are afraid to practice tonglen. They worry that if they visualize themselves taking on the suffering of others, then that suffering will ripen upon them. For tonglen meditation to be most effective, we do need to believe that we are taking on the suffering of others, but this does not actually occur. What happens instead is that our intention changes.

We start to care more for others and worry less about ourselves. Love and compassion increase, while disturbing emotions decrease. If we practice tonglen wholeheartedly, our positive qualities will grow, while negative thoughts and actions subside. Everyone benefits when kindheartedness grows within us. It transforms our whole life.

In addition, it's important to remember how cause and result works. It's not possible for another person's karma to ripen on us. We cannot experience the results of someone else's actions. This is the basic nature of karma. If it were possible to eliminate the negative karma of other beings, the buddhas and bodhisattvas would have already done it. Motivated by bodhichitta and without any hesitation, they would take on all of the suffering in the world if they could.

There are special cases when a bodhisattva may be able to take on the suffering of another being, but this involves the convergence of many specific causes and conditions. The bodhisattva's realization of bodhichitta and the power of their previous aspirations need to be linked to the karma of the suffering being in a specific way for this to occur. And because they have transcended conditioned existence, when bodhisattvas do take on the suffering of other beings, they do not experience it in the same way as ordinary sentient beings would.

It's rare for the circumstances to come together that would enable a bodhisattva to actually take on the suffering of another being, but there are stories of Buddhist saints where it is described. One example is Atisha's teacher, the great yogi Maitreya. One day, Maitreya was sitting on a throne teaching to a large audience, when someone nearby threw a rock at a stray dog. At that same moment the rock hit, Maitreya cried out, "Ah na na," an exclamation of pain, and he fell off his seat. His students were astonished, so he explained that someone had thrown a rock at a dog, and he took on the pain. To quell the doubt of skeptics in the audience, he pulled up his shirt to show the swollen red mark, right where the dog had been hit.

Once we have attained realization and become bodhisattvas ourselves, we will be ready and willing to take on suffering like this, but until then, as ordinary practitioners, we can feel safe doing the practice of tonglen. Still, we shouldn't underestimate the power of intention. Our intentions do have the power to affect the people around us and the objects of tonglen practice. Sometimes they can even feel it. The authenticity of our intentions determines our capacity to help others. And when we do help others and they feel the benefit, their positive experience is based on the power of our good intentions. The opposite is true as well. If we attempt to help others, but we're motivated by self-interest and disturbing emotions, the benefit of our actions will be greatly diminished.

So if you have a loved one who is sick and you do tonglen practice for them, they will benefit from your practice. But again, the benefit does not come from transferring the sick person's karmic causes and conditions to you, the practitioner. We aren't going to get cancer because we do tonglen for someone who has leukemia. But when we practice from our heart with genuine love and compassion, when our sole wish for the practice is to lessen the suffering of another being and to increase their happiness, then that being can feel soothed. We should never underestimate the power of a kind heart. If a doctor has genuine compassion for a patient, it helps the patient. If the doctor is arrogant, irritated, or uncaring, it can hinder recovery. I've seen this firsthand. When I was growing up in Tibet, there were two doctors in our village who practiced Tibetan medicine. One was famous for his knowledge of medicinal texts. But he was also arrogant and more focused on his reputation than on his patients. The other doctor was known for his compassion and kindness. He wasn't as knowledgeable, but he cared deeply about his patients and wanted them to heal. For a while, people flocked to the more educated physician, but it became apparent over time that his patients didn't fare as well, so many people changed to the more compassionate doctor.

Whatever we do physically, verbally, and mentally can be joined to love and compassion. If it is, then what we do will be more fulfilling and joyful. When we are selfishly focused, complete fulfillment and peace will never be reached. Problems will arise as a result of whatever it is that we have obtained, and there will always be a sense of needing something more. For this reason, always check your mind and see if love and compassion are expanding. At first, we might think it's hard to try to work for the benefit of others. But that's just because we haven't yet formed that habit; no one has uncontrived bodhichitta right from the start. It's important to be realistic and to start exactly where you are. Even if many of your actions are still mixed with self-centered interests, engage in the practices for increasing love and compassion. Put them into action to the best of your ability, because even if you wanted to, it wouldn't be possible to instantly drop self-clinging and only help others. Changing the mind is a process. It starts with introducing a way of thinking, acting, and reacting that is opposite to what we're used to. It takes time, patience, and persistence to succeed. So we start by contriving it through methods, by producing the mental states of love and compassion through contemplation and meditation, even while our motivations are mixed with selfishness, attachments, and expectations.

You can explore this by reflecting on how your thoughts and actions are almost always self-centered. Sometimes they're directly self-centered, sometimes indirectly, other times they're secretly or even unconsciously self-centered. Even when we're asleep, our dreams are all about ourselves. This is why we don't have to meditate on having concern for ourselves. It's already our first and most natural response. We don't have to produce this motivation by going through a process of reasoning. It's a very strong habit. But if you reflect deeply, you'll see that self-centeredness is at the root of all of our problems. It's as if we are building a wall between ourselves and others, and there is no way to find peace and happiness when we conduct our lives and our hearts in this way.

Over time, though, as love and compassion grow within us, our motivations will become more naturally pure and we won't have to contrive it anymore. At the same time, our attachments and selfish needs will decrease. Once we genuinely experience purer forms of love and compassion, we will really know how they are the source of all happiness and the means to benefit both ourselves and others. At that point, the motivation to benefit others will arise effortlessly and spontaneously in our minds, as our natural response to people and situations. The challenge for us is getting there.

CALM ABIDING IS PRESENT IN
EVERY MEDITATION

When practicing tonglen, we are cultivating the qualities of two meditation practices in one: bodhichitta, which is a necessary component for
taming the mind; and calm abiding, the one-pointed focus of meditative
absorption. All of the Buddha's Mahayana teachings are based upon bodhichitta. The ability to develop this intention depends on our capacity to
hold it with one-pointed focus.

Calm abiding is the support for all practices, but it is not the entire
path. One-pointed focus on any object will bring a cessation of thought
and give rise to a peaceful mental state. But merely resting in calm abiding, even for hours at a time without a single moment of distraction, will
not necessarily lead us to a freedom from suffering. In fact, the experience of peace that arises when thoughts cease to move is not even the ultimate goal of calm abiding. It's a side effect. The goal of calm abiding is
to develop the ability to hold the mind on whatever we are cultivating
without thinking of or paying attention to anything else, and without too
much effort or too much relaxation. In the case of tonglen meditation, we
are cultivating love and compassion. This meditative concentration will
then serve as a foundation for training in profound insight, the wisdom
that realizes true nature, also known as ultimate bodhichitta.

One of the main reasons we may not experience the positive effects
of meditation is because we're distracted. We may sit for thirty minutes
or even an hour, but how much of that time are we actually absorbed in
the practice? For many of us, we focus for a moment or two, think about
something else, then return to the practice. Our attention flits from one
thing to another, alighting on the object of meditation only fleetingly. This
is the natural state of the mind when you begin meditating, and even if
you've been at it for a while, it is still a major part of the process! So it isn't
a failing that we are distracted, it is just something that we need to begin
to notice so that we can guide our awareness back to the practice and keep
it there more consistently in order to develop the meditative absorption.

Every meditation session is different, and we have to adjust our practice according to the events in our lives, our moods, and our personality. We also need to know ourselves well. If we tend to be too relaxed, we may need to make a concerted effort to focus, sharpening our attention by sitting up straighter or lifting our gaze so that we aren't sleepy or dull during practice. If we feel tension and the mind is agitated and wandering, we need to relax our effort, loosen the posture, and lower our gaze. It's important to find just the right balance of effort and relaxation to remember loving-kindness and compassion. Think of strings on a guitar. If the strings are too tight, the pitch will be too high. If the strings are too loose, then the pitch will be too low. The best sound comes when the guitar is properly tuned. The same goes for meditation practice.

Progress in calm abiding develops gradually as we practice tonglen, just as it would if we practiced calm abiding alone. When we first start practicing tonglen, we use the breath as the focal point, joining our attention to the exhalation with thoughts of loving-kindness and to the inhalation with thoughts of compassion. Initially the breath helps us to develop one-pointed concentration on love and compassion. But as the practice deepens, we have less need for the support of our breath as we focus more on the experience of love and compassion. Eventually, we won't need to focus on the breath at all, but instead will rest effortlessly in the contemplation of love and compassion.

As ordinary beings, it's unrealistic to have no concern for ourselves and to only cherish the welfare of others. That's the experience of a bodhisattva. But even as ordinary beings, we can develop bodhichitta. If we train our mind through the formal practice of sitting meditation, then contemplate these mind trainings informally throughout the day and apply what we've learned to the best of our ability, we will experience deepening levels of bodhichitta that are sustained for longer periods. The practice has a cumulative effect. We'll start having moments when we see all beings as equally important to ourselves and eventually we'll find ourselves spontaneously wishing to take on others' suffering in exchange for our happiness. This practice powerfully transforms the mind. And as we practice, we commit to fully realizing bodhichitta so that one day, we too can become bodhisattvas, for the benefit of all.

APPLYING THE TRAININGS

We have the opportunity to practice each and every moment of our lives. Cultivating love and compassion during post-meditation is as important, if not more important, than formal sitting practice. Thoughts and actions are governed by habits. So, if we are to truly change our mind, we have to carry all circumstances onto the path, otherwise our formal practice will remain theoretical and won't take root in our thoughts and actions. Most of us spend a lot more time engaged in our daily work and activities than we do meditating on the lojong teachings. That's why, like a yo-yo, we revert to our usual thoughts and reactions when we face challenges.

In the "Preliminary Practices of the Heart Drop Essence," or *Longchen Nyingtik Ngondro*, it states, "Though there may be recognition of true nature, if we are not deeply familiar with it, that awareness will be lost to the enemy of ordinary thought patterns, like a baby on a battlefield." Our minds are not habituated toward bodhichitta, and therefore this state of mind is easily lost to the enemy of disturbing emotions. When we understand our susceptibility to habits, we realize how crucial it is that we put equal effort into formal and informal meditation practice. Once again, we need carefulness, vigilant guard, and mindfulness to succeed in practice. We need to carefully watch the mind to make sure we do not get carried away by disturbing emotions. We need vigilant guard to check the state of our thoughts and actions and catch when we forget to practice. And we need mindfulness to remember how to apply the right practice at any given moment.

Every situation is potentially dangerous because it might lead to disturbing emotions and actions that compound suffering. So it's important to employ carefulness at all times. Being careful is the same as being attentive. Just as we are attentive to our surroundings when we walk down an unlit street at night, so we need to be attentive to our own mind. This will provide an environment in which mindfulness and vigilance—and therefore practice—can flourish.

In addition, the more mindful and vigilant we are during formal sitting practice, the more effective our practice will be. It's the same for informal practice, post-meditation. Mindfulness is more than merely being aware in the moment. It's remembering what to practice and how to apply that practice properly.

The opposite of mindfulness is forgetting. In formal meditation, when we forget the focal point of the practice, we are not being mindful. This happens when we are distracted, or sleepy and dull. In everyday life, when we get carried away by emotions and forget to practice, we are not being mindful. But also, if we remember to practice in the moment but we can't recall enough of the details of the mind trainings, we won't be able to apply them effectively either. Practicing mindfulness is actually subsequent to vigilant guard, which is the awareness of the present moment. Mindfulness is when you remember the teachings and how to apply them at that moment. To gain skill at this, it's important to study the teachings again and again, to pore over them until they are committed to memory. Only then can we remember how to apply them when we need them.

Mindfulness is not our normal habit. Usually, we let our mind sink into the experience of whatever is happening, like water soaking into dry dirt. Our attention focuses on the objects of our perception—the forms, sounds, tastes, scents, and tactile sensations—or we get immersed in thoughts about the past, future, and everything else. Inundated by thoughts and perceptions, our time is spent in a state of complete distraction. We are captive to whatever is happening around us.

To have vigilant guard is to be alert. It's the act of occasionally checking the mind during sitting meditation to make sure we haven't forgotten the object of our practice. At all other times, it's our self-awareness when we ask, "What is my mind doing?" As soon as we become self-aware, we either see that mindfulness is present or we reinstate it. That is the job of vigilant guard. If we don't check our minds throughout the day, we may be overcome by disturbing emotions.

Carefulness, mindfulness, and vigilant guard work as a team. Together they give us the ability to apply the lojong trainings. Having carefulness throughout the day ensures that we are taming our mind no matter what situation we may be in, and we never want our state of mind to be separate from vigilance. If our vigilant guard is sporadic, then our mindfulness will only be occasional. And if we train the mind intermittently, we will not gain proficiency. So in every circumstance, no matter what is going on, ask yourself, "What is the state of my mind?" Then remember the appropriate mind training for that situation and practice it right on the spot. This is how practice becomes stronger and more effective in all situations.

7. Three objects, three poisons, three roots of virtue.

The *three objects* refers to the way we categorize the objects of our perception—any person, place, thing, or situation—as either good, bad, or neutral. The *three poisons* refers to our negative emotions, which can be summed up as attachment, aversion, and ignorance. These three are known as the root poisons of the mind because all of our disturbing thoughts and emotions arise from them. The *three roots of virtue* refers to the alchemy of transforming poisons into virtuous mental states and positive actions. So, the three objects and three poisons become the three sources, a.k.a. roots, of positive actions. All positive actions are then termed "virtue" since they produce positive results in the future.

The Three Objects

When we encounter something or someone that we find pleasant, attractive, or desirous, attachment and desire arise. We want to possess or hold on to that form, sound, taste, or tactile sensation. This is the object in relationship to which attachments form. When we encounter a situation that we don't like or perceive as unpleasant, painful, or unwanted, aversion or anger arises. This is the object in relationship to which aversion forms.

When the object or circumstance is neither pleasant nor unpleasant, we experience a neutral feeling. We are neither drawn toward the object nor do we feel a need to reject it. This bland feeling is ignorance. Although it is not marked by attachment or aversion, it is an almost imperceptible experience of mental dullness based on not recognizing our true nature.

The Three Poisons

These three root poisons—attachment, aversion, and ignorance—are called such because they are the source of all other disturbing emotions. They are disturbing because we suffer when we experience them. They also prompt us to act in ways that cause suffering to others, which creates the causes for future suffering. Usually, when we experience a disturbing emotion, we allow ourselves to fall under its power. We believe that we have a good reason for being upset, and we are swept away by emotion. When we feel desire, we pursue what we crave even at the cost of harming others or ourselves. When we get angry, we try to change the situation even at the cost of someone else's or our own well-being. When we experience ignorance, we simply believe in the appearance and fail to investigate the true nature of what we perceive.

The Three Roots of Virtue

By practicing these lojong trainings, we apply a new way of thinking that causes our perceptions to change, allowing us to drop our afflictive mental states and adopt a positive frame of mind. Practicing lojong allows us to take something toxic and transform it into something positive. Disturbing emotions become a catalyst for practice and a source for accumulating merit. We can develop love, compassion, and wisdom by using disturbing emotions as our support. Now we have three roots, or sources, of virtue! The beneficial effects from this practice are unfathomable.

THIS PRACTICE IN ACTION

Through these three objects, three poisons, and three roots of virtue, we rely on disturbing emotions to cultivate our positive potential. To do this, we first need to recognize the affliction. When you encounter something or someone that you want, identify the desire with a thought such as, "This is desire" or "This is attachment." Second, think about the negative effects of desire. Consider how getting what you want doesn't necessarily bring you happiness, and how the more you succeed at getting what you want, the more your desire grows. Our desires are endless, and pursuing them is ultimately unfulfilling and leads to dissatisfaction or worse. The pursuit of our desires can lead us to cause great harm.

Bring all this to mind, even if only briefly. It isn't necessary to go through a laborious analysis every time a disturbing emotion arises, but we should spend at least a few moments reflecting on the harmfulness of the affliction. This will motivate us to practice. Because we know the deleterious effects of desire, we will want to be free from it. Now, the final step is to do tonglen by recollecting how all beings suffer from desire and generating the compassion that wants them to be free of desire with the thought, "May the desire of all beings be gathered here within my experience of desire. By taking it on, may all beings be completely freed from desire and its results. May they never again be afflicted by desire, and may they reach ultimate happiness that is free from suffering."

If we do this, then in that moment of desire we gave rise to loving-kindness and compassion for all beings. Instead of focusing on ourselves and what we want, our mind turns toward the welfare of others. That is a profound step. It's how desire can serve as a catalyst, reminding us of others and of how they are afflicted as well. If in our own moments of affliction, we imagine taking on the suffering of all beings and freeing them from it, it will have a deep impact on our mind.

If taking on the suffering of others feels too overwhelming, you can generate the simplified wish that others find freedom by thinking, "May all beings be free from desire and the suffering that results from it. May they attain ultimate happiness, free from suffering."

For aversion, apply the same method. When your anger ignites, identify the feeling as aversion. Then, remember how anger harms you and others and think, "May the anger of all beings be gathered here within my experience of anger. By taking it on, may all beings be completely freed from anger and its results. May they never again be afflicted by anger, and may they reach ultimate happiness that is free from suffering."

Or if you prefer, think, "May all beings be free from anger and the suffering that results from it. May they attain ultimate happiness, free from suffering." Or, "May all beings be free from anger and its results."

Apply the same method to ignorance and to all of the afflictive thoughts and emotions that stem from the three poisons. For example, to transform jealousy, think, "May the jealousy of all beings be gathered here within my experience of jealousy. By taking it on, may all beings be completely freed from jealousy and its results. May they never again be afflicted by jealousy, and may they reach ultimate happiness that is free from suffering." You can use this method to transform any experience in your life. Even when you stub your toe you can think, "May the pain of all beings be gathered here within my experience of pain. By taking it on, may all beings be completely freed from pain, and may they reach ultimate happiness that is free from suffering."

Now instead of indulging in negative thought processes or focusing on our discomfort, we let go of that self-centered fixation and generate loving-kindness and compassion for others. It's a pure thought because we have no expectation that we will gain anything in return for it. We simply wish for others to be happy and free. With this practice, all of our disturbing emotions become companions on the path.

It may seem counterintuitive to take on more suffering when we already have plenty of our own. But it's not unlike an infected wound that needs to be lanced and cleaned in order to heal. Initially, the treatment causes more pain, but it's needed to heal the injury and end the pain. So when you face problems, take on the problems of all beings. When you suffer, take on the suffering of all beings. When you are afflicted, take on the afflictions of all beings. By taking them on, you will have embarked on the very path to healing, the path of profound inner peace that can only come from love and compassion.

THE THREE OPPORTUNITIES TO PRACTICE

Each time we have an afflictive mental state, there are three windows to transform it: the first moment it surfaces, while it is full blown, or after it has subsided. To become proficient, we have to take advantage of whichever window we can access as soon as we remember to practice.

Obviously, the first moment is the best because the emotion has not yet fully formed, and we have not yet built a habit for reacting to that specific circumstance. If in that moment we recognize that an affliction is forming and we remember to practice tonglen, the practice will have the greatest impact on our mind. When we miss that window, the mind becomes habituated to justifying the emotion, and it becomes harder and harder to change it and the negative actions that follow.

There is a Tibetan saying, "Wipe out the butter lamp while the vessel is still hot." We Tibetans have a lot of experience cleaning butter lamps—small candles offered in monasteries and on personal shrines. When the flame of a butter lamp burns out, if we take a cloth to the butter lamp cup right then, the residual butter is easily cleaned. But if we wait until the butter is cold, it hardens and becomes a hassle to remove. Similarly, if we practice tonglen the moment a disturbing emotion arises, we are more likely to succeed in transforming our minds.

If, however, that first moment has passed and now we are experiencing full-blown emotions, it isn't too late—it is just more difficult. Take intense anger, for example. Once anger is fully formed, we have an intense and often uncontrollable adrenaline rush. Our face becomes red, our veins bulge, and we might even shake. Some of us might start smashing or throwing things. At this point, it's going to be pretty tough to talk ourselves out of having an angry outburst, especially if we're already in the midst of one. We may manage to remember tonglen and even do the practice, but the anger won't necessarily subside. Still, even in moments like this, we should try to apply the practice because we don't want to develop the habit of anger or experience the consequences of actions based on it. Anger is a particularly challenging emotion to transform. It is often easier to practice tonglen with desire, attachment, jealousy, or any number of other afflictions that usually aren't as intense.

The final window to practice is after the emotion has subsided. In the midst of our anger, we might have said nasty things we regret, embarrassed ourselves, or hurt someone. Since all emotions are impermanent, the intensity of the anger eventually subsides, and then we are left with the aftermath.

At this point, we can still practice tonglen in the spirit of developing a habit that orients us toward love and compassion. It is better to remember the practice after the fact than not to remember it at all. Every time we practice tonglen, we are imprinting our mind with a habit to do it again. So once the emotion has subsided, recognize that you became angry—or whatever affliction arose—generate regret, resolve not to react that way in the future, and then practice tonglen. This will undermine the habit for negative mental states and will set the stage for good habits to replace the bad ones going forward.

We can also remedy disturbing emotions with the view of ultimate bodhichitta. First, identify the disturbing emotion, then recognize its empty nature and simply allow the mind to settle into that recognition. The essence of the emotion—whether it's attachment, aversion, or ignorance—is empty, and, by recognizing this, the emotion resolves of its own accord. Of course, this practice will only work if the practitioner has a good understanding of ultimate bodhichitta.

When we talk about applying a remedy to a disturbing emotion, it's important to be clear about what "remedy" means. It doesn't mean the suppression of emotions—something that we often worry about. When an antidote to a disturbing emotion—a remedy—is applied properly, that emotion resolves. We don't react to it, nor do we deny or suppress it. But if a disturbing emotion persists, even if we don't act on it or display it externally, it's still there. It has not been remedied. For lojong, this means doing the practice that corresponds to the situation so that instead of feeling disturbed or upset, we experience love, compassion, or wisdom.

At first, even if we apply the lines of reasoning from the lojong teachings to our disturbing emotions, we may not experience the remedy because our habit for afflictive mental states is stronger than our habit for love and compassion. If this happens, don't get discouraged. Keep going. Keep doing the practice. It takes time to develop skills and become good at new things. Over time, as we apply the tools of lojong both formally and informally, we will strengthen that habit in our minds, and love and compassion will grow.

The more committed we are to establishing a habit, the more success we will have. To build a habit, start with an intention and then reaffirm that intention. For example, you could make a general commitment with a thought such as, "I vow to tame my disturbing emotions with love, compassion, and wisdom." Then, when New Year's rolls around, you could make the commitment again, "This year, I vow to tame my disturbing emotions with bodhichitta." You can make that same commitment for a month, a week, or even just a day. It's also a good practice to make commitments like this before entering situations you know will be difficult. Imagine yourself in the challenging environment you're about to face, but instead of feeling disturbed, see yourself feeling love and compassion. Imagine yourself applying the lojong teachings and continue to make the commitment.

As the habit for mind training grows, it will become your natural response, and your actions and reactions will be shaped by it. There's a saying worth memorizing: "At first the practitioner holds the meditation. Later, the meditation holds the practitioner." We have to grab hold of these methods and diligently apply them again and again. As the habit forms, the practice will arise naturally with whatever occurs, even without our making an effort to remember the teachings and apply remedial factors. When we reach this stage, everything we experience brings us to meditation. The mind has become supremely flexible and pliant, and we begin to experience the true power of mind training.

8. *Train using sayings during all activities.*

Another way to train is to use the words and statements of tonglen throughout the day, in the middle of whatever is happening. "May all beings be happy, may all beings be free" is a powerful thought, but to say it at any given moment is transformative. For example, when we say, "I give all of my happiness and the causes of happiness to all beings, and I take on all of their suffering and the causes of suffering," we interrupt our self-clinging. Our words cause an intense moment of habit shifting that can't be achieved through contemplation and meditation alone. Language is an extraordinary tool.

There are lots of sayings you can use. For example, "I give all profit and gain to others, and I take all loss and blame upon myself." This is not how we were raised to think. It's ingrained in us to put ourselves first, to pursue what we want, even if it hurts someone else. In fact, we're regularly encouraged to put ourselves first. In our society, personal profit is celebrated, and it is common practice to let losses and blame fall on others. But when we say things like this, we start to reverse that thinking.

It's important to use common sense when applying this mind training. It wouldn't be appropriate to blurt out one of these statements when you are with others. They might think you're very strange, and your words might even disturb them if they don't understand the basis of mind training. When you remember a saying around others, say it in a whisper, or even silently to yourself. And when you are alone, say it aloud.

Throughout the day, say these sayings as much as possible. Say them while walking, talking, cleaning the house, relaxing, working, surfing the internet, watching the news, or even while you're texting on your phone. There are many great masters whose stories of mind training serve as inspiring examples as we attempt to emulate them. For example, in the monastery where I grew up, there was a lama, a renowned practitioner of the Kadam tradition, whom I greatly admired. His name was Lama Nangdor and he was a *cha-tralwa*, someone who gives up all material possessions and worldly aims and lives extremely simply. His clothes, for instance, were always ragged and had been repaired so many times that they were almost entirely made of patches. He was known for taking loving care of dogs and other animals. One day I went to visit him, and I could hear him muttering something under his breath, repeating words like they were a mantra. As I listened closer I realized he was saying "I give all profit and gain to others, and I take all loss and blame upon myself." Then I noticed he had even written the saying on the windowsill to remind him every time he looked out the window, and he had also written it on a beam above his bed to remind him whenever he lay down.

Still, sometimes people are leery of these sayings if they confuse the meaning with certain cultural concepts. For example, we know low self-esteem is detrimental and should be guarded against, and that we should not allow others to abuse us. Using these statements doesn't change that. It takes courage and confidence to engage in mind training. Someone who lives in an abusive situation may outwardly take on the loss, blame, and pain of another person, but their internal experience is of immense suffering. Their minds are disturbed by the experience, and they are forced to suppress their emotions. This is not the practice.

Lojong is based upon positive reinforcement and confidence. Practitioners do not suffer from doing the practice if they are doing it correctly. Instead, their disturbing emotions are replaced by love, compassion, wisdom, patience, and other positive mental states, which in turn inspires them to continue engaging in the practice.

It's important that we work within our capacity, which means we don't give beyond what we are capable of giving. So if one day you are feeling really inspired, and you think to yourself, "I don't need my car. That person over there needs a car," and you give away your car only to regret it the next day, then you weren't ready to put that thought into action. When we feel inspired like this to help someone else, it's important to first evaluate whether we can truly give without expectation or regret. If we can do that, then it's within our capacity. This will keep us from feeling bitterness and other disturbing emotions after the fact. But in terms of mind training— the practice of tonglen, the recitation of sayings, wishing others happiness—apply the practices enthusiastically and wholeheartedly. In your mind, give away all of your happiness and love with abandon. This will cause your capacity for actual giving to naturally increase.

9. Start by accepting your own suffering.

Sometimes people think, "I suffer so much already, how can I possibly take on the suffering of others as well?" That's why it's important, especially in the beginning, to begin the practice by accepting your own suffering. We have had the habit of self-clinging and all the disturbing emotions that come with it since time immemorial. Self-centered orientation is ingrained in us, which is why we may feel resistance when we imagine exchanging our happiness for the suffering of others. To be able to take on others' suffering, we first have to accept our own. So we start by taking on our own suffering. This is not tonglen practice, but it is a step toward it. The root text has been translated many times, and often this statement is somewhat erroneously translated as "Begin this process of training with yourself." This has led some to believe that it means you do love and compassion meditation for yourself, when in fact, the words are saying to start by accepting your own suffering. There is a subtle but key difference in meaning.

Bring to mind all of the negative thoughts and actions you have ever engaged in—not just in this life, but in past lives as well. All of these have caused suffering or will cause suffering in the future. Some of that suffering created by past negative actions will ripen through rebirth into less fortunate realms. Think, "May that suffering ripen on me right now, in this life. Through this power may it not become future suffering." Then consider the suffering created by past negative actions that will ripen in this life. Think, "May it ripen on me this year." Next, consider the suffering that will ripen this year and think, "May it ripen upon me this month." And then, "Whatever suffering will ripen this month, may it ripen on me today." And finally, "Whatever suffering is going to ripen into experience today, may it ripen on me this very second!"

When we practice in this way, we are accepting our karmic lot. This does not invite misfortune; rather, it is our recognition of suffering that is inevitable. Since we have already accumulated the causes and conditions for future suffering, we might as well accept it. It is inevitable that suffering will come sooner or later. This also gives us courage and helps to release fear and aversion, hence reducing how much we suffer over it. Practicing this teaches us to accept our suffering, and it helps us bring it onto the path where we can work with it. Accepting our own suffering will shift how our mind operates, and we will then be able to turn our attention to the suffering of others.

Another important point is that people often say "you need to love yourself first." Actually, this is just another way to focus on self, which continues the same patterns we have been stuck in for so long. In reality, doing tonglen, exchanging your happiness for others' suffering, is an act of true love for oneself. There is no greater self-love because the practice of tonglen will bring true happiness. It is the most effective and powerful way to experience joy, and it will benefit us both temporarily and ultimately.

For many people, love and compassion deepen in stages. The practices in this book—such as those previously taught for equalizing ourselves with others and later contemplations, such as training in the specific qualities of love and compassion and the four immeasurables—help us to progress. As we deepen love and compassion through these trainings, exchanging ourselves for others will come more naturally.

HOW TO PRACTICE

The Excellent Beginning

Sit in meditation posture to cultivate the key points of body and speech (see page 17 for a full explanation). Then, cultivate the key points of mind by setting your intention. Think, "I will cultivate love and compassion for all beings."

The Excellent Main Part

Review the following list of concepts introduced in this chapter by reading one point at a time, alternating between contemplative meditation and resting meditation.

Key Points to Contemplate

- What does it means to exchange yourself with others?
- What does it means to cherish others more than yourself?
- For a detailed guided practice of tonglen, use appendix 4. Read the practice aloud or silently until you reach the first class of beings or objects of compassion—"One person who has been very kind to you." Depending on your time, spend approximately five minutes doing the practice. Then, gradually move on to the remaining five categories of beings. Of course, you can do more or less, but five minutes for each category provides a thirty-minute meditation on tonglen. Each

time you change the object(s), first reflect on how those particular beings have suffered and/or are actively creating the causes of suffering. Likewise reflect on all the ways they lack happiness and/or the causes of happiness. Through this, generate compassion (wanting them to be free of suffering) and loving-kindness (wanting them to have true happiness). Then do tonglen with the breath and visualization.

- For a shorter practice of tonglen, simply bring to mind any person, group of people, or class of beings. Reflect on how they are suffering or are actively creating the causes of suffering. Similarly, reflect on all the ways beings lack happiness or the causes of happiness. In this way, generate compassion and loving-kindness, followed by tonglen using the breath and visualization.

The Excellent Conclusion

Dedicate the merit generated by this practice and make aspirations. Think, "I dedicate the merit of this tonglen practice to all beings that they may be freed from suffering and attain both temporary and ultimate happiness." Then, make aspirations such as, "May all beings be happy and may all beings be free. May everyone abide in loving kindness and compassion." (You can also use the dedication and aspiration prayers in appendix 5.)

Off the Cushion

Throughout the day, remember to do informal tonglen whenever you can by practicing the three objects, three poisons, and three roots of virtue. Use sayings during activities and, occasionally, start by accepting your own suffering.

You can do tonglen at any moment in relation to your situation or someone else's. If you see a person or animal with an injury, such as a broken foot (specificity is fine in each situation), you can think, "May the suffering of having a broken limb, and likewise the pain of all beings with broken bones, be gathered into me. Through this power may they and all beings be free from such pain." Or you could use a simpler version: "May they and all beings be free from such pain." For another example, if you stub your toe, think, "May I take on the suffering of all stubbed toes so that no being ever need experience this!" Be creative in your phrasing by making it personal and even funny if you like. Do tonglen for positive experiences as well. For instance, if you have a delicious meal, think, "May all beings have such an abundance of good food." If you visit a nice home, think, "May everyone have a beautiful and safe place to live." There are limitless situations and ways to practice this! Any time you are aware of a disturbing emotion arising, use the opportunity to practice with the three objects to transform the three poisons into the three roots of virtue.

Randomly throughout the day, say to yourself, "May all beings be happy, may all beings be free," or, "I give all profit and gain to others, and I take all loss and blame upon myself." And, occasionally, when you feel resistance to something challenging, start by accepting your own suffering.

Following any of these kindness and compassion practices, you can also bring to mind the wisdom aspect, remembering everything is like a dream or an illusion. Then allow your mind to rest for a moment within this recollection.

PART THREE

TRANSFORMING ADVERSITY: TURNING HARDSHIPS INTO OPPORTUNITIES

THE THIRD KEY POINT

Transforming Adverse Conditions into the Path to Awakening

We live in a degenerate age—a time when the world is filled with negativity. Externally, wars, famines, diseases, and natural disasters occur frequently. Internally, beings experience strong disturbing emotions, which cause a breakdown in ethical conduct and lead to even more harmful actions. While sentient beings suffer more in this degenerate age, it is because of these dark times that we practitioners have more opportunities to train our minds and alleviate the suffering of others.

*When the entire world and all living beings are filled
with negativity, transform all adversity into the path to awakening.*

A Buddhist proverb says, "More adversity brings more practice. More practice brings more positive qualities and realization." When we face adversity, we have abundant opportunities to apply the practice. Negative thoughts and actions will decrease, and positive thoughts and qualities will increase. Suffering becomes fuel for our practice, like dry wood on a fire. It lights the path and enhances spiritual progress.

If suffering occurs and we don't practice, it's just suffering, plain and simple. What's more, discursive thought processes compound the suffering with even more disturbing emotions. These emotions then push us to engage in harmful and negative actions. Now, in addition to the original suffering, we are also creating the causes for future suffering. This makes no sense at all! We spend so much time justifying our afflictions and negative actions, telling ourselves we are in the right. But really, we're just convincing ourselves that our actions, which create more suffering, are necessary. Wouldn't it be better to relate to suffering by decreasing our internal affliction and discarding the causes that perpetuate it? Why not experience the well-being of loving and compassionate mental states? Why not take up the causes of happiness? If we use the lojong teachings to transform adversity, our suffering will gain meaning. It will become ultimately beneficial to us. The focus of this third key point is to learn how to transform adverse conditions into positive ones. In chapter 6, the teaching about the three objects, three poisons, and three roots of virtue demonstrated how to focus on the internal object, the afflictive emotional reactions of the mind, as the means to practice. In this section, the teaching emphasizes the characteristics of the external object as the means to reduce disturbing emotions. Both of these approaches are important, since we need to tame the mind from multiple angles.

Using Relative Reality for Transformation

1. *Drive all blame into one.*

When something bad happens, we tend to blame others. Even when we know it was our actions that created or contributed to an unwanted situation, we often forget our role and complain about how someone else caused the problem. We think, "It's his fault," or, "I only did this because she did that." How often have we had thoughts like this? When we blame others, we ignore the fact that our current experiences are a direct result of our previous actions, and we reinforce our disturbing emotions. To *drive all blame into one* is instead a unique perspective that pushes us to go against our ingrained habits.

There is one root cause for all suffering: self-clinging. Since beginningless time, grasping to a self has caused us to have disturbing emotions. The notion of "I" leads us to think "I want" and "I don't want." It also gives rise to the perception of superiority: "I am more important than others." These thoughts of attachment and aversion lead to the full range of disturbing emotions and negative actions, including the willingness to cause harm in order to get what we want.

Other beings may provide the conditional circumstances for our problems, but we wouldn't suffer if we hadn't produced the specific causes for suffering in the first place. All of the suffering we have ever experienced in the past and all of the suffering that we currently endure began with intense self-clinging. Likewise, all the suffering that we may experience in the future will be produced because of our current attachments to our self. This is the true culprit, the creator of all of our problems. Self-clinging is the only perpetrator we have to blame for suffering.

Compounding this problem, our current selfishness and resulting mental afflictions provide the conditions for the causes of selfishness to grow. When something is happening that we don't like, we need to remember the role that selfishness has played in the past and present, and will play in the future. It is the great enabler that paves the way for our problems.

If someone is harming us in the present, it is because we have caused similar kinds of harm in a previous life. As we know, it is only possible to experience the results of the causes that we have created. The previous negative actions that produced our current suffering sprang from afflictive mental states. These mental states arose on account of deep-rooted selfishness.

For example, during a pandemic, because of self-clinging and a desire for immediate gratification, we might choose to go to a party, only to then catch the virus and all the hardship it entails, including for others. That we could get sick in the first place, though, is not only because of the self-centered choice we made to go to the party. At some point in the past, perhaps even in a previous lifetime, we operated out of selfishness and that is why we are vulnerable to harm now. Self-cherishing could have caused such a strong desire in us that we even harmed someone physically to get what we wanted. That action then imprinted our consciousness with the karma to experience the physical and mental pain we once inflicted on others. That is why we are susceptible to harm, why we can be hurt by others, get into accidents, or become ill. Our selfishness in the past and our selfishness in the present enables this to happen.

When we blame others, our blaming mind feeds our suffering. The more we cling to ourselves, and the more we focus on how our suffering is someone else's fault, the more disturbed and upset we become. Our suffering is caused by self-clinging and then magnified by it. For as long as we don't recognize the role that selfishness plays in this whole drama, we will continue to create the causes for suffering and the conditions for those causes to ripen.

We have a great responsibility right now to make choices that lessen our self-cherishing. If we are more careful in the present, we can render dormant the seeds of harm that may have been sowed by previous negative actions. Careful awareness can prevent all kinds of suffering.

It is important not to misunderstand the role that self-clinging plays in creating the causes and conditions for suffering. To *drive all blame into one* does not suggest that we should hate ourselves for our suffering. In fact, self-loathing and low self-esteem are actually a result of harboring too much selfishness.

Selfishness is not the self. It is a disturbing emotion created in relation to oneself, just like anger. We know that anger is not the self. Recognizing the harm anger causes and wanting to reduce and eventually eliminate it does not prompt self-hate. Rather, reducing anger helps us to improve ourselves in positive ways. It is the same with self-clinging. When we identify selfishness as a disturbing emotion that is a source of problems and strive to transform it, we are empowered. Rather than being a victim of selfishness, we actively participate in changing our experience. As our capacity for this change increases, so will our confidence.

So the moment you experience suffering, remember that the source of all problems is the belief in a self. Turn your attention to the root cause of the problem and begin to break the habit of always blaming others. By accepting personal responsibility for your role in suffering—by driving all blame into one—the whole dynamic changes, and your mind will have the space to practice. Do tonglen in that moment. Do this every time you find yourself blaming someone else. Then, not only will your suffering be greatly reduced, but it will become the catalyst for expanding love and compassion to all living beings. This is a turning point. It is a new way of relating to suffering. It enables us to stop making our problems worse and helps to cultivate positive actions and qualities. It ensures that our suffering will not be meaningless.

2. Meditate on the great kindness of all.

The Buddha said there is no living being who has not been our mother or father. He also said, there is not a handful of dirt where we have not been born. Wandering through the states of existence—sometimes as animals, sometimes as humans, sometimes as hungry ghosts or other types of beings—in most of these lifetimes we were born from parents, which means every being, at one time or another, has cared for us. In our many lives, we've been everywhere in cyclic existence, had every relationship, been in every possible circumstance. The Buddha, after clearing away the obscurations of ignorance and realizing the wisdom that knows true nature, saw with omniscience that all beings have been our mothers at some time and have taken care of us in countless ways. Remembering this kindness, we can generate gratitude.

Sometimes there are people in our lives whom we consider enemies. Yet even our enemies have, at some point in time, taken care of us when we were sick. They loved and protected us. We don't remember when because of our current conditions and karma, but still, if we recall their kindness, we will have yet another reason to generate love and compassion. This is gratitude from a worldly perspective.

Another way to generate gratitude is to remember the source of all positive qualities. Just as attachment to self is the source of suffering, caring for others is the source of happiness. We depend on others to develop the qualities of love and compassion. To love is to want another being to be happy. So without other sentient beings, we wouldn't have a basis for generating love. When we generate love, we are the first beneficiary of that virtuous act because it creates positive karma, the source of good fortune in the future.

This is how it is with all of the lojong trainings: They can only be practiced in relation to other beings. For example, how could we perfect the practice of generosity if there was no one to receive our generosity? How could we refrain from causing harm—the practice of ethical conduct—if there were no beings to protect? So when you encounter others, especially your adversaries, remember that it is in relation to them that you will develop positive qualities and create the causes of happiness. It's the ultimate win-win situation. We help others by being patient, generous, or kind, but we also reap the benefits from taming our mind and experience the positive results—all thanks to beings. If it were not for others, we could not attain the state of enlightenment. There is no greater kindness, and that is something to be truly grateful for. This is gratitude from a spiritual perspective.

It's especially important to realize how our enemies are kind to us. In Buddhist scriptures it is said, "There is no greater harm-doer than anger and no greater virtue than patience." The benefits and positive effects generated through the cultivation of patience, defined as the profoundly undisturbed mind, are immense. To generate true patience for even a single moment purifies countless obscurations and accumulates vast amounts of merit. The power of our practice is greatly magnified when training in relation to adversity versus when there is no adversity.

In time, if you diligently remember the kindness of everyone—especially your adversaries—situations that used to upset you no longer will. And when you do become upset, it will be less intense and easier to transform into practice. When someone does something you don't like, if you generate positive qualities in response, you will see that they are actually kind to you. The more we focus on the positive qualities that come from others, dwelling on their kindness, the more patience we will have. When we experience this profoundly undisturbed mind, we will know this to be the truth.

But these days, people get upset very easily and have little patience. Communication styles have dramatically changed, especially with various social media platforms, which has led to more sudden and intense mental afflictions. Even public figures react dramatically to situations, causing society as a whole to accept this type of behavior. It may only take a couple of words—not even spoken with malice—to trigger an explosive emotional reaction. A few harsh words and it might even come to blows.

Anger is also one of the greatest obstacles for awakening bodhichitta. It blocks us from feeling compassion. Compassion and anger cannot coexist, which is why anger is one of the most detrimental of the disturbing emotions and why, if we are able to generate patient forbearance in upsetting situations, great virtue will result. If we practice with anger instead of succumbing to it, the person who provoked us—our so-called adversary—transforms into one of our greatest companions in spiritual progress. This is why enemies are actually the kindest of all beings.

It's important to identify why we get angry in the first place. Anger arises because of self-clinging and the perception that someone is harming us or our loved ones. We might perceive this harm directly or indirectly, and it might occur to our face or behind our back. Maybe someone says something about us that we consider to be unkind. Or maybe someone does something that we think threatens our wealth, position, or reputation or that of our loved ones. Basically, we get angry because we either don't get what we want or get what we don't want.

We think of people who treat us badly or who get in the way of what we want as enemies. After that, even when they aren't causing us or our loved ones harm, if something good happens to them—if they gain greater wealth, reputation, or power—we feel unhappy about it because of our lingering resentment.

Understanding why we get angry and anticipating the situations that make us angry are the first steps to ridding ourselves of anger. Then, the more we understand and apply the practices of love and compassion, the less anger we will feel.

THREE TYPES OF PATIENCE

In addition to those methods for cultivating patient forbearance, there are three additional trainings called the three types of patience: the patience of accepting suffering, the patience of not blaming the harm-doer, and the patience of certainty in the true nature of phenomena.

The Patience of Accepting Suffering

The first type of patience is to accept suffering, which means to use it in a meaningful way. In other words, we relate to unwanted circumstances as opportunities to grow and develop wisdom, gain life skills, or increase our capacity for love and compassion. Someone who has developed the patience of accepting suffering has decided to take their pain and make it beneficial. They choose to dive into the ocean of bodhichitta and change their lives.

To engage in this practice, we must change our relationship with suffering. Suffering can be a catalyst that changes our lives in a way that is more positive and ultimately meaningful. Think about how some of the most challenging situations you've been through have helped you grow and gain insights. When I was seventeen years old, my father drowned in a nearby river. The burial ground was also not far from our home, and it was a "sky burial," which means the corpse was cut up and offered to vultures.[1] I witnessed his body being recovered from the water and watched the burial ceremony. As the eldest sibling of a large family, I also became responsible for my many brothers and sisters who were left behind. It was one of the single most painful ordeals in my life and my first deep experience with suffering. When I look back, it was at this time that I took my first steps on the path. This profound pain forged my resolve to pursue the path of inner qualities and wisdom that have made me the person I am today. So for me, the greatest challenge of my life was also what brought the greatest positive changes.

The doorway to the path also opens once we see and know the nature of suffering in all things. This leads us to develop the wish to be free. That is the power of suffering. It motivates us to find freedom. When we see this potential within suffering, we begin to appreciate it. Then, because of that appreciation, our suffering becomes easier to bear. When we feel less aversion to suffering, we also will feel less anger. When there is less anger, there is less suffering.

Suffering can also inspire us to help others. It often isn't until we endure a hardship that we really get a sense of what others feel when they struggle. Suffering deepens our empathy and compassion, and the benefits of such virtues are infinite. Compassion also cools anger and produces the undisturbed mind of patience, which enhances our acceptance of suffering.

In addition, we suffer because we have accumulated the causes and conditions for suffering in the past. But suffering can be a means through which we purify negative karma. By experiencing the fully ripened results of previous actions, we are exhausting those negative causes and conditions and will not have to undergo their results again. Resolve not to engage in negative actions in the future with the following commitment: "From today onward, I will refrain from harmful and negative actions, which produce suffering." If we approach suffering in this manner, not only will we exhaust past negative actions but we will also cease to perpetuate suffering.

Through the practice of tonglen, we can accept suffering with loving-kindness and compassion. In the immediacy of a painful moment, generate bodhichitta and remember how all living beings—our mothers throughout existence—are suffering in similar ways. It is likely that their suffering is even much worse. Contemplate this and then think, "May the suffering of all beings be gathered here within my experience of suffering. Through this power, may they be freed from all suffering and its causes."

The Patience of Not Blaming the Harm-Doer

The second type of patience is not blaming the harm-doer. Pause before you blame someone who has harmed you and begin by contemplating the statement, *Drive all blame into one.* Then reflect on how they want happiness just like you, but they don't know how to create its causes. Whatever they are doing is driven by the power of ignorance and other disturbing emotions. When they hurt you, hurt others, or even harm themselves, they don't realize they are driven by the power of ignorance and afflictions. Human beings are not fundamentally corrupt. The problem is that our disturbing emotions compel us to act.

Most people submit to the power of their disturbing emotions. They are "under the power of other." Whenever someone causes harm, they are motivated by disturbed mental states such as anger, desire, attachment, jealousy, pride, or other afflictions. Compelled by the power of these emotions, they become capable of harm. It is like being swept up by a fierce current in a river and lacking the strength to resist it. Without the tools of mind training, we are carried off by the river of our emotions.

How strong are these disturbing emotions? Think about what people cherish most in this world: their own lives. Yet under the power of disturbing emotions, people can even kill themselves. If disturbing emotions are strong enough to compel a person to commit suicide, of course they could compel a person to harm others. Understanding the strength of disturbing emotions should not be used as a license to hurt people or as an excuse for our negative actions. The purpose of this contemplation is to cultivate ways of thinking that help us counteract the tendency to respond with anger.

We don't choose to be angry. This state of mind, like any disturbing emotion, results from causes and conditions. These causes do not arise solely from what's going on in the moment. The current situation is simply a catalyst that prompts our anger. Behind every experience of anger lies a lifetime's worth of conditioning. Most people's mental states are completely dependent upon that conditioning and external circumstances because they lack the tools to change their minds. They don't realize anger is merely a way of thinking about something. It's a habit. They also don't realize they have the choice to change it.

So when a person causes you harm, think to yourself, "This problem is not caused by a flaw in the person; it's caused by the flaw of their disturbing emotions." Cultivating this understanding both prevents us from engaging in harmful actions and helps us to be compassionate instead of angry. Sometimes we rationalize that we need to retaliate so that the person causing harm doesn't get away with what they've done. But no one gets away with anything karmically, and to engage in negative actions only accumulates more causes of suffering.

When something happens that we don't like, we usually justify our anger by repeatedly focusing on the offenses of the person we deem to be at fault. Mind training involves going beyond this ordinary rationalization to reach a more sophisticated perception, one that is an actual cause for happiness. This change of perspective is what it means to engage in dharma practice. It means we are willing to apply wisdom to whatever takes place in our lives to tame the mind. We use our understanding of how things are to reduce afflictions and to increase positivity. Basically, we talk ourselves out of reacting with anger or other disturbing emotions.

It's up to us to make a conscious decision to use these methods instead of simply succumbing to our negative emotions. We should do our best to think about things from other people's perspectives. They are suffering enormously from their negative emotions, not to mention the causes of suffering they are creating. Have you ever watched someone get angry? Their skin reddens, their eyes narrow, and the veins on their temples bulge. Their hands might shake and their voice might quiver. Someone who is gentle under normal circumstances can turn into a monster when they get angry. It is torment to be overwhelmed by anger. Does it not warrant a compassionate response?

It is important to consider that the reason we use to justify the anger may be based on a misperception. Also, the object of our anger does not determine our experience. It's all on us. That is why three people can encounter the same situation and one person will get angry, another will feel compassion, and the third will feel nothing at all. When we change the way we think, we change our experience.

If someone hits us with a stick, we don't blame the stick—we blame the person wielding the stick even though it's actually the stick that hurts us. It's the same thing when someone says something we don't like. We don't blame their words—we blame the person. But we need to consider that when a person harms us, they are under the power of disturbing emotions. Contemplate this until you develop a new perspective and your mind is less disturbed. Once you decide not to react in anger when you are harmed, it will be much easier to apply the other mind trainings.

The Patience of Certainty in the True Nature of Phenomena

The third type of patience is the undisturbed mind that comes from certainty in the true nature of phenomena. When anger arises in someone with a genuine understanding of emptiness, the practitioner recognizes true nature, and an emotional reaction does not develop. Depending on the person's level of insight, the anger could dissipate right on the spot or have very little power over the mind. But we don't need to have complete realization to reduce the effect of our negative emotions. We should use whatever wisdom and methods we have to antidote afflictions.

Ordinary mind operates under a framework of three spheres: subject, object, and action. The subject is the perceiver; the object is what is perceived; and the action is the interaction that takes place between the subject and object. When accomplished practitioners see the empty nature of these three spheres, their disturbing emotions are resolved as they arise. Because their minds remain profoundly undisturbed, they experience patient forbearance. Practitioners who have not yet developed this degree of insight should examine the three spheres until they see that, although they appear, they are empty and are without any inherent existence.

Here's another way to think about it: When you feel upset, rather than thinking about why you feel angry, look directly at the essence of anger itself. Where is it? What is it like? What is its nature? At the moment of looking, relax and let go, and rest naturally. If you can do that and your mind remains undisturbed, the anger will resolve then and there. This can bring an experiential recognition of emptiness. But for this method to work, we have to be willing to let go of the reasons why we are angry.

Another way to generate patience is to recognize the dreamlike nature of experience. Our experiences, conjured by the interdependence of multiple causes and conditions, do not exist in their own right. They are no more real than a dream or an illusion. This perspective can help decrease the strength of disturbing emotions because it counteracts the belief that whatever we perceive is real.

HOW TO PRACTICE

The Excellent Beginning

Sit in meditation posture to cultivate the key points of body and speech (see page 17 for a full explanation). Then, cultivate the key points of mind by setting your intention. Think, "In order to benefit beings, I will transform all adversity into the path."

The Excellent Main Part

Review the following list of concepts introduced in this chapter by reading one point at a time, alternating between contemplative meditation and resting meditation.

Key Points to Contemplate

- What does it mean to *drive all blame into one*? How would this perspective decrease your mental afflictions and thereby decrease your suffering?
- Why *meditate on the great kindness of all*? What would it look like if you felt appreciation for everyone, even when you dislike them?
- What are the three types of patient forbearance? Try applying all three to one situation.

The Excellent Conclusion

Dedicate the merit generated by this practice and make aspirations. Think, "I dedicate the merit of this practice of transforming adversity to all beings that they may be freed from suffering and attain both temporary and ultimate happiness." Then, make aspirations such as, "May all beings be happy and may all beings be free. May everyone be able to transform adversity in their lives." (You can also conclude by reciting the dedication and aspiration prayers in appendix 5.)

Off the Cushion

Every time you encounter adversity, give yourself a moment before reacting. Pause, take a breath, and bring to mind the first or second statement or bring to mind any or all of the three types of patient forbearance. This will give your mind space and perspective. Follow that with informal tonglen practice. Design a saying that is specific to the situation. For instance, "May the pain of all beings who suffer in these ways be gathered here in my experience, through which power may they all be free from such suffering and its causes." If you can, briefly recollect ultimate bodhichitta by thinking about how the situation does not truly exist according to your perception or is no more real than a dream. Then allow the mind to rest for a moment.

When you don't have time, especially if you are in the middle of a tense situation, do just one—remember one of the statements or do tonglen. Follow either of these trainings with a moment of rest. This practice takes only a few seconds and can be done at any time, even in the middle of a conversation.

If the affliction persists or your mind dwells on the circumstance past the initial moments, continue to reflect on any of the points made in this book and apply them to your particular circumstance. You could even systematically think about each of the four thoughts that change the mind (the first key point of mind training) in relation to the situation, then cultivate wisdom that sees the ultimate nature. Or you might reflect on the meaning of driving all blame into one, considering the kindness of others, or remembering the value of practicing patience. Follow any contemplations with loving-kindness and compassion practice, such as tonglen. You already have an arsenal of tools to implement during challenging situations!

Using Ultimate Reality
for Transformation

3. *Meditating on the appearances of confusion as the four kayas is the unsurpassed protection of emptiness.*[1]

We suffer because we don't know the true nature of phenomena. All appearances are the result of this delusion. We believe things to be what they are not, and we suffer in relation to these perceptions. It's like a dream. In a dream, we experience myriad appearances. While sleeping, because of our mind's confusion, we believe the dream is truly happening to us. If it's a pleasant dream, we're happy; if it's unpleasant, we suffer. Either way, it's just a dream. The happiness or suffering only occurs as long as we believe the dream appearances to be true. So when we have a nightmare, if we recognize that it is just a dream, right there we are liberated from the nightmare. This is the same for waking experiences. If we realize their emptiness, their dreamlike nature, we are no longer under their power. At first, we may still experience suffering, but the intensity of the pain will be reduced, and we'll have fewer disturbing emotions. Over time, even physical pain will decrease. Since everything in cyclic existence is merely a perception—an appearance based upon confusion—as that confusion dissipates, liberation unfolds. This practice for transforming adversity and carrying it onto the path begins to unravel cyclic existence.

Each of us has a different level of understanding of the view of wisdom, so we should apply this third instruction to the best of our ability. Our understanding will deepen and blossom over time as we refine our mind with the practice of bodhichitta and study more texts on ultimate wisdom.

To understand this third instruction, we need to become familiar with the Sanskrit term *kaya*. *Kaya* can be translated literally as "dimension," "form," or "body." It is not referring to a physical form but rather to a body of qualities. It describes the ultimate nature in which everything is complete. In other words, the ultimate truth that encompasses all phenomena.

As practitioners, we can integrate the wisdom of emptiness—also called the four kayas—to transform adversity.[2] Whatever we experience, be it physical pain or mental fear and anxiety, these perceptions arise from delusion. In a dream, we might be burned by fire or carried off by a river, but these appearances manifest to our perception because we are confused; they do not exist in their own right. We can apply this view to our waking life by recognizing that, at any given moment, the appearances that arise have no inherent truth. They do not exist as we perceive them. By relaxing in this recognition of the empty nature of appearances, the mind is free of clinging to a perceiver and perceived. It is free from any fixed reference point. In that moment, everything in its entirety is experienced as empty essence or *dharmakaya*, the absolute dimension.

The mind that perceives and the objects it experiences are both empty, but that does not mean perceptions cease to appear. The very nature of appearance is emptiness. While being empty by nature, these appearances continue to occur and are experienced. This is called *nirmanakaya*, the dimension of manifestation.

The appearance is empty and emptiness is the appearance. Appearances and emptiness are timelessly one and the same. This primordial unity is referred to as *sambhogakaya*, the dimension of enjoyment.

Though we speak of these four kayas as if they are different things, they are, in fact, indivisible. We call this *svabhavikakaya*, the dimension of oneness. Think about it in terms of the house we explored in chapter 5. When we recognize the nature of a house as being empty of inherent existence, we know it's dharmakaya. The house cannot be established as real and yet it continues to appear, which is the nirmanakaya. When we recognize that the house and its empty nature are indivisible, that's the sambhogakaya. These dimensions are not three separate things but one single essence, svabhavikakaya.

When we recognize emptiness, we directly experience the four kayas. During adversity, if we rest in meditative absorption, that hardship becomes the cause for recognizing true nature. This is called transforming adversity into the path. Transformation occurs through seeing that what is appearing is the four kayas. This is the supreme method for cutting through deluded appearances, which makes it the unsurpassed protection from suffering. If we are able to practice in this way, our disturbing emotions will be transformed into wisdom.

So when we become angry, if we recognize the empty nature of the anger, we directly experience what it truly is, and it simply resolves by itself. If we rest the mind in that timelessly pure essence, it will no longer follow after the anger and succumb to it. There is no need to block, suppress, or stop the anger because simply by knowing its true nature, it dissipates in and of itself. There isn't anything else we need to do. Knowing its empty nature is sufficient. Just rest, and the anger will simply dissolve on its own. This method is called self-liberating the anger.

Most of the time we justify our feelings by repeating the reasons for them over and over again, convincing ourselves that we have a right to feel a certain way. This only causes us to suffer more. To engage in this practice, we have to first make the choice to do so and we have to be willing to let go of focusing on what's made us angry. Then, we can look at the true nature of anger itself. We need to build a habit for this, because the more we practice, the stronger it will become. As the practice becomes more powerful, it will become strong enough to antidote anger and other negative emotions.

Once we recognize experience as emptiness and we rest the mind within that recognition, the practice of the four kayas is complete. From this perspective, disturbing emotions are not seen as something inherently flawed that we need to eliminate. Their true nature is innately pure, so disturbing emotions will cause no harm if we are able to recognize their essence.

This is the most effective way to eliminate anger. If we recognize the true nature of anger, then anger is the path. This approach can be applied to any of the disturbing emotions.

Even if we don't yet understand emptiness, simply contemplating that whatever is occurring is like a dream can have profound effects. So can considering that things might not be what we believe them to be. This view starts us on the path of wisdom and helps us build the strength we need to overcome afflictions.

But why stop with disturbing emotions? This insight can be applied to anything and everything that occurs: all pain, suffering, and unwanted circumstances. No matter what you face, large or small, recognize that the ultimate nature of that experience is empty and allow the mind to rest. By letting go in that expanse, you will see that all of the problems in the world are a vast display of emptiness. They are simply a sequential drama of appearances, none of which ultimately exist. Their very nature becomes the means for finding freedom. Then we can say that negative emotions are our spiritual companions because the more adversity we face and the more we practice, the more we will bring about positive effects, both immediately in the moment and in the future.

So to recap, transforming the mind using the view of ultimate bodhichitta is a simple practice. Whenever you encounter something unwanted, stop focusing on what's making you upset. Stop thinking about what isn't right and drop your justifications for your reactions. Look at your response and the unpleasant sensation you're feeling. Focus on that emotional state, then look directly at its essence and rest your mind. Allow your mind to utterly relax in that moment. Take control of your negative emotions by seeing them for what they really are.

To give an example, here's a story about one of my students who was struggling with anger. Her husband's nephew kept borrowing their lawn mower without asking. He was careless and would mow over branches and clumps of dirt, repeatedly ruining the lawn mower's blade. She tried to meditate on kindness by thinking about how her husband's nephew, just like all beings, wanted to be happy, but it wasn't working and she was still angry. Then, one day, she spontaneously saw that her husband's nephew was made of parts, and the lawn mower blade was made of parts, and she too was made of parts! Her anger abated and she actually smiled. She had an unintentional recognition of emptiness. As discussed in chapter 5, we respond to situations with disturbing emotions because of the many layers of ignorance present in our mind. As our wisdom regarding the empty nature of our experience deepens, the persistent misapprehension of appearances decreases, less disturbing emotions arise over time, and the more effective a practice such as this will be at resolving them in each situation. This is also a reminder that sometimes we can see the fruition of these contemplations unexpectedly.

This book is filled with methods to help you change your perception. It's important to apply the practices to the best of your ability. There are multiple ways you can address any given situation. As practitioners we need to know which methods work most effectively for us, and if one method doesn't work, then we try another.

Every emotion, every thought—all suffering—can be transformed. If we recognize ultimate nature, adversity will be resolved on the spot. If we don't yet have this capacity, then we can resolve our difficulties with the trainings of relative bodhichitta, such as tonglen. The practices of relative and ultimate bodhichitta can be used to address our suffering and also the suffering of others. Every aspect of our experience can be carried onto the path using the practices of relative and ultimate bodhichitta.[3]

HOW TO PRACTICE

The Excellent Beginning

Sit in meditation posture to cultivate the key points of body, speech (see page 17 for a full explanation). Then, cultivate the key points of mind by setting your intention. Think, "In order to benefit beings, I will transform all adversity into wisdom."

The Excellent Main Part

Review the following list of concepts introduced in this chapter by reading one point at a time, alternating between contemplative meditation and resting meditation.

Key Points to Contemplate

- Slowly examine the instructions for *Meditating on the appearances of confusion as the four kayas is the unsurpassed protection of emptiness*, taking your time to digest the material.
- Rephrase each of the four kayas in a language that resonates with you.
- Imagine yourself in the middle of an unwanted situation and think about how you might apply this wisdom insight to successfully transform your perception and way of experiencing it.

The Excellent Conclusion

Dedicate the merit generated by this practice and make aspirations. Think, "I dedicate the merit of this practice of transforming adversity through wisdom to all beings that they may be freed from suffering and attain both temporary and ultimate happiness." Then, make aspirations such as, "May all beings be happy and may all beings be free. May everyone be able to transform adversity with wisdom in their lives." (You can also conclude by reciting the dedication and aspiration prayers in appendix 5.)

Off the Cushion

When you encounter something you don't like, pause. Bring to mind the wisdom insight that sees the true nature of reality. Depending on your personal understanding and experience, there are multiple methods for practicing ultimate bodhicitta. No one size fits all. You could apply the more experiential approach of looking directly at the essence of the mind that feels dislike, or you could go through the full process of investigating its nature. Utilize the advice given in this section. After any recollection of true nature, allow the mind to rest for a moment to more fully assimilate the wisdom.

Using Creative Methods
for Transformation

4. The four applications are the supreme method.

Whenever someone suffers from sickness, lack of success, or other obstacles, there are four additional practices to rely on. These actions are so
deeply embedded in Tibetan Buddhist culture that to respond by doing
them is typically a native Tibetan's instinctive way of working with adversity, even for non-practitioners. These are called the four applications:
gathering accumulations, purifying obscurations, offering *tormas* to gods
and demons, and offering tormas to the dakinis and dharma protectors.
These practices can be joined to all other practices of mind training.

GATHERING ACCUMULATIONS

If we want happiness, we must gather the causes for happiness. So when
we experience adversity, we should accumulate as many positive actions as possible.[1] It makes no sense to react to suffering with disturbing
emotions and negative actions. It's bad enough that we are forced to

endure pain. To compound our suffering by creating causes for future suffering is completely counterproductive.

To gather accumulations, think, "All suffering is the result of negative actions, so I will accumulate the causes for happiness—positive actions!" In Tibet, this way of thinking is part of our culture, because we relate to our experiences in terms of cause and result. The worse the circumstances, the more virtue we accumulate. Adversity is often the impetus for charity. In times of hardship, Tibetan people focus on practicing generosity and helping others.

There are endless possibilities as to how we can accumulate merit. We can do small things, such as speaking kindly to another person or even removing a worm from the sidewalk! Or we can do big things, such as taking on a large project that will benefit many beings. No positive act is too big or too small. Practicing generosity can mean donating to a charitable organization that you trust or volunteering with them. To accumulate merit, help others in any way that you can, look for every opportunity to be kind, and go out of your way to alleviate other beings' suffering.

For those who know these practices, we can also accumulate merit by making offerings to the buddhas and bodhisattvas. We can make shrine offerings, offer butter lamps, do prostrations, or circumambulate representations of the body, speech, and mind of the buddhas.[2] We can also save lives. This practice is common in Tibet. It is a very special practice of generosity that is potent in the face of adversity, particularly for people who are suffering with illness. To save—or *ransom*—lives means that we protect other living beings from suffering and death. As a commonplace practice in Tibet, for instance, we might purchase a yak or a sheep designated for slaughter and keep it in our herd for the rest of its life. We even brand the animal so no one will ever kill it for food. In coastal cities in China, Buddhist practitioners often buy live fish at the market and release them back into the sea. In Louisiana, Buddhist practitioners purchase crawfish and crabs and let them go. As practitioners, we can also rescue creatures that we happen upon, such as a worm in danger on the sidewalk. It only takes a moment to move it to safety.

Even though gathering accumulations is the best thing to do when we face hardships, it's not the normal thing to do. The normal thing is to think, "What about me?" We can't possibly focus on others while in the midst of our own personal crisis! But we need to remember that focusing on ourselves only makes our suffering worse, while devoting our time, energy, and resources to others is powerful. It changes everything.

In Tibet, adversity is often the impetus for charity. When a person or family experiences sickness, death, financial loss, or other obstacles, they look for ways to benefit others. Families will often sponsor food for a monastery, give alms to the poor, or help someone in need.

During our most difficult hours, we need virtue more than ever. Once we realize the nature of cause and result, we will be inspired to engage in it. Random acts of kindness don't need to be random. They can be deliberate because we know that actions that benefit others, benefit us. It is important to always appreciate the power of positive actions.

PURIFYING OBSCURATIONS

The practice of dharma can be summed up as gathering accumulations and purifying obscurations. When we gather accumulations, we accumulate the causes for happiness. When we purify obscurations, we rid ourselves of the causes of suffering by refining away the habitual imprints of suffering that exist in our minds.

Negative actions from our past can affect us in one of two ways. Either we will experience their full result in the future, or we can purify these actions before they ripen. When we commit a negative act, we plant a seed in our mind. Once the conditions come together for that seed to grow, we experience the result of the action, like a plant bearing fruit. If, before these actions ripen in our experience, we burn those negative seeds, we can render them harmless and unable to bear fruit. We can do this by antidoting the habitual imprints in our mind.

The great Indian master Nagarjuna[3] said, "The only good thing about negative actions is that they can be purified." When we experience suffering, the cause of that suffering—a past negative action—is exhausted.

This process is very different from purification. The exhaustion of karma is like drinking poison and being sickened by it. But if we drink poison and realize that it's going to make us sick, we can take an antidote and reduce or even eliminate the harmful effect. So we have a choice. We can experience the full results of our past negative actions until they are exhausted, or we can purify them and eliminate their potential to cause suffering.

The Four Powers

The most direct way to purify past negative actions is to rely on the four powers. They are the power of regret, the power of resolve, the power of the support, and the power of the remedy.

We begin with the *power of regret*. When we engage in purification practice, the first thing to do is to bring to mind all of the harmful, negative actions that we have committed with our body, speech, and mind. These include physical acts, harsh words, negative thoughts—everything we know we've done, things we've done that we didn't know were harmful, and even actions we can't remember. We may not remember the negative actions we committed in previous lives, but we should consider them too. We should also contemplate the actions we engaged in that may have caused our current suffering. Think of the disturbing emotions at their root—the ignorance, anger, and self-cherishing. Reflect on how these emotions are the source of suffering for ourselves and others and how all negative actions stem from them. Then, generate a feeling of deep regret for these actions. This counteracts the habit of mind that gave rise to them. The power of regret weakens the habitual imprints of our negative actions. But it's not a guilt-based exercise intended to make us feel bad about ourselves. In fact, there is no word for "guilt" in the Tibetan language. Regret is actually a healthy mental state because it motivates us to improve ourselves and to grow from our mistakes.

Next comes the second power, the *power of resolve*. Generate the determination to never commit these negative actions again. When we generate the power of resolve, we commit to overcoming the disturbing emotions that caused us to act negatively. The power of resolve disrupts our negative tendencies and further undermines the habitual imprints in our mind that would otherwise bear fruit.

Our resolve needs to be strong so that it can overcome the negative habits we've developed. The stronger our resolve is, the more powerful an antidote it will be. So after cultivating sincere regret, think, "Even at the cost of my life, I will not engage in these harmful actions again." Be decisive and imagine how you will act differently in the future.

Some people express concern about making strong resolutions. They worry that they might regress and commit the same negative action again after vowing not to do so. "What if the habit for this mistake is so strong that, even though I want to change, I cannot resist these disturbing emotions or actions?" We don't need to worry about sliding backward. The very reason we make strong vows and aspirations is that they help us to overcome our bad habits. How can we ever change our negative habits if we don't make a commitment to do so? The more that we make a positive resolve to overcome negative actions, the more likely we will be to change. We need to keep vowing to change our thoughts and actions until we succeed. We have to start somewhere. Even if we don't have the capacity to change yet, generating the sincere wish to improve ourselves helps us to build strength of mind and the habit that will lead us in the right direction. We should not fear developing a feeling of resolve just because we might not be able to change our behavior immediately.

Next, rely on the third power, the *power of support*, an authentic source of refuge. A refuge is something that we can rely upon to protect us from suffering. Ideally the refuge is infallible. Buddhist practitioners take refuge in the buddhas, the dharma, and the sangha of bodhisattvas. The buddhas and bodhisattvas support us, but what directly protects us from suffering is the dharma—the teachings and the actual practices, such as these mind trainings. So practitioners of mind training can rely on the teachings on relative and ultimate bodhichitta as the support.

Finally we come to the fourth power, the *power of the remedy*. This is the antidote we use to transform the mind.[4] We could use the relative bodhichitta meditations on love and compassion, such as tonglen, or we might meditate on emptiness. Whichever meditation practice we choose, when we apply it with the specific intention of purifying our minds, we have employed the power of the remedy.

To do a formal purification practice, start by sitting down and settling the mind. When you are ready, cultivate your motivation by generating bodhichitta, then develop the intention to purify the causes of your hardship. Acknowledge that your current circumstances are the result of past negative actions, and set your intention to purify them. Generate the power of the support, of regret, and of resolve, and then meditate on relative or absolute bodhichitta as the power of the remedy. Conclude with dedication and aspirations. Dedicate the merit of your practice to all living beings, then dedicate it specifically to purify the causes of your hardship. This is called the application of purifying obscurations.

OFFERING TORMAS TO GODS AND DEMONS[5]

Making food offerings, or tormas,[6] to local deities, spirits, hindrance-causing ghosts, or formless beings is a common practice for Tibetans. Westerners may not immediately identify with these practices as they are not commonplace, but they can still be of great benefit. It's possible that when we face obstacles, they are caused by local beings or other negative formless beings with whom we have a karmic debt. Making ritual offerings to these beings can help us avoid their negative influences and overcome whatever adversity we may be facing.

OFFERING TORMAS TO DAKINIS AND DHARMA PROTECTORS

Dharma protectors and dakinis are wisdom beings who have sworn to protect the dharma and the practitioners of the teachings. By making offerings to these protectors, we form a direct connection to them. This can help us overcome our problems and have greater success in our practice.

While we all may not be ready to engage in protector practice, it can be a powerful support when adversity arises.

5. *Immediately join whatever you encounter to the training.*

When someone falls ill, the illness can last for days, months, or even years. In cases of chronic adversity like that, there may be long periods of time when we can contemplate and apply different mind-training practices. We can also ask our teachers for guidance.

But we have a tendency to forget the practice when something happens suddenly. We get so caught up in the drama of the situation that we forget to join everything to love, compassion, and wisdom. The purpose of this fifth instruction is to remind us to build a habit of practicing right on the spot. To do this, we need to prepare our mind-training tools so they are ready to use no matter what happens. Then, when something unexpected does happen, we will more readily remember to use them.

To train with this fifth point, focus on the stuff that pops up out of nowhere, like when you get elbowed while walking down a busy street or when someone gives you news you don't like. Because it's unexpected, you react without thinking.

Until the habit of mind training is strong, unexpected circumstances are going to be tricky to deal with. We have such a long-standing tendency to react with disturbing emotions and negative actions. So, every morning set the intention to immediately join whatever you encounter to mind training and check it throughout the day. When necessary, reset your commitment. Visualize yourself reacting to surprising circumstances with mind training. If something happens and you forget to practice, imagine yourself back in that situation, but this time see yourself remembering to apply the mind training. Train continuously in this way, and, over time, a good habit will form. It will become easier and easier to practice when unexpected things happen. But you must train over and over again. Just keep going.

Conditioned existence is full of unwanted things that happen unexpectedly. That's why it's crucial we learn how to relate to everything constructively. Don't let surprise be your excuse for reacting badly. For as long as we cycle through samsara, such surprises will occur. All beings are in this same boat.

If we expect unwanted things to happen and learn to accept the surprises, they won't overwhelm us. If we don't anticipate the unexpected, then what starts as a bad situation can easily turn into a terrible one. The unfolding is predictable. We suffer over something that's happened. Then we react with anger or jealousy or another disturbing emotion. We forget that suffering and dissatisfaction are the nature of samsara. We can't believe this is happening to us. We think, "This isn't fair!" and justify our disturbing emotions. Then, to top it all off, we're anxious about what's happened, which blows the situation out of proportion even more. Everything is made worse by our reaction. Wouldn't it be better to just practice? We can, if we prepare in advance.

No matter what happens, join it to practice. The kind of experience doesn't matter—anger, anguish, pain, desire, even joy or happiness—if you don't like something, practice. Think, "May the suffering of all beings be gathered here within my suffering. By this power, may they be freed from suffering and the causes of suffering." If you do like something, practice! Think, "May all beings have such joy, and may they have even greater happiness and the causes for happiness." Join everything to practice. No situation is too small. Nothing is insignificant. And no situation—no matter how serious or intense it may be—makes practice irrelevant. Do this, and you will be practicing tonglen in the moment.

There are countless ways to apply this method. If you feel physical pain, think, "May the physical pain of all beings be gathered here within my experience. By this power, may sentient beings be completely freed from such pain and the causes of pain." Or if you feel a negative emotion, think, "By my experience of this afflictive mental state, may the mental suffering of all beings be gathered here. By this power may they all be freed from disturbing emotions now and in the future." Even if you find yourself doing something harmful, you can think, "May the harmful actions of all beings be gathered here within my own negative actions. By this power may they never engage in negative actions again and cease creating the causes of future suffering."

It's important to remember to train when things are good, too. Think, "May all beings have even greater happiness than this and create the causes for more happiness." If you are enjoying a delicious meal, think, "May all beings have wonderful and delicious food. May they always have the causes for abundance and never suffer from hunger." When you engage in positive actions and create the causes for happiness, think, "I give away the merit of this action to all beings. May all beings have the causes for both temporary and ultimate happiness."

We don't have to limit our training to our own life experiences, we can also train as we witness the joy and suffering that others experience. When you see other beings in pain, think, "May they be free from suffering and the causes for suffering." Then, when you see someone who is happy or successful, or when you see someone who is engaging in virtuous actions, think, "May they never be separate from such happiness, and may they have even greater happiness and all the causes for happiness." You can craft these statements to fit any and every situation.

The opportunities for practicing mind training are endless. And yet the practice boils down to this: In each moment and in every situation, think of all living beings. If the conditions for yourself or others are painful, generate compassion. If the conditions for yourself or others are joyful, generate loving-kindness. In this way, shift the focus of your mind from yourself to others.

If we practice mind training in all situations, then no matter what happens, we can create happiness and the causes for happiness. If we join all of our experiences to this meditation, then no experience is wasted. All experiences are meaningful. Renowned masters of mind training throughout history, the great saints of the past, have demonstrated this attitude in their actions and their teachings. In "Finding Joy No Matter What Occurs," Gyalse Ngulchu Togmey, an exemplary mind-training practitioner and the author of the *Thirty-Seven Practices of a Bodhisattva*, wrote:

If I am sick, I am happy, because I exhaust past negative actions.
If I am healthy, I am happy, because I have a clear mind and body to serve as a vessel for practice and engaging in virtuous actions.

He also wrote an aspiration prayer for overcoming hope and fear:

> If this sickness benefits beings,
> I pray to the Three Jewels that I may be sick.[7]
> If being cured from this sickness benefits beings,
> I pray to the Three Jewels that I may be cured.
> If my death benefits beings, I pray that I may die.
> If living benefits beings, I pray that I may live.

In Tibet, we have a rich history of practitioners who immersed themselves in the lojong teachings. The stories of how they trained their minds give us inspiring examples of people who were able to overcome adversity, transform everything into the path, and find joy no matter what occurred. During the Cultural Revolution in China, which brought immense change to Tibet, there was a time when many lamas were imprisoned in work camps. One of my teachers, Guru Lama Thupten Tsering, was one of those lamas. The prisoners were required to do extremely hard labor, but even when they worked hard, some of the guards just didn't like them and would verbally and physically punish them. And of course if they didn't work hard, they would be punished too. Reflecting on this, Guru Thupten Tsering determined that it didn't matter if they did a good job or not, there were no actions they could take to avoid punishment. It became clear to him that the only thing to do was practice. So he decided that every time he was yelled at or beaten, right there in that moment, he would train. Then, no matter what occurred, he would be okay. Every day, he set the intention to disregard whatever unkindness was directed at him by training right there and then. At the end of the day, he would count all of the times he was reprimanded and reflect on how he did mind training in that moment. Because each scolding or beating became a practice, he not only stopped disliking the punishments, but at the end of the day they became a source of joy for him. In this way, adversity arose as his spiritual companion because he immediately joined everything to practice. When we look at the difficulties practitioners like Guru Thupten Tsering have faced, on the surface they may seem to have suffered intensely. But they did not actually experience suffering in the same way as someone who did not have practice because they transformed their experience through mind training.

Take sickness, for example. A sick person who does not practice mind training will feel uncomfortable, maybe they'll even have pain. They will also suffer mentally with worry, fear, anger, and other disturbed emotions. But if an accomplished mind-training practitioner ends up in the same situation, they won't suffer mentally, and their lack of disturbing emotions will even reduce their discomfort and pain. In some cases, they won't experience discomfort at all. If you find this hard to believe, think about how people experience pain differently, determined by habit, culture, or other factors. Physical pain is subjective, and it's strongly influenced by our attitude.

Imagine you have a scale that can weigh painful sensations. Piled on one side of the scale is the physical and mental suffering of a person who doesn't do mind training. On the other side is the suffering of an adept mind trainer. It would be as if a hundred-pound rock weighed down one side of the scale, while the other side held just a few feathers. This is because even though they may have the same amount of adverse experiences, an adept practitioner of mind training experiences far less mental anguish and even less physical pain than a non-practitioner.

While mind training is deeply transformative, most of us will still need to combine our practice with practical solutions to address our problems. Common sense is key. We should, for example, go to the doctor when we're sick. But we should also know that our practice has the power to overcome the causes of suffering that gave rise to the illness in the first place.

In order to tame the mind and overcome our greatest enemy—our disturbing emotions—we should avail ourselves of the full arsenal of practices and apply whatever we know. Study as many methods for working with the mind as possible. Study and contemplate the teachings until you remember them clearly and you are convinced of their value and benefit. Develop a conviction in the efficacy of the teachings that is strong enough to override any justifications for indulging in disturbing emotions. Commit yourself to practicing the teachings in all situations, no matter how unexpected they may be. Make that commitment again and again. Accept the inevitability of adversity, keep the tools of mind training at hand, and reinforce your intention to use those methods whenever trouble arises. Facing difficult circumstances becomes much easier when we know that we can transform them into the path and make them the source of positive qualities and beneficial actions.

Developing the skill of mind training takes time and determination, but with practice you will succeed. Apply these methods again and again, and over time you will develop a strong habit. Also, every time you remember the practice, be sure to rejoice. This will help reinforce the antidote and it will deepen your appreciation of the teaching.

HOW TO PRACTICE

The Excellent Beginning

Sit in meditation posture to cultivate the key points of body and speech (see page 17 for a full explanation). Then, cultivate the key points of mind by setting your intention. Think, "In order to benefit beings, I will practice the four applications as a means to transform all adversity into the path."

The Excellent Main Part

Review the following list of concepts introduced in this chapter by reading one point at a time, alternating between contemplative meditation and resting meditation.

Key Points to Contemplate

- What are the four applications? Consider if rephrasing any of these would make them easier to remember at the moment of need.
- Which ones can you start to apply right now? Which ones do you feel need further study and understanding if you were to apply them yourself?

- Consider the importance of immediately joining every adversity you encounter to mind training, and imagine what your life would be like if you did so.

The Excellent Conclusion

Dedicate the merit generated by this practice and make aspirations. Think, "I dedicate the merit of this practice of these four applications to all beings that they may be freed from suffering and attain both temporary and ultimate happiness." Then, make aspirations such as, "May all beings be happy and may all beings be free. May everyone be able to transform adversity through applications such as these." (You can also conclude by reciting the dedication and aspiration prayers in appendix 5.)

Off the Cushion

When facing adversity, remember that everything you experience is a result produced from its specific cause, and everything you do is a cause, which will produce a future result. Therefore, actively participate in the causes of happiness by engaging in positive, loving, and compassionate actions. Go out and commit random acts of kindness. Give your time, energy, or resources to people who need help or to organizations that help others. Purposefully compliment people you encounter in all walks of life and look for opportunities to practice kindness.

Acknowledge that the causes for all unwanted circumstances are negative thoughts and actions. Then, counteract those habitual imprints by engaging in the purification practice following the steps provided in this chapter. If you have teachings and understanding of the last two applications, you may add them to your activities as well. Otherwise, it is sufficient to focus on just the first two applications.

PART FOUR

TRAINING IN LIVING AND DYING: APPLYING THE PRACTICE IN ALL CIRCUMSTANCES

THE FOURTH KEY POINT
Integrating Practice into Your Whole Life

Immersion in the five forces is the heart of mind training: the propelling force, the force of familiarization, the force of planting positive seeds, the force of regret, and the force of aspirations. These teachings show us how to bring all elements of the practice into every aspect of our life, including our death. Applying this guidance is the difference between having theoretical knowledge of the profound mind trainings and completely transforming every experience through this knowledge. Using the five forces changes everything.

10

How to Train during This Life

**1. *A concise explanation of the heart essence of
pith instructions: train in the five forces.***

The methods for integrating the teachings explored in this book into our
lives are contained in a practice known as the five forces: the propelling
force, the force of familiarization, the force of planting positive seeds, the
force of regret, and the force of aspirations. In this chapter, we will explore
how to apply all five forces in daily life.

THE PROPELLING FORCE

The propelling force is our resolve to tame the mind. When we make a
formal commitment, the likelihood that we will follow through on our
intention increases. So we vow to do mind training, and our resolve becomes the springboard for practice. It is a force that propels us.

If our ambition is to attain total purification and ultimate realization,
or buddhahood, then we should vow to train the mind comprehensively.
Think to yourself, or even say aloud, "From this moment onward, until I

reach enlightenment, I will practice the mind trainings of relative and ultimate bodhichitta." Make this vow regularly. The more you do, the more the commitment will propel you forward. So while walking, talking, eating, or even brushing your teeth, recite this vow. And if you have a daily meditation practice, make this vow at the beginning of the session when cultivating your motivation of bodhichitta.

Don't forget to make the vow when you need it most, such as when you are entering a challenging situation. Vow to maintain bodhichitta no matter what occurs. When we practice in this way, the power of resolve carries us through into the most difficult situations, giving us more capacity to remember the mind trainings and to apply them. Our commitment keeps the teachings close to our hearts and propels us toward the practice of relative and ultimate bodhichitta.

THE FORCE OF FAMILIARIZATION

Just as we vow again and again to practice mind training, so too we must actually do the practices over and over again. Through repetition, we make training in bodhichitta our habit. So use the tools of mindfulness and vigilant guard to develop the force of familiarization. Whether you are eating, lying down, walking, sitting, working, relaxing, talking, being silent, or meditating, join everything to mind training. There is no circumstance that cannot be embraced by these trainings.

THE FORCE OF PLANTING POSITIVE SEEDS

Life is like a garden in which we should sow as many positive seeds as possible. Each seed is a cause for future happiness and a means for benefiting others. By engaging in beneficial actions, we develop the force of planting positive seeds.

The dharma provides various methods for the accumulation of merit depending upon a practitioner's disposition, preferences, spiritual faculties, and so forth. We have the unparalleled signature approach of the

Mahayana tradition, which includes, among many methods, the Six Per-fections, or Six Paramitas. These are the practices of generosity, ethical discipline,[1] patience, diligence, meditative concentration, and profound wisdom.

Within the countless methods of the Mantrayana tradition, we have the preliminary set of practices referred to as *ngondro*. This series of trainings includes prostrations, offerings, and other meditations, all of which prompt us to engage in positive actions of body, speech, and mind. When we train in relative and ultimate bodhichitta, we develop the quali-ties of loving-kindness and compassion, and gain profound insights into the ultimate nature of all phenomena. In other words, we develop skill-ful means and wisdom. These aspects of the teachings encompass the en-tirety of dharma practice. Each is like the wing of a bird. Both are needed to fly.

The result of practice is that we come to see every situation as a chance to help others. Each moment we have an opportunity to put love and compassion into practice. However big or small, joyfully seize these op-portunities to benefit others physically, verbally, or mentally. Every posi-tive action is precious. Even things as simple as smiling or offering a few kind words can help others. There is great power in practicing virtue.

Tibetan Buddhism is fortunate to have a rich history of saints who have shown us many ways to benefit beings. Within the Nyingma tra-dition, masters such as Longchen Rabjam[2] and Rigdzin Jigmé Lingpa[3] were great bodhisattvas whose actions to benefit others produced immeasurable benefit that continues to impact us today. In the Kagyu tradition, we have the example of Milarepa,[4] who as a young man sought revenge for his family's misfortunes. Later, he became a dharma practitioner, and he diligently strove to accumulate merit and wisdom. It was through the force of planting positive seeds that he transformed the course of his life to become one of the most famous saints in Tibetan history. By reading the teachings of these masters, we gain insight into the meaning of bodhichitta. By reading their life stories, we see examples of their teachings in action.

One recent example is the teacher Patrul Rinpoche,[5] who accumulated an awe-inspiring amount of merit. He was one of the great masters of his time and a teacher to many lamas in the Nyingma lineage. He had tremendous diligence and completed the entire cycle of ngondro practices twenty-five times, using the extended versions of the teachings, not the concise texts often used in the West. For an ordinary practitioner, it can take several years to complete the ngondro just once. Twenty-five times is mind-boggling.

Patrul Rinpoche also carved into rock the entire Buddhist canon—more than one hundred volumes of scripture containing the Buddha's words. Each volume is four hundred to five hundred pages! With the help of students, he carved the teachings onto flat slabs and then stacked them to create a mountainous reliquary. It is called the Patrul Rinpoche Do-kah. Patrul Rinpoche also made hundreds of thousands of clay images of buddhas, called *tsa-tsas*. These are made with molds, and on occasion the ashes of the deceased are mixed with the clay so the tsa-tsas become small reliquaries. You can find them in sacred places all over Tibet, as well as in caves and rock overhangs.

Patrul Rinpoche also encouraged people to show compassion for animals. In eastern Tibet there were many butchers and hunters who regularly killed animals for food. But Patrul Rinpoche taught them about the importance of doing no harm. It was said that his teachings converted so many people to vegetarianism that an entire region stopped eating meat.

One of the most treasured texts that Patrul Rinpoche taught on was *The Way of a Bodhisattva*, a seminal text on loving-kindness and compassionate action written by Shantideva. It's one of the most beloved Buddhist texts from India. Patrul Rinpoche taught on this text every year in a field in eastern Tibet, and in that field sprouted a profusion of rare flowers. Many Tibetans saw this as another sign that Patrul Rinpoche must be a reincarnation of Shantideva. He was certainly a living example of Shantideva's teachings.

While we may not have the capacity to practice virtue to the same extent as Patrul Rinpoche, his example helps us to understand what it means to accumulate virtue. Always strive to do as much good as you can, to the best of your capacity, throughout your entire life. When we plant positive seeds, we create a fertile field where our practice can grow, be sustained, strengthen, and finally blossom into realization.

THE FORCE OF REGRET

The next force is called regret, but not in the typical sense. Because the point of mind training is to uproot the fixation on a self, here the chief regret is self-cherishing. This unique approach goes right to the heart of the matter—to the starting point of all our issues. As mind-training practitioners, we should become skilled at identifying when we become intensely attached to ourselves.

We won't be able to relinquish self-clinging right away, but there are steps we can take to move in that direction. It's important to become aware of when we have self-centered thoughts. Think, "I only feel this way because I'm motivated by self-clinging." Then contemplate the harm that self-clinging has caused you and others. Consider how since beginningless time until this moment, all hardships—disturbing emotions, issues, difficulties, struggles, and so on—come about because of our self-centered fixation on the self. All harmful actions that anyone has ever engaged in throughout history came from self-clinging and self-righteousness. It is the source of all wars, strife, arguments, and disagreements, and it propels people to kill, steal, lie, cheat, and so on. Self-clinging is the root cause of our past suffering and our present suffering. Every issue or problem we have now, or ever will have, arises from the concept of self and our attachment to it. What we own, who we love—it's all about self.

Recognizing the troubles selfishness has caused, strive to feel regret for this attachment and think, "I vow to overcome selfishness," and "I will do whatever I can do to destroy this fixation on the self." Generate this feeling of regret as much as possible. The force of this regret undermines our habitual orientation to self.

To practice the force of regret, become skilled at recognizing when you are overtaken by intense attachment to self. If you use this contemplation in that moment, it will antidote your self-clinging. It also helps to set aside a time to give rise to this regret at least once a day. At the end of the day is a really good time. Reflect on how the day went, how well you applied mind training to your thoughts, words, and actions. Think about the difficulties that you encountered and recognize how self-clinging played a role in them. In this way, train in the force of regret.

THE FORCE OF ASPIRATIONS

As practitioners, we aspire to develop positive qualities. We aim to deepen our understanding of relative and ultimate bodhichitta and to increase our capacity for benefiting beings. Fortunately, there are countless ways to make aspirations. It's good to recite aspiration prayers when we engage in formal meditation practice, and we should make aspirations when we engage in positive actions or when we successfully apply mind-training techniques. We can also make aspirations at a particular time of day, such as before going to bed at night.

It's valuable to use aspiration prayers that were made by saints of the past so that we can then follow in their footsteps. Their prayers are important because they aspired to qualities we often don't even think about. By making these aspirations, we create interdependence with both the saints that help us realize these qualities and the qualities themselves. These kinds of aspiration prayers can be found in other sources, as well as in appendix 5. However, we can also make our own simple mind-training aspirations such as, "Through the power of this merit, may I have the capacity to guide all living beings without exception to the state of enlightenment." Or, "Through the power of this merit, may I never be separate from relative and ultimate bodhichitta, not even for a moment, not even when I'm dreaming." Or, "May I be able to carry all circumstances, whether they're good or bad, onto the path." Or, "May I transform everything into the path of awakening." In this way, make strong prayers and aspirations and then dedicate the merit to the welfare of others. If we pray like this, the force of aspiration will point our mind in the right direction and help us to connect with the positive qualities we hope to emulate.

HOW TO PRACTICE: A DAILY ROUTINE

In a single day, it is simple to integrate mind training using the five forces. If you practice in this way, your entire day will unfold within the context of mind training, and the practice will be integrated into the fabric of your life.

Beginning the Day

As soon as your alarm goes off, start your day with the thought, "I vow not to be separate from bodhichitta all day," or "I vow not to be separate from love, compassion, and wisdom today."[6] That is *the propelling force*. Start your day with a strong intention.

During the Day

- **The propelling force.** Set your intention before starting any significant activity, such as work. For example, think, "From when I begin work until I'm done, I vow to not be separate from relative and ultimate bodhichitta."
- **The force of familiarization.** If you can, make some time in the morning to sit and meditate on love and compassion or on wisdom, even if it's only for a few minutes. If you can't meditate in the morning, try to find another time during the day. Throughout the day, practice tonglen and recognize everything to be like a dream. Both formal and informal practice are the force of familiarization. Remember to practice as many times as you can—in the midst of positive, negative, or neutral situations. For example, if you see someone suffering, think, "May they and all beings be free from that suffering and from the causes of suffering." Then immediately follow the thought by recognizing that it's like a dream and let go, allowing the mind to rest right there. Or when you see something good for someone else, think, "May they and all beings always have such happiness and may they never be separate from it." Then

recognize its dreamlike nature and rest for a moment there. You can do all of this in less than fifteen seconds without stopping what you are doing, or you can take a break for a couple of minutes and spend more time with it.

- **The force of planting positive seeds.** Do as many positive things as you can during the day. No action is too small. Smiling, talking to someone kindly, or offering others compliments all count. For example, say something kind to a cashier, or ask for the manager at a restaurant when your server did something special to share your appreciation with them. These can be big or small acts, but take advantage of the small ones to build the habit for random acts of kindness. Look for opportunities to help others and consider this a daily goal.

Concluding the Day

- **The force of regret.** At the end of the day, before you go to bed, review your day. If you acted selfishly at any point during the day, if you engaged in harmful actions, had disturbing emotions or forgot to practice, generate regret and resolve to do better the next time. Pay particular attention to the moments of self-centeredness. Where you forgot to practice, you may even imagine yourself in that same situation and go through the stages of mind training.
- **The force of aspirations.** Acknowledge your successes at using the five forces and rejoice by bringing to mind all of the positive thoughts and actions you engaged in and the moments when you remembered to apply the practice. Finally, make aspirations and dedicate the merit to the welfare of all beings. Think, "I dedicate all the merit generated today to all beings that they may be free from suffering and find true and complete happiness."

Special Advice for Difficult Situations

1. If you are going into a tough situation or meeting someone with whom you have a difficult time, start with *the propelling force* by setting your intention with, "From the moment I encounter this person (or until such and such a situation ends), I vow not be separate from relative and ultimate bodhichitta."

2. During that time, for *the force of familiarization*, watch your mind carefully with vigilant guard. If you see yourself feeling agitated, do tonglen with that emotion right in the midst of the conversation and then remember its dreamlike nature. Apply any and all of the techniques given in this book.

3. After the situation, give yourself a few moments to self-debrief. How did it go? Where you didn't practice or were unable to refrain from being disturbed, cultivate regret and then resolve to do better the next time. Envision yourself in that same situation successfully training your mind and not becoming upset. This is *the force of regret*.

4. Think about where you succeeded and what you did well and rejoice. Then apply *the force of aspirations* by dedicating the merit to all beings that they may be free from suffering. And make the aspiration to always be able to practice in the midst of adversity.

11

How to Train While Dying

2. The Mahayana oral instruction for transferring consciousness at the time of death is the five forces. Conduct is important.

The previous chapter explores applying the five forces to daily life. But for a practitioner who is serious about training the mind through lojong practice, the five forces are also indispensable to the process of dying. Once we know that death is imminent—if, perhaps, we have been diagnosed with a terminal illness or are in the waning years of life—that is the time to rely on the five forces for dying. These instructions do not pertain to sudden death, such as from an accident, but instead are meant for someone who is dying gradually.

THE FORCE OF PLANTING POSITIVE SEEDS

As we prepare for death, it's crucial to let go of any attachments or fixations and to use whatever wealth and possessions we have to accumulate merit. Giving away our possessions without grasping—especially things of value—will help us to gather virtue and purify obscurations. Taking this step not only plants seeds but it makes dying easier. If we give away all that we have with a mind of generosity, we leave this life with a clean slate, free of attachment to our material possessions. The less grasping we have, the less suffering there will be. But if we don't let go of what we own, our attachment to our possessions will hinder us at the time of death, and our suffering will be much worse.

When I was growing up in Tibet, there was a very rich man who was renowned for his stinginess, just like Ebenezer Scrooge in Charles Dickens's *A Christmas Carol*. I was quite young at the time, and I remember being impressed by his valuable possessions. When he was dying, his family requested a group of monks and lamas to come to the house to recite the traditional prayers for someone approaching death. I was one of the monks. As the dying man was lying in his bed, suffering from a terrible illness, he requested to see all of the possessions he had acquired during his life. The flaps to his nomadic tent were lifted so that he could gaze at his yaks, horses, and sheep. He then asked to see his trunks of precious jewels, including gold, coral, and turquoise. I remember the pained expression on his face as he looked at his things. It was unbearable for him to be separated from them, and his attachment made it incredibly hard for him to die.

We don't want to die like that! It is so much better to die with a clean slate and to plant positive seeds that will bear fruit in a future harvest. When we give away money and possessions, the purpose of that wealth is fulfilled. We have extracted its essence by using it to benefit ourselves and others. As we prepare for death and consider giving away our wealth, we should think about who will benefit from it the most. Whatever we can do to support the dharma teachings is immeasurably valuable. Making offerings to the three jewels, great sources of benefit in themselves, is one of the most beneficial things we can do. We should also be generous to those who have been kind to us and who have helped us in our lives, so making donations that will alleviate the suffering of people who are deprived of their basic needs is also enormously beneficial. If we practice the force of planting positive seeds once we know we only have a little more time to live, it will be so much easier for us when death does come. If we can enter the next life without even a speck of attachment, our suffering will be greatly reduced.

THE FORCE OF ASPIRATIONS

During the days or months leading up to death, dedicate merit and make aspirations daily. Think about all of the virtue you have accumulated and are still accumulating, all of the positive things you have done, even the virtuous actions you may have forgotten, and think about all of the good things you would like to do in the future. Imagine the limitless number of positive actions made by other sentient beings and by the buddhas and bodhisattvas of the past, present, and future. Gather this vast accumulation of merit in your mind and then dedicate it to all sentient beings, praying that they be freed from suffering and never be separated from temporary and ultimate happiness. Throughout the dying process, dedicate merit in this way and make aspirations. In particular, pray that you will never be separate from relative and ultimate bodhichitta, and that in your next life, you again will have the good fortune to meet with a qualified spiritual teacher and receive teachings such as these so that you can continue to work for the welfare of beings.

THE FORCE OF REGRET

As we are dying, we also want to generate regret for the self-clinging that has dominated our lives. Think about how all suffering stems from a fixation on oneself. Self-clinging has caused us to suffer in the past, it is causing us to suffer now as we die, and it will cause us to suffer in the future. If we don't free ourselves from this fixation, then we will never be able to find true, ultimate happiness that is free of suffering. Self-clinging is the source of all of our mistakes and the reason why we have harmed others. Generate regret for this and resolve to overcome self-clinging.

THE PROPELLING FORCE

The propelling force is our strong commitment to never be separated from relative and ultimate bodhichitta. As you prepare for death, make this vow: "I shall never be separate from the two kinds of bodhichitta while dying, in the bardo, or in my future lives." The Tibetan word *bardo* means "in between," and in this case it refers to the intermediate state between death and life. We vow never to be separate from bodhichitta as we transition from this life to the next, and we carry this vow with us throughout all time and in all situations. If we make this vow again and again, it will act as a propelling force that will drive our mind on the path to enlightenment.

THE FORCE OF FAMILIARIZATION

As death approaches, we need to remember all we have done to develop relative and ultimate bodhichitta and to recall the understanding we have gained as a result of our training. Immerse your mind in the practice and continue to familiarize yourself with bodhichitta. If you can, enlist the support of a practitioner experienced in mind training who can gently remind you of the instructions at this critical juncture in your life. This becomes even more important as the moment of death draws near, when the support of a spiritual friend can help you apply the teachings no matter what you suffer.

CONDUCT IS IMPORTANT

How we physically and mentally approach the moment of death is important. The ideal is to be able to practice mind training as our consciousness leaves our body.

Dying in a sitting position is the most supportive for practice. In the best-case scenario, a practitioner sits cross-legged or sits while being propped up from behind. Sitting is not always possible though, so the second-best posture is to lie on your right side with your right palm under your right cheek, holding up your head while the left arm and hand rests naturally along the left side of the body, palm facing down on the leg. The Buddha Shakyamuni left samsara in this posture, which we can see in images that depict his *parinirvana*. If you are unable to adopt either of these postures, then position yourself however is most comfortable.

Begin with tonglen. If you're lying on your right side with your right palm under your cheek, close off the right nostril with your right pinky. Breathe through the left nostril and generate relative bodhichitta—the mind of love and compassion—by practicing tonglen. Then move into the practice of ultimate bodhichitta and meditate on emptiness. While your mind and body undergo the dying process, hold your attention on bodhichitta. Ideally, in the last conscious moments, you will recognize true nature and rest in the view of emptiness. It is here, while recognizing ultimate nature, that your consciousness passes from this life.

This lojong practice of generating relative and ultimate bodhichitta at the time of death is called *phowa*, the transference of consciousness. There are many practices that can be done to transfer one's consciousness at the time of death, but this meditation, using tonglen at the time of death, is particularly profound. It's especially effective if we have trained in tonglen and lojong throughout our life. But because it is quite simple, anyone can do it at the time of death.

HOW TO PRACTICE

The Excellent Beginning

Sit in meditation posture to cultivate the key points of body and speech (see page 17 for a full explanation). Then, cultivate the key points of mind by setting your intention. Think, "In order to benefit my loved ones and all beings, I will make the necessary preparations for death and dying."

The Excellent Main Part

Review the following list of concepts introduced in this chapter by reading one point at a time, alternating between contemplative meditation and resting meditation.

Key Points to Contemplate

- What does it mean to plant positive seeds at the time of dying? What kinds of positive actions could you take during this time, and how does that relate to making legal documents such as a trust or will?

- How do you practice the force of aspirations while dying? What kinds of aspirations do you envision yourself making during this time?
- What is a healthy way to integrate the force of regret while dying? Envision yourself at this stage of life and see how practicing healthy regret allows you to let go and focus on the future without being bogged down by the past.
- What is the propelling force in this context? How do you think making commitments helps to focus your attention on what is positive and propel you forward as you would wish to go?
- How do you practice the force of familiarization during this stage of life? Envision how you would integrate mind-training practice at the time of dying.
- Follow the instructions for practicing the section on "conduct" as you go to sleep at night.

The Excellent Conclusion

Dedicate the merit generated by this practice and make aspirations. Think, "I dedicate the merit of this practice on death and dying to all beings that they may be freed from suffering and attain both temporary and ultimate happiness." Then, make aspirations such as, "May all beings be happy and may all beings be free. May everyone have a peaceful death." (You can also conclude by reciting the dedication and aspiration prayers in appendix 5.)

Off the Cushion

Strive to generate a keen awareness of death throughout the day in order to live your life in relation to death. In particular, whenever you remember death, reflect on whether you will regret your current actions or rejoice in them. Likewise consider, if you were to die in this moment, would you be prepared? Have you done the work on your mind you set out to do?

In addition to practice, the best way to prepare for death is to have all your affairs in order while you are healthy and well. This includes creating a will or trust, making a living will (also called advance directive), and finding a secure way to communicate all the information about bills and accounts that your designated loved ones will need to access at that time. Have conversations about it! This is one of the greatest acts of kindness for your loved ones. Then, if you die suddenly, you don't leave a confusing mess for them to figure out. This is a true gift of generosity. Likewise, if you are diagnosed with a terminal illness, you can focus on spending quality time with loved ones and doing mind-training practices instead of dwelling on paperwork during this most precious time of your life.

PART FIVE

ASSESSING PROFICIENCY: RECOGNIZING THE SIGNS OF PROGRESS

THE FIFTH KEY POINT
The Measure of Mind Training

Mind-training practice transforms the way we think and act. To be proficient means the training becomes our direct experience. But how do we gauge our progress? By our own experience. If we practice love, compassion, and wisdom consistently, over time our reactions to people and situations will change. As love and compassion increase, selfishness and other disturbing emotions decrease. The teachings in this chapter are designed to help us recognize signs of progress and instill confidence that we are practicing correctly.

12

Four Ways to Measure Your Growth

1. *All dharmas have a single, unified purpose.*

Whether we're training in relative or ultimate bodhichitta, practicing the Six Perfections, or sitting down on a cushion to meditate, all positive actions of body, speech, and mind are aimed at a single point: to tame the mind. As we practice, our attachment to self should decrease, which in turn will cause our disturbing emotions to wane. We will experience fewer and fewer attachments, and our feelings of anger, jealousy, pride, and so forth will diminish. As a result, we will engage in fewer harmful actions, and our ability to benefit others will increase. Love and compassion will steadily grow within us, and our actions and the way we relate to others will become more positive. If the process of mind training unfolds in this way, it is a sign that we are on track. The greater the positive effects, the more proficient we have become in our practice.

But if we notice that self-clinging, disturbing emotions, and harmful behaviors have not decreased or that love, compassion, and patience have not increased, then that's a sign that something is amiss in our practice. Either we aren't applying the mind trainings with enough diligence or we are practicing incorrectly. It could also be that we haven't studied the teachings well enough, which makes it hard to apply them effectively. If we feel that our practice is off track, we need to look at ourselves to figure out where the problem lies. Then, we need to do whatever it takes to remedy it.

Hearing teachings on love, compassion, and wisdom is not enough, nor is it enough to merely appreciate these qualities. Even contemplating the teachings will not be enough to bring about radical change if they are not taken to heart. Although hearing the teachings and contemplating their meaning are indispensable to cultivating practice, we need to take one more very important step. We need to join the meaning of the teachings to all experiences. This is what it means to practice, to experience the teachings by merging them with our mind.

If we get into the habit of listening to teachings but not applying them, we are in danger of becoming desensitized to the dharma. In Tibet, we say such people have become *chötrey*, that is, blasé, or hardened to the dharma. Such people might think, "Oh, I've already heard this teaching," or they might think they already know what's being taught. If, for example, we're sitting in a teaching about the four thoughts but saying to ourselves, "I've already gotten this message on precious human birth. I know everything is impermanent. I wish this lama would talk about something more profound," that's not a good sign. It suggests that we have become jaded. If the teachings feel dry and hard instead of juicy and inspiring, then it will be difficult to use them to tame the mind.

Milarepa said a person who has become hardened to the dharma is like a butter bag. In Tibet, we store butter in bags made of leather. When the bag is new, the leather is pliable, but over time it hardens because of the constant exposure to oil. Similarly, a person who receives teachings but does not practice becomes like a piece of leather that has been hardened by overexposure to oil. And just as this leather won't be made softer by applying more oil to it, no matter how many teachings a person receives, the dharma won't soften or tame their mind.

If we practice the teachings, the dharma will infuse our hearts, and our enthusiasm for study and practice will be unending. When we hear a teaching we've heard before, rather than feeling bored, a new level of understanding will unfold. Because our mind is open, the teaching will reinforce and deepen whatever experience of it we already have. The dharma is like ambrosia, an elixir for the mind. Each time we taste it, it refreshes us, nourishes us, and tames our negative emotions—the sole purpose of practice.

2. Of the two witnesses, rely on the primary one.

Another way to measure progress is to observe changes in behavior. Here, the two witnesses are oneself and others. As we tame our mind, our words and actions will shift. Our friends and family will notice if we become more loving, compassionate, patient, and generous. In other words, it is possible for others to witness our growth.

But while others can see changes in our behavior, they are not the primary witness to our proficiency in mind training. People can only see what appears on the outside. In addition, their perceptions are colored by their own habits and projections, and while they may be able to infer what we are thinking or feeling based on our expressions, our mind and motivations remain hidden from view. We might present ourselves as being kind and good, while inside we are actually focused solely on ourselves and teeming with disturbing emotions.

We are the sole witness to our own thoughts and emotions. Only we know the extent to which our self-clinging has decreased and loving-kindness and compassion have increased. Only we know the depth to which our mind has been tamed.

To witness our own mind we need an unconventional level of self-reflection and honesty. So in every situation, look at your expectations, hopes, and attachments. Examine the degree to which your actions are motivated by loving-kindness and compassion for others.

As ordinary people, there is always some measure of personal gain involved. Maybe we're expecting to be acknowledged, to gain financially, or to advance socially or professionally. Perhaps our expectations are more subtle than that. We may hope to feel good from helping someone. But what if we fail to help them? What if we don't get the gratification we were hoping for? Then, we might regret trying to help in the first place. We might get angry and resentful and look for someone to blame. If we experience this or anything like this when our expectations aren't met, it's a guarantee that we are not motivated by a pure heart. If we had no attachment to ourselves, we would be happy to engage in good deeds, regardless of the outcome. But if we become upset when our hopes are not fulfilled, it's because we are clinging to the self.

To be the principal witness means to honestly appraise our disturbing emotions and selfishness. It's the only way to truly gauge the extent to which our mind is tamed. To do so, check your intentions regularly and notice whether they align with the teachings. Check your conduct too. If you are at ease and feel no shame or regret after taking a positive action, even if that action seems to fail, then you will know that your mind training is moving in the right direction. Do not measure your success by the immediate outcome of actions. Instead, look at your state of mind and conduct in the process.

When our intentions and actions are in harmony with the dharma, we will experience fewer disturbing emotions. When we experience that purity regularly, our mind will have greater and greater ease, regardless of the circumstances. A mind motivated by pure, unselfish love and compassion is always at peace.

3. *Always keep a joyful mind.*

When we first begin to train our mind, the negative thoughts and emotions are so strong that they override the practice. Though we may apply the trainings when we face adversity, our mind will still be disturbed because our practice hasn't yet gained sufficient strength. But persevere. Apply the teachings again and again, and over time the strength of positive thoughts and emotions will gain traction until, eventually, the scales will tip. Positive mental states will be much stronger than negative ones. Once we reach this stage, we will begin to experience joy continuously.

At first, this joy arises because we know we can train our mind in all circumstances. We can train through physical pain, mental upheaval, loss, or gain—any positive or negative situation. In this way, all of life's experiences are brought onto the path. We have ceased compounding our suffering. We are making our lives ultimately meaningful.

Over time, this joy grows. It transforms from an intellectual appreciation of our success in mind training into a continuous state of mental strength. Upsetting things may happen, but we won't become disturbed. We won't even see it as a big deal. Even physical pain will be diminished, flooded by our abiding sense of well-being. As Gyalse Ngulchu Togmey,[1] a bodhisattva from Tibet who lived in the thirteenth century, wrote in the prayer "Finding Joy No Matter What Occurs," once we have gained proficiency in mind training, we are okay in all circumstances. If we are sick, we are okay. If we suffer, we are okay. If we get what we want, we are okay. If we don't get what we want, we are okay.

Having reached this level of proficiency, joy is our ever-present companion on the path. It is not dependent on outer circumstances. It provides peace and happiness that outer circumstances cannot. When everything is brought onto the path, everything becomes meaningful and a source of benefit. This is a measure of practice.

4. *There is proficiency if we can train while distracted.*

If we train our mind well, there will come a point where we no longer need to purposefully train. Without effort, our reactions will flow from a place of love, compassion, and wisdom. In expected and unexpected situations, pleasant and unpleasant ones, we will not need to work to apply the teachings. We will simply react with mind training because it has become our natural response. Relative or ultimate bodhichitta will pervade our thoughts, no matter how distracted and caught up in a situation we may appear to be. The practice is automatic.

Once we develop proficiency, that does not mean we have finished training the mind and no longer need to practice. It's the exact opposite. These instructions, or statements, also serve as reminders to keep us on track.

HOW TO PRACTICE

The Excellent Beginning

Sit in meditation posture to cultivate the key points of body and speech (see page 17 for a full explanation). Then, cultivate the key points of mind by setting your intention. Think, "In order to benefit all beings, I will practice diligently to experience these signs indicating the presence of mind training."

The Excellent Main Part

Review the following list of concepts introduced in this chapter by reading one point at a time, alternating between contemplative meditation and resting meditation.

Key Points to Contemplate

- What is the single, unified purpose of all dharmas? Can you see this in your own personal practice?
- Of the two witnesses, which one is the primary one? Consider how this understanding shifts your focus and gives you more personal awareness.
- How it is possible to always have a joyful frame of mind? Can you imagine yourself experiencing this?
- What is proficiency? How could you train even while distracted?

The Excellent Conclusion

Dedicate the merit generated by this practice and make aspirations. Think, "I dedicate the merit of this practice on gaining proficiency in mind training to all beings that they may be freed from suffering and attain both temporary and ultimate happiness." Then, make aspirations such as, "May all beings be happy and may all beings be free. May all beings be proficient in training their minds." (You can also conclude by reciting the dedication and aspiration prayers in appendix 5.)

Off the Cushion

Technically, these are not considered meditations per say, but they are important points that highlight the potential for developing our mind and for correcting and adjusting our practice. Knowing intimately the four key statements of the fifth point will enrich your mind training. To become more familiar with them, spend a day or two with each one, reciting it throughout the day. Reflect on what that purpose is and repeat the statements as many times as you can throughout the day. You can follow each recitation with tonglen and then wisdom insight.

PART SIX

LIVING IN HARMONY WITH PRACTICE: COMMITMENTS OF THE PATH

THE SIXTH KEY POINT
The Commitments of Mind Training

As practitioners, we need a framework to support mind training. So we make commitments—*samayas* in Sanskrit—that help us to uphold the practice. This series of resolutions show us when our actions align with practice or when they do not. If our actions consistently contradict mind training, our progress in mind training will be impeded. The good qualities we have developed will decline and the qualities of the practice we have yet to generate won't arise. These commitments protect and nurture our mind training. For example, if we plant a flower, we need protective parameters, such as a good fence to prevent deer from eating it. If we leave the flower unprotected, deer may eat its first shoots, so it doesn't grow at all; or they may eat it when it's partially grown, causing the plant to wither; or they will nibble it bit by bit, which will stunt its growth. The statements in this chapter bring a keen awareness to our actions and intentions and how they affect our practice and personal growth. Maintaining these commitments empowers us to live according to the mind-training teachings.

13

Sixteen Actions to Avoid That Contradict Mind Training

1. *Continually train in the three universal principles.*

At all times it is important that our actions uphold three basic principles: that they don't contradict the commitments of mind training, that they don't become confused, and that our mind training isn't biased. These commitments include vows to refrain from harmful thoughts, words, and actions that undermine mind training while upholding other actions that support it. When we lapse in our commitments—even once with a single thought or action—we compromise the intention of mind training. But when we keep these commitments, we are in harmony with the practice. Of course, this is a work in progress, and no one starts out perfectly aligned, but we must begin by acknowledging the effect that each action has on our practice and then work to refine them one action at a time. In this way, each commitment is a crucial aspect of practice. It makes us aware of the many subtle ways that we can trip up and cause ourselves to regress. We need to be vigilant and to keep these commitments in mind to ensure our thoughts and actions are in accord with our practice and aspirations.

THE FIRST UNIVERSAL PRINCIPLE: DON'T CONTRADICT THE COMMITMENTS OF MIND TRAINING

The commitments of mind training include all of the commitments comprising this section as well as the three vows.[1] To uphold our commitments is the first of all commitments because the structure of the entire path is supported by them. Essentially we are making a vow to keep our commitments because when our behavior contradicts these lojong commitments, it directly contradicts the mind-training practices. This is a universal principle because it pertains to every mind training.

There are additional formal commitments called vows that Buddhist practitioners make to support their practice. The foundation of all commitments is the refuge vow. The Buddhist path formally begins when we go for refuge in the buddha, dharma, and sangha. Going for refuge in the buddha means to rely on buddhas as authentic teachers who can show us the entire path to awakening. Going for refuge in the dharma means to rely on the dharma as our path, what we will practice to tame our mind. And going for refuge in the sangha means to rely on realized bodhisattvas and qualified spiritual teachers as our guides and examples for how to practice.

Once a practitioner has gone for refuge, it serves as the foundation for the three vows that practitioners take as the support for the path and practice. These three are the vow to do no harm, called *pratimoksha precepts*; the vow to benefit beings, called the *bodhisattva vows*; and the vows of pure perception based on ultimate wisdom, called *vajrayana samayas*.

Vows are taken from a teacher who holds the vows purely and who is qualified to give precepts. Traditionally, students would request these of their teacher when they have studied the vows and are inspired to keep them. The first vow to do no harm is the practice of ethical discipline, which is one of the Six Perfections. Once we commit not to harm others, we are able to commit to the second vow to benefit beings, the bodhisattva vow. By making this commitment to train in bodhichitta, we formally begin the Mahayana path. This is a natural progression as we practice.

The third vow is that of the samayas, the precepts of the Mantrayana, to uphold the pure view of wisdom. These precepts are taken by receiving initiation into this method of practice through empowerment.[2]

To continually train in these every day and in all situations, remember you have these commitments. In other words, practice mindfulness and be vigilant about checking the state of your body, speech, and mind to make sure they are in harmony with the vows. If you see your actions are not in harmony, apply whatever mind training is relevant so that you can uphold the commitments you have made on the path. Bring this carefulness to everything you do under all circumstances.

THE SECOND UNIVERSAL PRINCIPLE: DON'T ALLOW CONDUCT TO BECOME CONFUSED

Sometimes, practitioners misunderstand teachings they've received on the ultimate nature of phenomena. When that happens, their conduct can become confused, and they risk falling into the extreme of nihilism. They may think they have realized the ultimate view, and therefore erroneously believe that they have transcended cause and result. To prove that they are an accomplished yogi, they may then behave recklessly without fear of consequences. For example, someone who imagines they have realized that there is no self may go to a place where there's an outbreak of contagious diseases to demonstrate their realization. Their ego is so big that they feel compelled to show others how spiritually advanced they are, so they pretend to be fearless when, in fact, they are just being foolish. Then, if they get sick, they regret that decision. Their conduct is confused because they are confused.

When we truly understand ultimate nature, we become even more conscientious of our actions and how we affect others. We become acutely aware of karma—how every action is a cause that produces a result. Our conduct becomes even more careful and refined. If someone goes out of their way to show off their realization through a lack of concern for conventionally accepted behavior, that is an automatic sign that something isn't right. Somewhere along the way they became confused.

You might wonder why a person would think they could display realization by acting strangely. It's probably because they've heard of "crazy wisdom."[3] Sometimes, a truly realized master will see that they can benefit others by acting unconventionally, so they engage in what's called "crazy conduct." These beings have already demonstrated signs of realization. They have the ability to perform what we in the West call "miracles," which is to say that they have the capacity to do things that ordinary individuals cannot do, benefiting beings in inconceivable ways. If someone pretends to be a practitioner at this level, it not only isn't beneficial but it can also be immediately harmful to themselves and others. Such conduct is antithetical to genuine practice. That's why, as practitioners of mind training, it is important to guard against conduct that is confused.

THE THIRD UNIVERSAL PRINCIPLE:
DON'T ALLOW THE MIND TRAINING
TO BECOME BIASED

Mind training only works when it is unbiased, which means we should practice faithfully in all situations. We may be willing to try very hard to cultivate patience with our loved ones because we fear losing them. But when it comes to practicing with someone we don't like, that's a different story. We shouldn't pick and choose when we train the mind and when we don't. Patient forbearance should be unbiased. Every single time the mind is disturbed, we need to apply the trainings, no matter what the situation is or who we are relating to. One-sided patience based on personal preferences is not going to bring forth the forbearance of a profoundly undisturbed mind.

We can also be biased in our practice if we train when we face adversity but forget to train when we are happy. I meet a lot of people who do this. They apply themselves diligently when they are having a difficult time, especially since it's often suffering that brought them to the dharma in the first place. Then, when their lives improve, they become distracted by the pleasures of samsara and they practice less and less. It's easy to remember the trainings when we suffer because they help reduce disturbing emotions and increase positive reactions. But when things are going our way and we feel good, we often neglect to practice. This is one of the most common forms of biased practice. Another is practicing after we've had a good night's sleep and feel well rested, but then not practicing when we are tired. We use our tired, cloudy, or disturbed mind as an excuse not to practice. Engaging in such one-sided training will greatly limit the power and efficacy of practice. To practice without bias means to train no matter how we feel. That is the only way to reach mastery. So if things are bad, train. If things are good, train. If you're happy, train. If you're sad, train. If something delights you, train. If something bores you, train. If you tame the mind in all circumstances, whatever you wish for will be accomplished.

2. *Change your intention, but act naturally.*

Mind training profoundly changes our intention. It's like turning a piece of clothing inside out. We transform our habitual self-cherishing into a cherishing of others' well-being. It's a shift that fills our mind with loving-kindness and compassion.

As our mind changes, we should act naturally. There's no need to show off how we've changed. It isn't necessary to act differently, or alter our personality, or stand on a pedestal and look down on others. If, after practicing mind training, our family and friends can no longer relate to us, that is a problem.

Sometimes when we begin to practice, we feel a surge of love and compassion, but then the ego jumps in and wants others to know about our great qualities. So we behave in ways that promote our accomplishments. For example, in the midst of an ordinary conversation we might blurt out, "Oh, poor things. May all sentient beings be happy!" While we may be practicing tonglen or doing other mind trainings in that moment, it isn't appropriate to say things just so others can hear and admire us.

Even in a monastery, sometimes practitioners desire to be noticed. When I was young, I remember one monk who wanted all of us to know how compassionate he was. We would all be roughhousing and playing, as young monks do, and then suddenly he would say, "Nying-jey!" and make a big show of looking pious. *Nying-jey* is sort of like saying "poor thing" in English. It's something we might utter if we encountered a wounded animal or another painful situation. But even in a monastery, it was an odd thing to say out loud. Although everyone had training in these practices, we knew they weren't meant to be shown off. Dramatically acting out the practice is annoying to others and not the purpose of training.

It is important to remember the teachings and to develop compassion in all circumstances, but we don't need to demonstrate our state of mind to others. Mind training is an internal process that completely transforms us. If we make our mind training an external act, it can put people off. The ways that we've changed will be clear enough when we don't react to problems with anger or other disturbing emotions. There's no need to point it out as well. Change your intention in every way, but always act naturally.

3. Don't speak about others' defects.

It's important to speak carefully and to express ourselves with kindness, gentleness, and compassion. We shouldn't speak about others in a derogatory way, or about their mistakes, downfalls, or anything that might be wrong with them. On an internal level, such expressions reflect the fact that we may look down on other people, as if the challenges they face make them lesser beings in our mind. This belittling or scornful attitude is what this statement addresses. By making a commitment to refrain from using unkind expressions that point out the defects of others, we become aware of our own habits of negative thinking. We can then use the antidote of loving-kindness and compassion to develop a caring attitude toward others.

People from different cultures use different derogatory expressions. In Tibet, for example, it is considered inappropriate to refer to someone as "the man with no legs," or "the woman who can't see," or "the slow one." Think of the expressions that are considered belittling in your own language and culture and notice the attitude and mental state that compels us to say these things. Are these words ever motivated by loving-kindness and compassion? Referring to someone based on a physical or mental handicap contradicts our commitment to benefit them and all beings. Love and compassion are the core of mind training, which means that how we speak of others should reflect those qualities.

4. *Don't concern yourself with others' affairs.*

We could have a flaw the size of a mountain and not be aware of it, while at the same time we could be totally obsessed with a flaw the size of a single atom in another person. As practitioners of love and compassion, we need to overcome our tendency to focus on what is wrong with others. Our perceptions are colored by pride because of our strong self-cherishing. Pride obscures us from seeing what we actually need to work on—our own flaws. It makes us think that we are better than others and that our perception is the right one. It also blocks us from appreciating other people's good qualities. Once we're aware of pride's role in self-c herishing, we can start to see how we focus on other people's flaws. They may not even have those flaws, but we perceive them because we are habituated to seeing what's wrong with others and not with ourselves. The truth is that other people's problems are not our business, and our perception is simply our own projection. Whether the flaws we perceive are real or imagined, the only mind we can tame is our own.

During the time of the Buddha Shakyamuni, there were people who could not appreciate or even recognize his qualities. He was a fully awakened being who had purified all flaws and realized all positive qualities, yet some people saw only faults in the Buddha. They slandered him, not realizing that their perceptions had nothing to do with him.

So how do we break this insidious habit of fixating on other people's flaws? Every time you catch yourself judging another person, stop and look at yourself. Do it immediately. Think, "This person may not even have this flaw, but I have the habit of seeing flaws in others, and the flaws I see are a reflection of my own mind." Or think, "It's only because of my ignorance, pride, and disturbing emotions that I notice flaws like this in others." Then, practice whatever mind training is appropriate for the situation. In this way, you can break the habit of seeing flaws in others and replace it with a habit of seeing the good in them. You will be rewiring the mind, changing impure perception into pure perception.

5. Train in the most obvious afflictive emotion first.

We each have something different that we need to work on. As we become more aware of our mind, we'll start to see not only how disturbed our mind is, but which of the disturbing emotions are predominant. For some, desire will predominate, while for others anger, selfishness, jealousy, or pride will be the strongest.

Once you see which of your emotions is the strongest, make a plan to work with it by using the entire arsenal of mind-training tools. It's like going into battle. First, you strategize and try to anticipate as many scenarios as possible. Then, when it's time, you use all your weapons.

In the battle to tame the mind, we use the special weapons of relative and ultimate bodhichitta. Relative bodhichitta is what begins to wear down disturbing emotions at the more coarse and obvious levels, and ultimate bodhichitta is what addresses their source and disrupts the continuity of the emotions so that their seeds are eliminated. Strategize about how you will use them. Anticipate the different circumstances that give rise to your most disturbing emotion and pay attention to the specific situations when it is most inflamed. Every time it crops up, unleash your weapons.

For example, if anger is your main antagonist, focus on anger. Reflect on how much suffering it creates in your life. Think about how it makes you feel and how it causes you to make mistakes when it carries you away. Look at how anger causes harm to yourself and to others. Resolve to overcome it. Generate relative bodhichitta with this thought: "May the anger of all living beings be gathered here within my own anger. May my experience of anger take the place of the anger of others so that no living being ever has to suffer from it again." Then generate ultimate bodhichitta by looking at the nature of anger and recognizing its empty essence. Don't focus on the reasons you feel angry—that will just feed the affliction. Instead, look at the anger itself. If you can recognize the empty nature of the emotion, it will dissolve.

It's important to use both formal meditation sessions and the time in between to train in taming your most disturbing emotion. For formal sessions, bring to mind a situation that simulates the feeling, then antidote it with each and every one of the mind-training practices. Imagine yourself successfully applying the practices in different situations. Reflect in this way again and again. In between sessions, regularly make vows to succeed in mind training whenever the emotion arises. Every time you feel even a flickering of that negative mental state, apply relative and ultimate bodhichitta. And before you enter a situation that you know will exacerbate the emotion, remember the mind-training methods, set your intention to apply them, and go in prepared. It's also important to do purification practices, gather accumulations, and make aspirations. By doing all of this, you will hit the emotion from every direction until eventually, its power to affect you is weaker than the remedy.

By consistently heaping all of the mind trainings on top of the most intense disturbing emotion, we will begin to see our patterns change. The emotion that plagues us will occur less frequently, and it will have less power to dominate our mind. Then we can use our arsenal on the next disturbing emotion that plagues us most, until we've tamed our mind completely. So start with the most obvious disturbing emotion and train using everything you've got!

6. *Give up all hope for a result.*

It is possible that we might be deceiving ourselves about our true motivation for practice. Although we believe we are practicing mind training, we might actually be harboring a secret hope for personal gain.

It's important to practice with the pure and genuine intention to bring all beings happiness and to free them from suffering. But if we are not careful, self-cherishing will sneak in and undermine the practice. When that happens, we'll find we are practicing for selfish reasons, wrapped up in hope and fear about how the practice will benefit us. This will not bring about the transformation we truly seek.

Many people practice mind training with short-term goals in mind. If they get sick, they might practice in hopes of recovering or to lessen their fear of mortality. Others might practice because they want to manage stressful situations more effectively. Some might also hope they'll be recognized and praised for how well they are handling things. If we find ourselves doing mind training just to get through one difficult situation or to gain status or wealth, the true aim of practice is lost. Giving up the hope for a result is like a compass that keeps us on track. It reminds us to maintain a pure motivation so that we practice dharma according to the purpose of dharma.

This is not to say that we shouldn't appreciate the sense of well-being that mind training brings. As we practice, we suffer over things less, we are able to overcome challenges without getting upset, we enjoy greater peace and happiness, and we don't accumulate future causes of suffering. But these results come about because we feel genuine love and compassion for others. We are successful in practice when we don't lose sight of this perspective.

7. Avoid poisoned food.

When we practice incorrectly, the results of practice won't come. This is analogous to eating poisoned food, which may make us sick and will not nourish us as healthy food should. To avoid poisoned food, we must discard incorrect or incomplete methods of practice, which is ensured when both relative and ultimate bodhichitta are present.

We know that our practice should always be motivated by the unselfish wish to benefit others, and yet it's easy to slide back into a self-centered orientation. We might be practicing tonglen, but when we check our mind, we find that our real reason for cultivating love and compassion is our self.

That's why it's important to examine our motivation. Any time you see that it is "all about me," remember that holding a self-centered focus is the very reason we have suffered since time immemorial, and that love and compassion for others is the source of true happiness for oneself and all beings. Recommit yourself to that unself-centered intention and continue to train.

Another way to practice incorrectly is to view things as truly existent: thinking that we ultimately exist, that others exist, and that the situations we find ourselves in are real. During meditation and throughout the day, check to see if you have this belief. As long as we continue to operate under ignorance, we are perpetuating cyclic existence and will not find true freedom. Remember that you, others, and all appearances are like a dream. In this way, correct the practice by infusing it with ultimate bodhichitta.

The analogy to poisoned food has its limits, of course. If we eat rotten food, we will get sick right away. But if our practice is flawed, we are unlikely to experience immediate harm. The mind training will just not produce results and may continue to perpetuate worldly existence. This doesn't mean that if our motivation and wisdom are lacking, we shouldn't train. It is better to do imperfect mind training than not to do it. After all, practice makes perfect. It is only by practicing that the two aspects of bodhichitta will develop. If we had perfect bodhichitta always present in our mind, we wouldn't need to practice! The reminder to give up poisoned food helps us make the most of our efforts. If our motivation is pure and we apply the view of emptiness, then, just like eating healthy food, nothing will contaminate the practice or undermine its power.

8. *Don't be dependable.*

A loyal person is someone who is dependable, has a generous heart, and takes care of people. They can be relied on, and no matter how many years have passed, they will never forget a friend. In Tibetan, we call such a person *zhung-zangpo*. It's a great compliment to be described in this way.

But that positive quality is not what's being addressed in the statement "Don't be dependable." What's being addressed is our grudges. We should not be loyal to them. We should strive to let go of anger and resentment. Some people remember every disagreement they have ever had with someone and choose to hold it against them forever. This kind of dependability is nothing like *zhung-zangpo*. It's the worst kind, detrimental to our well-being and directly opposed to mind training. If someone has harmed us and we continue to resent them for it, our resentment will prevent us from developing patient forbearance. It will undermine all of the loving-kindness and compassion we are working to generate. It is crucial to learn how to let go.

9. Don't retaliate against nasty words.

When we hear things we don't like, it can feel like a thorn piercing our skin. Harsh speech, criticism, unkind words—we are easily affected when we hear them. Usually, we respond in the most ordinary way by lashing out or saying something equally unkind. But to return harm with harm is a habit that benefits no one. This statement reminds us that we need to pay extra attention to the words we use. How we respond to nasty words is a part of our mind training.

If someone says something harsh to you, reflect on how much negativity exists in the world and respond with kindness. Find what's good and express it. Perhaps you could praise the person. When people say mean things, it gives us an opportunity to express compassion for them. At the very least, if you are unable to say something nice, stay neutral and say nothing at all. However, on occasion it may be appropriate to respond to someone if they say something that is unethical or demeaning to others, such as using a racist slur. Before you speak, though, always examine your mind first to be sure you are responding from a kind heart. And choose your words with care. If you are upset by what was said and you can't speak kindly in that moment, wait until a time when you can.

If you succeed at this, your experience will transform. The situation won't escalate because you won't be providing fuel to the person saying unkind things. Over time, if you speak kindly about the person to others, they may even stop speaking harshly altogether. You'll feel good because you won't have caused unnecessary harm or said something you might later regret, and you won't have planted negative seeds that will ripen into future suffering.

Ordinarily we think that we have acted weakly or that we have lost the argument if we don't respond to nasty words with nasty words. But to return harm with harm is a lose-lose situation. It doesn't matter who started it or whose fault it is, once we have lashed out, we are equally wrong. As the saying goes, "Two wrongs don't make a right." It's unpleasant in the moment, and the karmic result will be unpleasant as well. But returning harm with kindness is a win-win. We win now and in the future. In the *Thirty-Seven Practices of a Bodhisattva*, Ngulchu Togme Zangpo explains how the most effective spiritual advice for taming the mind is the advice that exposes our hidden flaws. He encourages us to view all criticism and hurtful words as an opportunity to see our own weaknesses and to remedy those dark places through practice. From this perspective, if nasty words expose our hidden flaws, we should consider them a gift—the best of all spiritual advice.

10. *Don't wait in ambush.*

Imagine that someone has hurt you. You realize that you can't do anything about it, so you adopt the posture of patient forbearance and treat the person kindly. Only your patience doesn't flow from a recognition of the harmful effects of expressing anger, nor are you motivated by loving care for others. Rather, you figure that if you bear this small hurt now, you'll gain something in the future. Maybe you pretend to be okay but plan to seek revenge. You may appear to be practicing, but you're not.

When someone upsets us, we might not react right away, but that's not necessarily because we have tamed our mind and are generating loving thoughts toward the person who hurt us. We might be thinking it would be better to get even with the person later. So we control our negative reaction in the moment, but in truth, our mind is disturbed. Maybe we refuse to forgive the person and then later on refuse to help them. In other words, we wait in ambush. If you realize you are holding on to perceived slights this way, come back to mind training. Remember your commitment to practicing with the pure and genuine intention to bring all beings happiness and to free them from suffering.

11. *Don't strike at a vulnerable point.*

We often know exactly how to hurt others, especially those who are close to us. When it comes to our parents, siblings, children, or partner, we know them so well that we're able to suss out their sensitivities, and it's not hard to say something that will penetrate a tender spot. We might speak harshly, sarcastically, or even gently, but regardless of our tone, our intent is to hurt the person we're speaking to. One Tibetan proverb says, "Though words may not be sharp like weapons, they can destroy a person's mind." Be especially aware of this when something is happening that you don't like or that you don't agree with. At those times we are most likely to lash out with the most hurtful words. So, when you face unwanted situations, prepare your tools of mindfulness and vigilant guard and take ownership of your mind with the intention not to strike the vital point. Always remember—to say things intended to hurt someone is the opposite of love, and it's antithetical to mind training.

12. *Don't put the oxen's load on a cow.*

In Tibet, livestock are equivalent to wealth. Oxen are considered more valuable than cows because they are bigger and stronger.[4] Owners who have them covet them. But when nomads move camp and load their belongings onto their livestock for travel, they sometimes try to protect their oxen by putting the ox's load on the back of a cow. It's not an ethical practice because the cows are burdened with an oversized load.

This statement reminds us not to burden others with our own responsibilities. We have a habit of blaming others for our mistakes, always ready with a reason why something went wrong that justifies how the problem isn't our fault. When we make excuses for our choices, we fail to take responsibility for our actions.

For example, if we get caught in traffic and are late for a meeting, we'll blame the traffic, even though we perhaps left later than we should have, neglecting to anticipate the cars on the road during rush hour. We conveniently forget the part we played in being late.

Our ego will go to great lengths to avoid blame, to shirk its load of responsibility and place it on someone or something else. We may even blame someone for a problem we know they didn't cause. But then when things go well, we're keen to take credit, even if we weren't actually responsible for the success. When we stop making excuses or overlooking how our choices shape our experience, we take responsibility for our own mistakes, which is also when we will begin to grow from them.

13. *Don't place your sole attention on the fastest.*

When people watch a horse race, they place their bets on the horse they think will be the fastest. But mind training is not a horse race. If we compete with other practitioners, we will lose our way.

Sometimes we compare ourselves to others. We notice their positive qualities, their diligence in practice, the praise they receive from others. But our progress will be undermined if we bring a competitive attitude to the practice.

Remember that the sole purpose of practice is to refine away negative thoughts and emotions and to increase positive ones. The wish to look as good as, or even better than, someone else directly opposes the spirit of mind training. Competitiveness increases pride and jealousy. We may think we are better than others or that we do more than they do. In the context of dharma practice, we may feel jealous or unhappy if we see another practitioner who is able to go to more teachings than we can, or who does more practice, or who receives more attention from our teacher. An increase in either pride or jealousy is not a good sign for any practitioner, as these are the very afflictions we are working to reduce!

To counteract competitiveness, come back to the pure motivation of bodhichitta each day. Mind training is not about who gets there first. The only comparison we should be making is between what our mind was like before mind training and what our mind is like now.

14. *Don't misapply ceremonial practice.*

The dharma contains as many methods to tame the mind as there are negative thoughts and emotions—in other words, a lot! In the Tibetan Buddhist tradition, some techniques include visualizations, mantras, mudras, and other forms of ritual that are intended to bring about swift spiritual progress. The purpose of these rituals is to generate bodhichitta and wisdom in order to benefit all sentient beings. Some practitioners are inspired by the profound methods contained within ceremonial practices that can effectively tame the mind.

But some practitioners forget the main purpose of ritual practice and instead use them solely to cope with unwanted situations, such as an illness, or to increase longevity, power, success in business, or other desired outcomes. When people engage in ritual practice without an altruistic motivation, they lose sight of the goal to achieve enlightenment for the benefit of all sentient beings. The practice becomes ordinary and self-centered and does not work as intended. Such rituals may appear to be dharma, but we should not deceive ourselves into thinking that we are spiritual practitioners if our main goal is personal, short-term gain. There are even those who go so far as to perform rituals in an effort to harm others, which is the most egregious misuse of the practice.

It's important to understand that this doesn't mean that doing a ceremonial practice to avert obstacles is a misapplication of practice. While on the path, sometimes it is appropriate to engage in practice to overcome illnesses or to dispel obstacles. The key is to keep the primary goal in mind: to purify ourselves of flaws and realize our true nature in order to ultimately benefit others. As long as we keep sight of that goal, it's fine to use ritual practice to overcome obstacles and provide the conditions we need to accomplish the dharma.

15. *Don't allow the divine to be reduced to the demonic.*

In Tibet, many people make offerings to and rely upon local gods, spirits, or god-realm beings. They view these beings as divine and turn to them for aid and power. But when the wrong kind of spirit is called upon, those same beings in whom they seek refuge may become a demonic influence in their lives.

In the same way, we need to be careful not to allow that which is divine—mind training—to be reduced to something demonic, because it is possible to practice incorrectly and, as a result, pervert the teachings. Sometimes when people practice, they begin to see themselves as very special. They use the teachings not to reduce the ego but to self-aggrandize.

As a result, pride and arrogance begin to multiply. The demon of pride is one of the greatest downfalls for a practitioner. Once it has taken over, a practitioner will look down on others and feel jealousy toward people who possess genuine qualities. If you ever catch yourself longing for recognition because of your practice, remember that such an attitude contradicts genuine dharma practice. A true practitioner is someone who experiences humility and great respect toward others and who rejoices in their good qualities.

People who have been around the teachings for a while need to pay special attention to avoid this pitfall. They might think that because they've been practicing for a long time that they know more than others and deserve respect. Then when they don't get the recognition they're hoping for, they might get jealous or angry. They might even delude themselves into thinking that their anger is wrathful compassion.[5] But if we use mind training to feed the ego, then even a hundred years of practice won't do us any good.

If we have genuine experience with the dharma, we should have fewer disturbing emotions, not more, and we should not expect others to acknowledge and respect us for our practice. Our minds should be relaxed and open, and our actions should demonstrate obvious signs that we are taming the mind.

So drop any self-centered thoughts about your level of experience and try, with humility, to be of service to everyone. Always be aware of the demon of self-clinging and stop it from creeping into your mind. Do not let your guard down. Don't let the ego twist the practice into something it is not.

16. *Don't seek others' suffering as a component of happiness.*

Our commitment as practitioners is to work for the benefit of all living beings, but sometimes we stand to gain from another person's loss. Here then is yet another avenue to deviate from mind training. Wishing for another person's misfortune because it will benefit us runs counter to the precepts of mind training. For example, if we are named as the beneficiary in a loved one's will, we may find ourselves looking forward to that person's death. But it's important that we don't put our interests first. Instead, we should consider the suffering our loved one will undergo when they die and hope that they receive whatever they need.

This kind of thinking—the seeking of another's suffering for our benefit—can easily crop up. We might see it in the stock market, where we'll gain from another person's loss. Or we might hope that a competing business will close so that our business can thrive. I have even seen it among practitioners in a monastery. In Tibet, when someone becomes ill or dies, their family will make offerings to monks and lamas, requesting that they perform special prayers. These offerings feed mendicant practitioners who live on very little. Sometimes a hungry monk will secretly look forward to the hardships of others because it will lead to sponsors providing food, clothes, and other necessary provisions. Most monks do not harbor these kinds of thoughts. But all practitioners—monks, nuns, and laypeople—need to watch out for this attitude and prevent it from creeping in.

HOW TO PRACTICE

The Excellent Beginning

Sit in meditation posture to cultivate the key points of body and speech (see page 17 for a full explanation). Then, cultivate the key points of mind by setting your intention. Think, "In order to support this mind training, I will make commitments to refrain from actions that contradict wisdom, love, and compassion."

The Excellent Main Part

Review the concepts introduced in this chapter by reading one statement at a time. Alternate between contemplative meditation and resting meditation. At the end of each meditation, make a commitment to uphold the specific conduct associated with the statement so that your actions aren't in opposition to your intentions. You can contemplate just one statement per meditation session or a few, depending on your time and inspiration. Likewise, you can practice these methodically, in the order they are presented, or randomly choose different ones to focus on in any given session.

The Excellent Conclusion

Dedicate the merit generated by this practice and make aspirations. Think, "I dedicate the merit of this practice on upholding commitments to all beings that they may be freed from suffering and attain both temporary and ultimate happiness." Then, make aspirations such as, "May all beings be happy and may all beings be free. May all beings uphold commitments for the benefit of all." (You can also conclude by reciting the dedication and aspiration prayers in appendix 5.)

Off the Cushion

Choose one statement to focus on each day, or commit a few days to each statement and repeat it as many times as you can remember throughout the day. When you have time, think about its meaning and reflect on whether any of your actions contradict it. If you feel able, make a commitment to uphold this particular aspect of training. If you think it is beyond your capacity at this moment, make an aspiration that in the future it will be easy and natural for you to keep this commitment. You can follow each recitation of the statement with tonglen and then wisdom insight.

PART SEVEN

SUPPORT FOR TAMING THE MIND: KEY ADVICE

THE SEVENTH KEY POINT
Advice for Mind Training

This collection of twenty-one pieces of advice reinforces mind-training practice. When we incorporate this advice, mind training benefits every aspect of our lives. Pore over each of these statements. Memorize them. Examine them to see if they are present in your life and actions. When they are present, rejoice and commit to practicing even more. When they are not present, or barely present, commit to doing better.

14

Twenty-One Actions to Adopt
That Support Mind Training

1. *Make all yogas one.*

Yoga is the Sanskrit term for practice.[1] In this context it means to immerse the mind in positive qualities. Make the goal of all yogas to free all living beings from suffering and to bring them true happiness. This is called "the single path to be traversed." As practitioners of mind training, everything we do can be motivated by the single aspiration of bodhichitta. Always check your practice to make sure that it is based on bodhichitta. Wherever this motivation is absent, focus on cultivating it.

2. *Use one method of correction for everything.*

It is inevitable that we will experience obstacles and suffering throughout life. Sometimes we won't feel like practicing, we'll have physical pain, or we'll be overwhelmed by mental upheavals. But no matter what occurs, no matter what we face, we should bring to mind the suffering of others and practice tonglen with the thought, "May the suffering of all beings be gathered within our suffering, and may they all be released from suffering."

When we are sick and need to undergo a painful medical treatment that could cure us, though the treatment is undesirable, we go through with it because we know it could free us of pain. It may seem counterintuitive to take on suffering when we suffer, but this is the most effective response to adversity. The moment you suffer, stop thinking about yourself and start thinking about others. It will change everything. It sounds hard to do because you are already hurting. But if you develop a strong practice, your suffering will become meaningful. This practice transforms painful experiences into the path to freedom. It enables us to extract the highest potential from every situation. It will increase our capacity to overcome difficulties and decrease the power that negative circumstances have over us. It will make us more patient. In other words, this one remedy will bring great value to our lives.

3. *In the beginning and the end, there are two things to do.*

It is important to begin the day by generating bodhichitta and to end the day by reflecting on how well we upheld that commitment.

The moment you wake, think, "Today, I will not be separated from relative and ultimate bodhichitta." Then, right before you go to bed, reflect on your day. Acknowledge when you didn't practice successfully or simply forgot to practice. Generate regret for any times you became upset, harbored negative thoughts, or engaged in harmful actions. Commit to refrain from negative thoughts, words, and actions in the future. Then resolve to cultivate bodhichitta and apply the practice next time. Acknowledging mistakes undermines the continuity of negative mental habits, sets a resolve to think and act differently, and helps establish positive habits.

Next, think about the times during the day when you upheld the aspiration of bodhichitta and were successful in practice and in benefiting others. Rejoice in this virtue. Acknowledging moments when you practiced well reinforces positive habits and increases joy. Conclude by dedicating any virtue you've accumulated during the day to the welfare of others.

4. *Whichever of the two occurs, be patient.*

Happiness and suffering—*the two*—arise one after the other. But no matter which occurs, be patient and use the experience as an opportunity to cultivate bodhichitta.

When suffering occurs, think beyond your suffering in the moment and consider the suffering that you and all living beings have endured throughout time. All of it resulted from negative causes. By experiencing this suffering now, you exhaust the karma for suffering in the future. Thinking about this helps cultivate the patience needed to accept the suffering. It also provides the mental space to practice relative or ultimate bodhichitta. Now practice tonglen and use compassion to take on others' suffering.

When happiness occurs, don't forget to practice! We can endure a lot of suffering, but then we can get carried away by good circumstances and waste those positive causes and conditions. We might even act carelessly and make mistakes with serious consequences. We've all heard stories of people who severely injure themselves or even die doing something fun.

It's also common for people who've had a windfall of wealth or who have gained power to experience arrogance and jealousy. This increase in disturbing emotions leads them to have less empathy for others and to be less caring. Over time, their positive conditions wind up harming many people. Instead, use happiness to create more happiness. Rejoice in your good fortune and use it to make aspirations for all beings. Think, "May all beings share in this happiness, and may they have even greater happiness."

Whether joy or sorrow comes your way, use every circumstance as an opportunity to generate bodhichitta. This is the true meaning of patience: to forbear whichever of the two occurs, and to not lose yourself in disturbing emotions. Strive to practice in this way no matter which of the two occurs.

5. *Observe these two, even at the risk of life.*

In every circumstance, we make an effort to protect our life. We never let that guard down because if we did, we might be harmed. This is the same attitude we need to adopt with respect to the commitments and the vows outlined in the sixth key point of mind training (see part 6).[2]

If our actions contradict these precepts, we gather causes that will directly harm our well-being and conflict with love, compassion, and wisdom. Always be aware of the commitments. Transgressing any of them not only undermines practice but it also involves negative emotions and actions that produce suffering. Strive to uphold the commitments and vows just as you would strive to protect your own life.

6. Train in the three challenges.

Three distinct challenges we face are recognizing disturbing emotions, applying the remedies, and stopping the habits that lead them to recur. It is important to be aware of these challenges so that you can set your intention to overcome them.

Sometimes people wonder why it seems so difficult to change. It seems that way because we don't train in the three challenges. When we get angry, we don't acknowledge that it's not the situation that's making us suffer, it's our anger. We justify the anger, feed it, and create more suffering—the opposite of what we want. To recognize this dynamic is to be aware of the anger and to acknowledge its negative impact.

If we behave in ways that reinforce our bad habits, we won't be able to cut the stream of negativity. It takes diligence to apply antidotes to disturbing emotions. First, we need to understand the problem, which is to recognize the disturbing emotions. Then, we need the will to solve it by applying the necessary tools, which are the remedies. And finally, we need to end the habits through continued application of that recognition and application. By working to overcome these three challenges, we reduce the power of disturbing emotions.

THE CHALLENGE OF RECOGNIZING DISTURBING EMOTIONS

At first, it's challenging to recognize when our mind is disturbed. It is our habit to feel emotions, not to be aware of them. We often get so caught up reacting to situations that we don't diagnose our disturbing emotions or the harm that they cause. Instead of identifying with the emotions, we should recognize them as quickly as possible. If anger arises, recognize it. If you feel pride, jealousy, desire—name it. Commit yourself to this task.

THE CHALLENGE OF APPLYING THE REMEDIES

Once we're aware of our disturbing emotions, the next challenge is to apply remedies to alleviate them. We won't be able to overcome our emotions by suppressing them. We need to apply one or more mind-training methods until the disturbing emotions resolve. At first it's hard to do this because our disturbing emotions are stronger than the remedies. That's why we need to practice mind training again and again. Eventually, the remedies we apply will be stronger than our emotions and our capacity to transform the mind will increase.

THE CHALLENGE OF STOPPING THE HABITS

Our final challenge is to stop responding to situations with disturbing emotions. We need to cut through the stream of negativity. This will happen as we work on overcoming the first two challenges, and even more so when we make a firm commitment not to be disturbed. Think over and over again that you will completely eliminate the disturbing emotions. Say to yourself, "I will cut through the stream of disturbing emotions!" Vow again and again not to react to unpleasant circumstances with disturbing emotions. Resolve to be free of them. Vowing to destroy disturbing emotions at their root is essential to taming the mind. This is how we overcome our demons.

7. Adopt the three principal requisites.

To practice the dharma correctly and gain freedom from suffering, we need to rely on a qualified spiritual teacher, practice correctly with a mind that is open to the dharma, and have the right conditions for practice. These are the three principal requisites. They are the primary factors that enable us to practice, but it's important to note that they are not the only requisites. For example, time is also a factor. It takes time to blend our mind with the dharma, which means we need to make time to practice.

RELYING ON A QUALIFIED SPIRITUAL TEACHER

A qualified spiritual teacher is someone who has the capacity to guide us through the entire spiritual path. This is an extraordinarily important relationship. It is not just a short-term support we use to cope with a difficult situation, nor is it like studying with a teacher in school. A spiritual teacher provides us with the foundation for the entire path and guides us to the very heart of awakening. It's not a relationship just for this life; it lasts all the way to the end of the path, however many lifetimes that may take. If a teacher is not fully qualified, then the path they show us will be incomplete or incorrect and will eventually cause us to lose our way. This has profound implications. So our primary teacher, or *root guru*, must have outstanding qualities. They must be spiritually qualified.

I cannot emphasize enough the importance of studying with a qualified spiritual teacher. Some teachers know a lot about a specific topic or text or may be able to provide basic advice, but they aren't qualified. While they can, to a limited degree, support our spiritual growth, they lack the capacity to fully guide us along the entire path.

There are three qualities that are the minimum requirements for a spiritual guide. First, they need to know the entire path. This means having acquired sufficient teachings on authentic scriptures and having received all of the necessary transmissions from their teachers so that they are able to provide students with the unique methods that they may need. Second, they must have direct personal experience of practicing those teachings so that they have experiential wisdom guiding them. Third, they must be motivated by pure bodhichitta—genuine love and compassion for their students. There are many more specific qualifications that pertain to particular practices, but these three are universal to all approaches to the path.

In terms of how and when to seek out a spiritual guide, it is best to first hear teachings and read authentic texts on Buddhist philosophy until you are familiar with the path and basic dharma principles. The second step is to learn more, through reading and hearing teachings, about what qualifications a teacher must have to serve as a guide for you. And finally, once you have enough information and have decided that you want to practice the Buddhist path, you begin to search, through whatever means you have, for a teacher that you feel connected to and are drawn toward. Go to teachings with them, meet them in person, look into their training and history and examine if they have the necessary qualifications. When you find someone you feel deeply connected to who fits all the criteria, request them to be your teacher, and if they accept you as a student, follow their guidance.

PRACTICING CORRECTLY WITH A MIND THAT IS OPEN TO THE DHARMA

The teachings become a part of our experience when we are able to blend them with our mind. Learning how to join the mind with the instructions is an indispensable skill. To do this, we need to be willing to follow through with the process. So, for example, if you have met a qualified spiritual teacher and they have advised you to do a certain practice, do it exactly as they suggest. Be like clay placed in a *tsa-tsa* mold that comes out exactly like the mold. This is how the qualities taught in the scriptures and the realization exhibited by our teachers and the great saints become our qualities.

Every good quality we hear about is intended to arise in our mind and become our direct experience. Meeting a qualified teacher and even accumulating all of the necessary provisions for practice is not enough. If our mind remains closed to the dharma and we don't practice it precisely as it is taught, its purpose will not be fulfilled. A mind that is open to the dharma is one that is willing to change. It is one that is open to awakening the potential qualities within by training in the methods taught by our teacher.

ACCUMULATING THE NECESSARY
PROVISIONS FOR PRACTICE

If our basic needs are not met—if we don't have sufficient food, clothing, or shelter—it's very difficult to practice. This does not mean a practitioner has to be wealthy; having too many resources isn't necessarily beneficial either. We need to find a balance between having too much and having too little. If we have too little, all of our time will be spent on survival. We won't have the means to travel to seek out the teachings or to spend time in retreat dedicating ourselves to practice. If we have too much wealth, all of our time will be consumed by accumulating and protecting our money, and there will be no time or mental space for practice.

Examine your life and ask yourself if you possess these three principal requisites: Have you found a qualified teacher, are you practicing correctly with an open mind, and do you have the necessary provisions? If you do, rejoice. Make the aspiration that all beings possess the three principal requisites. If you discover that you are lacking any of these supports, put special emphasis on cultivating the cause you lack. Make aspirations and prayers to help create these causes. When you see a person who possesses them, rejoice in their good fortune and think, "May they always have them!" And if you meet someone who does not have the supportive conditions for practice, meditate on compassion and make aspirations that everyone may possess the three principal requisites for accomplishing the path.

8. *Meditate without these three deteriorating.*

In order to tame the mind, there are three qualities that we need to foster: devotion to the teacher, enthusiasm for the trainings, and conviction in upholding the vows. It is vital to prevent these virtues from deteriorating.

DEVOTION TO THE TEACHER

As for the first, devotion, it's important not to allow our connection with our spiritual guide to weaken. All the qualities and realization that come from the Mahayana dharma depend upon a positive connection between student and teacher. The more we learn about the student-teacher relationship, the more we will appreciate its role in our spiritual growth. Over time, as we practice the teachings we've received, our devotion will expand as our faults decrease and positive qualities grow. On a deeper level, devotion enables us to experience our true nature, from which even more trust naturally blossoms. As trust increases, so does our practice and realization. Devotion opens us up to all that our teacher transmits. To foster devotion, keep learning and practicing, and let your heart be open.

ENTHUSIASM FOR THE TRAININGS

Enthusiasm for mind training is also important. It's essential if we're going to consistently apply the teachings. Strive to cultivate joy for mind training by appreciating its value. When you find that your enthusiasm for practice is diminishing, there are two things that will help to restore it: hearing teachings and contemplating the four thoughts. Attending dharma teachings will help reignite enthusiasm, and it will remind us of the value of practice. Contemplating precious human birth, impermanence, karma, and suffering will also increase our enthusiasm, so revisit the preliminaries practice frequently to keep remembering the purpose and value of mind training.

UPHOLDING THE VOWS

Finally, uphold the three vows: the pratimoksha, bodhisattva, and Mantrayana samayas, which form the framework for the path. Notice how this point comes up in different contexts within the sixth key point, commitments, and seventh key point, advice. The reason this is emphasized is because on many levels, upholding the commitment to the vows sustains and strengthens everything we practice. Anytime our commitment weakens, the spirit of practice is compromised. It is important not to allow our vows to degenerate in any way.

9. *Act without the three being separated.*

Body, speech, and mind—these three constitute who we are as human beings. Never allow them to be separate from what is positive and virtuous, and always refrain from actions that are negative.

Our actions can be summed up into ten negative actions to be eliminated and ten positive actions to be adopted. The ten negative actions include three that are physical, four that are verbal, and three that are mental. The ten positive actions are their opposites. So for the physical actions, instead of killing, strive to protect life; instead of stealing, strive to practice generosity; instead of sexual misconduct, strive to maintain good morals.

For actions of speech, instead of lying, strive to be truthful; instead of sowing discord, speak in a way that leads to greater harmony between people; instead of using harsh words, say kind things; instead of gossiping, speak about what is meaningful.

For actions of the mind, instead of feeling covetousness, cultivate the wish that others have and enjoy what they need; instead of thinking unkind thoughts, develop a kind heart; instead of holding incorrect views, adopt views that accord with the way things are. If our actions of body, speech, and mind accord with the ten positive actions, then we will have the conduct of a bodhisattva.

10. *Train impartially toward all objects.*
Extensive and deep training in everything is crucial.

Impartial mind training is the only way to bring true transformation. If we pick and choose to train our mind in some circumstances but not in others, our practice will never become strong enough to deeply change us. Partiality can take many forms. We might choose to practice when we're with loved ones, but then ignore it with people we don't know or like. Or maybe our practice depends on our mood. We might practice after we've slept well, but not after a restless night.

To be impartial means to generate relative and ultimate bodhichitta in relation to everyone and in every circumstance, without exception. For the training to be pervasive, it can't be done occasionally.

To train in ultimate bodhichitta is to remember the empty nature of all things as they come to mind or directly appear to our senses. This means that we know that everything we think or perceive is like an illusion. The depth to which we remember true nature at any given moment depends on how much we've studied emptiness. But no matter where our understanding may be, we should apply the knowledge we have pervasively and without partiality. The same goes for relative bodhichitta. Anytime we relate to other living beings, whoever they are, we should generate the wish, "May they find happiness and be free from suffering."

Train using inanimate objects, such as flowers or mountains, too. Obviously we aren't developing love and compassion toward these objects per se, but we can use them to work on our attachment, aversion, and indifference. Use relative bodhichitta to develop the wish that all beings enjoy a particular object, or perhaps be free of its harmful influence. For example, wish that all beings enjoy the beautiful flowers or wish that everyone be free from perils while climbing a mountain. Or remember the view of ultimate bodhichitta to see an object's true nature. Make everything that arises in your perception a component of mind training. This is what it means to train without partiality.

To train extensively and deeply means to take the practice to the point where it profoundly penetrates your mind. Many people hear teachings, but don't go much further. While they gain knowledge from having listened to the dharma, they merely take it as good information. Some people take a further step and reflect on the meaning. They think, "Yes, this is true." But the knowledge that comes from contemplation is also not enough. If the teachings remain mere theory, stuck in the realm of intellectual knowledge, they will not tame the mind.

The entire purpose of gaining knowledge through hearing the words of the dharma and contemplating their meaning is to make those qualities our direct experience. The point is to apply the methods during formal meditation and throughout the day until the qualities of the teachings deeply penetrate our mind and infiltrate our heart. When this happens, we become those qualities.

Applying the practice is a bit like baking a cake. It's not enough for it to look cooked on the outside. If the inside is gooey, we can't eat it. We need to allow enough time for the heat to penetrate and cook the cake all the way through. Many of us get stuck before we're cooked all the way through. We've heard the teachings and perhaps have even contemplated their meaning and trust that they work, but even though we have the knowledge, we haven't sufficiently applied the practice. As a result, it hasn't penetrated the mind to the core and become a part of us.

Knowledge alone will not tame our mind. We need to take the necessary steps to change how our mind thinks and operates. It's like reprogramming a system. Our current mental operating system is self-centered. Even when we help others, we are motivated by how helping makes us feel. Selfishness drives us and compels us to act. We don't have to think about it or meditate on it. It is simply the assumption from which we operate.

But what if we were driven by a truly unself-centered concern for others? What if we cherished others' welfare more than anything else? If we take these trainings to heart and practice them thoroughly, they will lead us to have a concern for others as deep as our concern is now for ourselves. Love and compassion will thoroughly penetrate our mind, and the wish to benefit others will propel us into action. This shift in perspective is what makes one a bodhisattva.

This process is gradual. It's accomplished slowly in stages. That's why we have so many trainings to develop bodhichitta. In the beginning, we train in love and compassion because we know it benefits us. At this stage, our love and compassion are surface level. But if we continue to practice, bodhichitta slowly penetrates deeper and deeper until our whole mind is permeated by it. This level of understanding bears no resemblance to merely having developed some confidence in the benefits of practice after hearing teachings.

It reminds me of learning to swim. It takes time to be able to do it effortlessly. Many of you have been swimming all your lives, but I learned as an adult after I came to the United States. First, I had to learn how to float. If someone didn't hold me, I would sink. Then, as I became more comfortable in the water, I learned how to kick my feet and move my arms, but I could only swim a couple of feet before I'd start to sink. I kept at it though, and I took more swimming lessons. Now when I get in the water I can swim as many laps as I feel like, no problem. As it has become natural, my body knows exactly what to do without thinking about it.

Mind training is just like that. If we keep practicing, eventually love and compassion will come naturally. When the dharma permeates our entire experience, it changes our life from within.

11. *Always train in the most difficult points.*

It's important to identify what triggers you. When do you lose control of your emotions and act in ways that you'll regret later? Once you figure out the people and situations that provoke you, you can deliberately mind-train when you encounter them. Maybe there's someone at work who has upset you or who is preventing you from getting what you want. Maybe you have been kind to someone and in return, they hurt you. Whatever the case may be, generate an awareness of who and what challenges you, and resolve to train your mind. It will take special effort, but if you sincerely try to cultivate bodhichitta for those you find most difficult, your reactions will become more and more positive.

It is particularly important to avoid harmful actions toward those with whom we have important relationships, such as our parents or spiritual teachers. This is because of the role they play in our lives and the kindness they have shown us. A parent gives us the greatest gift of this life—precious human birth. An authentic spiritual guide gives us the gift of a path to finding freedom.

Once you've identified the situations that challenge you, apply yourself enthusiastically to using the tools of mind training. In the morning, start the day by setting your intention. Make a vow by thinking, "If such and such challenging situation crops up, I vow not to be separate from relative and ultimate bodhichitta in that moment." It's also good to imagine yourself in challenging situations. See yourself not being triggered, instead responding with love, compassion, and wisdom. Likewise, if you are about to enter that situation, make a commitment to yourself to apply the mind trainings. During formal meditation sessions, or informally throughout the day, do tonglen toward the person or people associated with that difficult situation and meditate on the empty nature of all aspects of it. At the end of the day, think about how you did. If you reacted badly, generate regret and resolve to do better next time. Contemplate impermanence and karma to reinforce your commitment. You might think it is too difficult, that your disturbing emotions are just too strong in this situation, but that is just your mind. If you choose to work with all of the tools at your disposal, your perceptions—and consequently your entire experience—will change.

12. *Don't be dependent upon other conditions.*

Some people practice only when they feel good, while others practice only when they are having a hard time. But practice should not depend on how we feel in a given moment or whether our external conditions are supportive. If we're happy, that is a good time to practice. If we're struggling, that is also a good time to practice. Don't allow the mind training to be dependent upon conditions. Instead, bring everything onto the path— be it good, bad, or neutral.

Whenever you find yourself hesitating to practice for any reason, apply mind training immediately. Think, "Through my experience of feeling unable to do practice—an activity that is ultimately beneficial— may the challenges of all beings be gathered within my own challenge, and through that power may all beings be free from the suffering of being dependent on conditions." Then, meditate on the empty nature of the challenging conditions. In this way, even a perceived inability to practice becomes practice!

13. *This time, practice the indispensable point.*

Since beginningless time, lifetime after lifetime, we have wandered from one state of existence to another. But this time—in this human life—we have the chance to do what will be ultimately meaningful. This precious human life is the greatest support for achieving our true wish, to be free from suffering and never separate from happiness. But if we don't make use of this opportunity, it will be even harder to come by in the future. So, while enjoying these freedoms and advantages of body and mind, it is crucial to apply ourselves to the indispensable point—to tame the mind. To do this, we must consider practice to be the most important thing in this life.

Look at your priorities. Do you prioritize spending time on worldly pursuits? If so, you will not spend sufficient time using this life for what is ultimately beneficial. You must change your priorities. Make practice your primary objective.

This life is a vessel that can ferry us across the ocean of suffering. With it we can purify all obscurations and become completely realized. But this can only happen if we practice the path, generating relative and ultimate bodhichitta again and again.

Think of this life as being at a crossroads: We can take the transformative road that leads to ultimate happiness, or we can take the confused road that leads to more suffering, now and in the future. We have the power to make this choice. This time, practice the dharma.

14. *Don't misunderstand.*

It's possible to misunderstand—and consequently to misapply—the mind-training teachings. When the practice is misapplied, it doesn't tame the mind.

If you patiently bear hardships just so you can take revenge on someone later, you are misunderstanding the practice of patience. If you are diligent in your pursuit of worldly pleasures but indifferent about benefiting others, you are misunderstanding the practice of diligence. If you feel happy when another person experiences misfortune, you are misunderstanding the practice of rejoicing.

While many people will grit their teeth and endure discomfort to achieve selfish aims, many practitioners are unwilling to patiently bear even small discomforts that arise in the pursuit of dharma. To be lazy about the dharma is another way to misunderstand practice.

Even compassion can be misapplied. We could be misunderstanding the practice by having compassion for someone who is undergoing hardships to practice the dharma, where instead we should be rejoicing for them! Someone, for example, might feel sorry for Milarepa (see page 157) when they read about the hardships he endured for the sake of the path. Or we could lack compassion for someone who harms others, even though they are actively creating the causes of suffering and are just as worthy of compassion as their victims. There are many ways to misunderstand and misapply the practice of mind training. That is why it is so valuable to review the teachings repeatedly to avoid such mistakes.

15. *Don't be sporadic.*

If we train our mind sporadically, it will be difficult to gain competence. When we practice in spurts or apply the trainings in some situations but not in others, the mind training doesn't take root in our being. Occasional practice won't bring about the change we seek.

It's much more effective to be consistent. To develop consistency, most people need to hear more teachings. Dharma teachings inspire us to practice, and the more we practice, the stronger our practice will grow. The positive effects of practice will further inspire us, and we will become even more consistent. This is the dharma practice snowball effect.

16. *Train wholeheartedly.*

Focus wholeheartedly on taming the mind. Do this without distraction. Our habit is to do the very opposite of this, that is, to be in a state of constant distraction. At any given moment, our attention is directed toward external objects—forms, sounds, tastes, scents, tactile sensations—or we dwell on the past or on the future. We spend most of our waking hours having neutral or negative thoughts toward objects and our perceptions of them, and very little time focused on mind training.

We can begin to change this habit by remembering to integrate mind training once or twice a day. That will gradually increase to four or five times a day. Eventually we will remember to train our minds half of the time, then most of the time, and then, with enough diligence, all of the time.

When sitting in a formal practice session, focus all of your attention on the aspect of mind training you are cultivating. Then, when practicing informally during the day, vow to train your mind no matter what occurs. This is how you tame your mind wholeheartedly.

17. *Find freedom through both investigation and examination.*

When we begin to practice lojong, we need to investigate for obvious disturbing emotions. For example, we may find that we flare up with anger every time we're stuck in traffic. With practice, our disturbing emotions will become less coarse, and then in specific instances that previously upset us, such as traffic, we no longer get so frustrated. But that's when we need to examine ourselves more carefully to free ourselves from subtler negative emotions. Taking our traffic example, look carefully for underlying levels of agitation or aggression and continue to refine them by applying the trainings until they resolve. Investigation and examination seem like synonymous terms, but they are used to explain different aspects of the process of mental investigation. First, we investigate our mind for obvious mental afflictions. Later, as the afflictions grow less coarse, the process becomes subtler and we have to examine ourselves more carefully to free ourselves of negative emotions.

As our training progresses, there may be times when we experience no disturbing emotions. But just because we feel at peace, that doesn't mean we should become complacent. Even then we need to continue to refine and deepen the mind training.

The best way to find out if our afflictions are really gone is to purposefully put ourselves in situations that will incite emotional responses. This may sound silly now, but there will come a time when, if we want to progress in our practice, we will need to seek out unfavorable conditions, such as situations that could make us feel angry, jealous, or desirous. The point in those situations is to immediately apply the mind trainings to root out the disturbing emotions.

You can also bring to mind a person or situation that upset you in the past. Stay with this memory until it provokes your emotions, then monitor the mind closely. If aversion, dislike, or righteousness arises, apply a strong antidote immediately. Be particularly mindful of self-cherishing. Our attachment to self is so pervasive that it can be hard to recognize when it isn't blatantly expressing itself. We need to examine carefully to cut this attachment.

Investigation and examination are indispensable to mind-training practice. These two levels of inquiry ensure that we are not only resolving the surface-level disturbing emotions but also the less perceptible ones at their root. This is how we find true freedom from all of the poisons of the mind.

18. *Don't be self-congratulatory.*

If we practice, inevitably we will find ourselves helping others. We will be more generous toward those in need and more patient with those who are upset. We will avoid harming others and instead seek to protect them from harm. Our capacity will continue to grow as we cultivate love and compassion, and this will naturally manifest into actions.

The problem is we tend to reinforce our ego and become arrogant over our successes. We might begin to feel self-important because of our good deeds or be motivated out of a desire to demonstrate our positive qualities, a motivation that will only increase our sense of self-importance.

Watch out for this trap! If you find yourself thinking, "I've been so kind to them," or "I'm so amazing," remember the core of these trainings is to increase concern for others while also reducing ego-clinging. There is nothing wrong with acknowledging when you succeed in helping others, but don't use that success to reinforce pride.

To overcome this tendency, remember: We may be kind to others, but they are even more kind to us. If sentient beings weren't present in our life, how could we develop love and compassion? How could we cultivate patient forbearance or practice generosity? Only in relation to others can we perfect positive qualities. Therefore, think that sentient beings are kind to you because they provide the opportunity to accumulate positive actions, which are the causes for happiness, and to develop qualities and insights, which are the causes for liberation.

The path begins with the wish to benefit beings and on that basis both temporary and ultimate happiness are accomplished. So don't be self-congratulatory—it undermines everything you are striving for.

19. *Restrain jealousy.*

Many of us don't realize we have a habitual inability to feel happy for others when something good happens to them. For example, when you board an airplane and you file past the people in the comfortable first-class seats, are you happy for them? Or does a subtle—or not-so-subtle—negativity arise in you? The comfort they are enjoying is a perfect reason to rejoice. May they never be separate from such enjoyments! The person who thinks this, the person who genuinely rejoices in their comfort, may get more joy from that attitude than the person actually sitting in first class. Don't allow yourself to succumb to petty jealousy. Instead, uphold the integrity of practice and rejoice whenever you witness someone else's happiness.

20. *Don't be dramatic.*

As practitioners, we strive to become more and more aware of how our actions and reactions affect others so that we can increase our capacity to benefit them. But many of us react strongly to the most insignificant circumstances. We are excitable, fickle even. When something good happens, we might gasp, jump up and down, and gush excitedly. When something bad happens, we might quickly become downtrodden or angry.

When we react dramatically to every little thing, it's hard on those around us. Our mood swings strain our relationships, especially with family, friends, coworkers, and the sangha. People get the feeling they can't depend on us. We have a saying in Tibet: "Don't be like a goat's nose!" When you touch a goat's nose with the end of a stick even gently, they snort, jump up and down, and run away. When you practice mind training, don't be like that!

It is particularly important to be aware of this in relationships in small communities. Being dramatic can be especially hard in dharma centers, which often consist of people from diverse backgrounds who don't share blood relationships; nor do we get to choose them as we do our close friends or partners. Yet we come together because we share the dharma in common. When we initially gather for an event, people who haven't seen each other for a while may get very excited, but then perhaps the next day or in the middle of the retreat, someone might say or do something that we don't like, and we get upset. Being easily elated or easily disturbed makes us unreliable. In a spiritual community, dramatic behavior can be a major impediment to developing strong and healthy relationships with people who could help support our practice. No one is ever going to say everything we want them to say or do everything we want them to do. It is necessary to acknowledge this fact as we form friendships. Otherwise, none of these relationships will last. In addition, our spiritual growth depends upon the sangha—they are our support for cultivating positive qualities and realization. So place special emphasis on patiently bearing the small things that arise and understand that we are a diverse group of people coming together for the dharma.

With all of this in mind, set your intention to be steadfast in the face of ups and downs. Don't allow yourself to get easily excited or to swing with your moods. Strive to cultivate an expansive mind that remains stable despite surprises, disappointments, and change. In this way, cultivate new habits so that, while positive and negative conditions come and go, you can remain steady.

21. *Don't seek acknowledgment.*

The more we train our minds, the more we will be able to benefit beings, but the meaning of the practice is undermined if we expect reward for our efforts. Watch out for the desire for recognition. As soon as we expect praise for our spiritual accomplishments, we are no longer motivated by the pure intention to benefit others. Instead, we bounce back to self-centered square one. Ego is always looking for opportunities to worm its way into our mind and practice, and so it crops up again and again, subversively. This is why we need to always watch out for selfishness. So this is the final piece of advice: always watch out for selfishness. Continuously strive to avoid practicing with the hope that you will impress others or gain a good reputation. Practicing with pure motivation will refine the mind training and enrich the path.

HOW TO PRACTICE

The Excellent Beginning

Sit in meditation posture to cultivate the key points of body and speech (see page 17 for a full explanation). Then, cultivate the key points of mind by setting your intention. Think, "To deepen this mind training, I will assimilate this advice in order to reinforce wisdom, love, and compassion."

The Excellent Main Part

Review the concepts introduced in this chapter by reading one piece of advice at a time. Alternate between contemplative meditation and resting meditation. At the end of each point, reflect on how it relates to you personally. Is this something you already do, or that you could do? Look for creative ways to follow this advice by integrating it into different situations in your life. You can contemplate just one statement per meditation session or a few, depending on your time and inspiration. Likewise, you can practice these methodically, in the order they are presented, or randomly choose different ones to focus on in any given session.

The Excellent Conclusion

Dedicate the merit generated by this practice and make aspirations. Think, "I dedicate the merit of practicing this advice to all beings that they may be freed from suffering and attain both temporary and ultimate happiness." Then, make aspirations such as, "May all beings be happy and may all beings be free. May all beings follow advice that benefits others." (You can also conclude by reciting the dedication and aspiration prayers in appendix 5.)

Off the Cushion

Choose one statement to focus on each day, or commit a few days to each statement and repeat it as many times as you can remember throughout the day. When you have time, reflect on its meaning, consider whether you are actively following the advice, and think about how to more fully integrate it into your actions. Take, for example, the statement "Act without the three being separated." Repeat it as many times as you can remember throughout the day, immediately following with the introspective thought, "Are my body, speech, or mind separate from positive thoughts or actions?" You can follow each recitation of the statement with tonglen and then wisdom insight.

The Excellent Conclusion

Now we come to the final words from the root text, the colophon, beginning with

"This quintessential elixir of heart advice, which transforms the five kinds of rampant degeneration into the path of enlightenment, is a transmission from Serlingpa."

The great master Atisha compiled these lojong teachings after receiving them from his teacher Serlingpa.[1] These were passed on orally until, close to a century later, the practitioner Chekawa Yeshe Dorje arranged them as this text called "The Seven Key Points of Mind Training."[2] Chekawa Yeshe Dorje's own words appear in the colophon to indicate the source of the teachings and to authenticate their composition. Because these teachings are a distillation of heart advice shared orally from teacher to student, Chekawa Yeshe Dorje calls them "quintessential." Because they are a method for transforming all unwanted circumstances into something good, he calls them an "elixir."

In today's world we need the elixir of mind training. We're living in what's referred to in dharma teachings as "a period of degeneration," an era when sentient beings experience great adversity. There are five different kinds of degeneration, and each one affects our quality of life. The *degeneration of life span* refers to the many beings whose lives are cut short because of violence and poor living conditions. The *degeneration of afflictive mental states* refers to an increase in negative thoughts and emotions. The *degeneration of the quality of beings* refers to the selfish inclination of beings and their willingness to harm others, as well as society's devaluing of positive qualities such as honesty, consideration, and kindness. The *degeneration of views* refers to the radical views that dominate people's minds, which are not in harmony with the way things are. The *degeneration of time period* refers to environmental pollution, natural disasters, and the rampant deterioration of the world, which greatly reduce the quality of life for all of the planet's inhabitants.

But there's good news. These degenerating times provide unlimited opportunities for us to apply the methods of mind training. In fact, the more adversity, the more mind training. The trainings are like fire, and adverse conditions are like firewood. The more firewood you pile on, the stronger the fire burns. That's why this is the perfect teaching for right now. As adversity fuels our practice, we become better practitioners and better people.

There are many profound and effective methods for taming the mind within the dharma, but some of them take a long time to cultivate. The methods of mind training explained in this book, however, can bring immediate results when applied properly. They can be used by any practitioner to transform adverse conditions into the path of awakening. Whether you are old or young, experienced or inexperienced, have a highly evolved practice or are just beginning, it makes no difference. These methods work.

In his conclusion to the colophon, Chekawa Yeshe Dorje says,

"The awakening of the karmic energy of previous training aroused intense interest in me. Therefore, I ignored suffering and criticism and sought instruction for subduing self-clinging. Now, I can die, and I'll regret nothing."

And in this way, he joins Atisha's words with his own experience of mind training. He explains that the karma from his previous life inspired him to seek out these instructions, and despite discouragement from others and many hardships, he worked to overcome all obstacles. He practiced Atisha's instructions diligently, taming his self-clinging and reducing his disturbing emotions. In the end, he mastered the trainings. He reached the point of no regrets.

The root text is a series of condensed pith instructions that speak directly to our hearts. It is difficult to find a teaching that is more life changing in so few words. If we adopt these seven key points of mind training as the main practice for the rest of our lives, we will succeed in making our lives meaningful. Everything we need is here. This is one of the most detailed explanations on how to generate relative bodhichitta, the mind of awakening. And while other texts contain more detailed explorations of ultimate bodhichitta, the quintessential points on the ultimate nature of reality are contained within the seven key points. In other words, the entire path of Mahayana Buddhism is contained within this teaching.

Everything in this book will benefit your mind, but it is difficult to internalize all of the key points if you read them only once. So study the root text and commentary at least three times. Try the sitting meditations and take the "off the cushion" instructions to heart, making them your own over time. The more you pore over these teachings, the deeper they go, and as you integrate each point into practice, your understanding and experience will become more profound.

It is up to you to realize relative and ultimate bodhichitta. Study the teachings, contemplate them and meditate on them. Only then will you come to know how truly transformative these teachings are.

It is time to offer one final act of generosity by dedicating the merit we've gained by contemplating and meditating upon these lojong teachings. When we dedicate the merit, we give away all of the virtue we've generated to others. Imagine all of the causes of happiness and freedom we and others have created in the past, present, and future. Imagine the positive activities of not just ordinary beings but of buddhas and bodhisattvas too. Then, give all of that virtue away to sentient beings.

> I dedicate this study and practice to all sentient beings who fill the vast limits of space. May they be free from suffering and the causes of suffering, and may they find temporary and ultimate happiness. May they give rise to bodhichitta, and may they overcome all obstacles to practice along the way. May the wishes of all sentient beings be fulfilled. May everyone attain true liberation from suffering—the ultimate state of buddhahood. Until that time, I pray that beings are spared the suffering of natural disasters, war, famine, sickness, and poverty and that they experience safety, peace, abundance, good health, and well-being.

Dedicate the merit to the welfare of all beings every time you practice or do anything positive. By giving away the virtue, you seal your efforts with the great aspiration of bodhichitta. Practice begins with pure motivation and ends with pure aspirations. Let us dedicate the merit to all. May all beings be happy and free.

ACKNOWLEDGMENTS

Just as the saying goes, "It takes a village to raise a child," so too it takes a community of editors and readers to capture Rinpoche's oral teachings and share them with the world through the written word. We are grateful to all of Rinpoche's students who contributed to this fruition in various ways. Thank you especially to Paul Gustafson, whose vision galvanized a core group of Katog Vajra Ling's sangha in Connecticut to come together and participate in transcribing Rinpoche's teachings, and then who spent more than six years organizing, editing, and compiling the original draft with me. Thanks to everyone who transcribed this—Kathleen Hayes, Mike Larini, Roxy Pickering, Susan Shellard, Kris Yaggi, Karen Kernan, Laura West, and Paul Gustafson. Scott and Carly Casper's early support gave the project the jump start it needed. Cynthia Shumway provided feedback on the first draft and got us started on the endnotes and glossary. Lavinia Spalding provided kind and professional guidance on the introduction and biography. Ibby Caputo, our final editor, helped transform the first draft into a completed book with patience for both me and our vast learning curve. This was no small endeavor! Shamelle Gonzalez provided additional advice and insights, Shelley Jackson reviewed and helped polish the final draft, and Cyndi and Travis Wong helped us with some finishing touches. Jacqui Merrell copyedited the book, Kim Corrette and Susan Galligan contributed to last-minute edits, and Wyk Parish provided technical support. And special thanks to our agent Stephanie Tade who was so inspired by Rinpoche's vision that she accepted him as a client and shepherded this book to its best home in Shambhala. Our appreciation for the team of competent and inspired staff at Shambhala has no bounds. They gave this book far more time and attention than we expected in the process of making it a reality—so a huge thanks to acquiring editor Sarah Stanton, associate editor Audra Figgins, production manager Lora Zorian, interior designer Greta D. Sibley, marketer Johnnie Dina, publicist Michael Henton, copy editor Cannon Labrie, proofreader Emily Wichland, and indexer L. S. Summer. So many, many thanks to you all for helping bring Rinpoche's teachings to a wider audience. And finally, to the humble yet magnificent monk at the center of all thank-yous, who inspired all of our efforts and who gave us this teaching, Khentrul Lodrö T'hayé, may we repay your kindness by putting these instructions into practice ourselves and by sharing the opportunity to do so with others. All the merit accumulated through this process, we dedicate to taming the mind. May all beings be happy and may all beings be free.

—Paloma Lopez Landry

APPENDIX 1

ATISHA'S LIFE STORY AND
THE LINEAGE OF MIND TRAINING

Jowo Je Palden Atisha was born in eastern India in a Buddhist kingdom known as Zahor in the Western calendar year 982. His father was a king and his family was very rich and influential. Many families depended on them. In that region and at that time in history, there were a lot of realized masters in India. It was common for such wise men or women to go and examine a child just after birth to see if the child had the special marks or signs of a realized being. Many such masters came to see Atisha after his birth and they all gave a similar prophecy. They said he was a very special child. If he became a king, he would be a great ruler, but if he entered the path of dharma, he would become a realized saint who would propagate the Buddha's teachings across the world and benefit numberless beings.

At a young age Atisha went to the great Buddhist university Nalanda in the ancient kingdom of Magadha in modern-day Bihar. There he studied and practiced under many qualified spiritual teachers. Later he continued his studies and served as an abbot in Vikramashila, another prominent Buddhist university also in Bihar. Through his training he became renowned as a pandita, a distinguished scholar of Buddhist philosophy, and a realized being. He was respected from the east to the west in India as one of the most learned scholars in the entire path of sutra and tantra. Thus was his scope of knowledge.

Yet Atisha was not satisfied with this study alone. He had heard of teachings called lojong, which combine all of the key points of relative and ultimate bodhichitta into an extraordinary style of instructions based on direct experiential application. The most well-known teacher of this approach was the master Jowo Serlingpa.

Jowo Serlingpa lived in what is now present-day Indonesia. It is far from India—across the ocean. It was not an easy or safe passage at that time, but this did not deter Atisha. He was determined to seek out Serlingpa and receive his special instructions. Atisha embarked on a ship with a hundred other practitioners in pursuit of the teachings. Livestock and many other provisions were also loaded onto the boat. The journey took almost a year. During that time there were multiple storms, and they nearly lost the ship and their lives on several occasions. But the natural elements were not the only danger they encountered; there were many nonhuman beings—spirits and formless beings—who tried to thwart their journey to prevent them from receiving such profound dharma.

Even though Atisha had never met Jowo Serlingpa, he had great faith in him and prayed to him to dispel the dangers that arose. He also saved twenty-one women aboard the ship who almost fell into the sea. Later it was said that those women were emanations of the deity Tara, who were accompanying Atisha. Due to the power of Atisha's personal deity practice, the presence of Tara, and his prayers to Jowo Serlingpa, he was able to surmount all of the obstacles and dangers and reach his destination.

Once in Indonesia, Atisha set out in search of Jowo Serlingpa. Everywhere he went he asked if anyone knew Serlingpa or where he might reside. After a few months of searching, a messenger reached Serlingpa and told him that an Indian pandita named Atisha had come to meet him. Serlingpa was delighted and together with a retinue of a hundred students went to greet Atisha.

Atisha supplicated him, saying, "I heard you have a very special teaching on mind training. I have come to receive and practice those instructions." At the same time, he made a great mandala offering[1] to the master and said, "I will stay as long as it takes."

Serlingpa was very happy and invited Atisha back to his home. Atisha stayed there and served Serlingpa for twelve years, receiving all of the instructions and practicing diligently. They stayed in one room the entire time and even shared a pillow. And so they were together day and night as Atisha trained. The teachings were given in what is called "the ripening instruction approach" for taming self-clinging, whereby Serlingpa imparted one piece of advice at a time so that Atisha could fully practice and realize each point as he received it.[2] In this way, Atisha received all of the instructions on relative and ultimate bodhichitta in the most profound and extensive manner. Finally, he became a master in taming his mind through the mind-training approach, equal to his teacher, Jowo Serlingpa. It was then that Atisha returned to India.

Once in India, Atisha taught mind training extensively to the ordained practitioners and laypeople before he decided to leave for Tibet in the Western calendar year 1039. He entered Tibet through the region of Tö Ngari. On the road he met with a Buddhist scholar and translator who asked him many questions about Buddhist philosophy. Atisha said to him, "Perhaps there is no need for me to come to Tibet since there are learned scholars like yourself, but I have one last question for you. When you practice, how do you do it?" The translator replied, "You practice however it is explained in each text." With that Atisha exclaimed, "Rotten translator! Perhaps there is a need for me here after all!" Atisha knew that when we practice, we have to know how to synthesize the key points of all the teachings into a single practice.[3] This is what was transmitted through Serlingpa's oral instructions, and it's how Atisha came to stay in the Land of Snows.[4]

Even though Atisha was one of the most learned scholars of India and had studied the highest and most complex dharmas, mind training was the teaching he chose to impart throughout Tibet with a special emphasis on going for refuge. He taught on this so much, in fact, that he was nicknamed "the refuge pandita." The mind-training approach spread like wildfire. His students became known as practitioners of *ka-dam*, a tradition later called *kadampas*. *Ka* means the words of the Buddha Shakyamuni. *Dam* means oral instructions that synthesize the meaning of all of the teachings without a single word left out. Oral instructions also implicitly suggest something that is easy to apply and at the same time profoundly effective, an approach that anyone can implement regardless of their education or status that will fully and effectively tame the mind.

In summary, although Atisha had many teachers, three of whom taught him mind-training techniques, it is apparent who had the greatest influence on his practice and teaching style. The other teachers he learned mind training from were in India. One was Lama Dharmaraksita, who was renowned for giving away his own flesh. He was known for having gained realization of the empty nature of phenomena solely through the power of his great compassion and loving-kindness, the practices of bodhichitta alone. The other teacher in India from whom Atisha received instructions was the great yogi Maitreya, who was able to directly take on the suffering of others. The third and most influential was Jowo Serlingpa in Indonesia. It was under Serlingpa that Atisha received the majority of instructions and training. These teachings, called "The Seven Key Points of Mind Training," came from Serlingpa's style of instruction.

Before giving teachings, Atisha would supplicate his root and lineage gurus, reciting each name in sequence. Whenever he got to Serlingpa's name, he would bring his hands to his heart and his eyes would fill with tears. Sometimes he got so choked up he couldn't continue for a while. His students asked him, "Why do you cry whenever you reach Serlingpa's name and at no other time?" Atisha replied, "I have only a small amount of bodhichitta, but what little I have is due to the great kindness of Jowo Serlingpa." What we can understand from this is that the key to all practice is through a kind heart, bodhichitta. Even though Atisha was a realized master of the entire path, as erudite as they come, he knew that the most important practice of all began with giving rise to this awakened intention.

At all times Atisha demonstrated in his actions his great appreciation for a kind heart. For example, when someone came to meet him, instead of saying something like, "How are you?" as we would do, he would say, "Have you cultivated a kind heart?" and when people left, instead of saying goodbye he'd say, "Generate a kind heart." All of the time, no matter what he did, all of his actions were an expression of love and compassion. In that way he was able to benefit many.

The value Atisha placed on kindheartedness was apparent in how he related to his hundreds of students who became masters of their minds and gained realization by training in just this way. One of his most renowned students was Dromtönpa Gyalway Jungnay, who was known for having an especially kind heart. One day Atisha injured his hand, and he asked Dromtönpa to blow on it and give him a blessing to heal. Dromtönpa said to him, "You are my teacher! How could I ever be able to help you?" and Atisha replied, "If one has a kind heart, anything they do will benefit." He then insisted Dromtönpa blow on the injury. There are many such teachings exemplifying Atisha's qualities and how he embodied these trainings. It was in this way that Atisha stayed in Tibet, guiding students until the time of his death in 1054.

The mind trainers following Atisha's teachings became known as the Kadampas. Some of the transmissions he passed on were extensive and others were more concise. As the lineages spread like streams from a river in every direction of Tibet, they were given various names such as the "Father Dharmas" and "Son Dharmas." The "Son Dharmas" included detailed descriptions of who Atisha was, stating that he was actually an emanation of Guru Rinpoche.[5] This was also based on Guru Rinpoche's own prophecies from the time when he was in Tibet serving the dharma king Trisong Detsen. Guru Rinpoche stated that in the future he would come again as a very special spiritual teacher with unique methods of training. There are also several other source references found in the sutras that prophesy the coming of an incarnate master named Atisha. This is why many of us consider Atisha to be an emanation of Guru Rinpoche.

This tradition of summarizing the trainings into seven key points was the lineage that Chekawa Yeshe Dorje recorded. It has become widely known as "The Seven Key Points of Mind Training." Chekawa Yeshe Dorje was not a direct student of Atisha, nor was he a direct student of Dromtönpa. Rather, the trainings came to him some years later, after being passed on from teacher to disciple in an unbroken line. Chekawa Yeshe Dorje received many instructions from the lineage of practitioners of Atisha, synthesized them, and wrote them down in seven key points.

It is his written record of the key points that we use as the root mind-training text today.

Chekawa Yeshe Dorje was born into a family that held the ancient dharma tradition called Nyingma in Tibetan. His family was known to be practitioners of the Mantrayana of the Nyingma tradition. Chekawa Yeshe Dorje also studied the newer tradition called Sarma, and he had great knowledge in both lineages. His first encounter with the mind-training approach was at the bedside of a Geshey[6] who had written the following words next to his pillow: "I give all profit and gain to others, I take all loss and blame upon myself." Chekawa was profoundly affected when he read the statement. It awoke in him a great desire to study the teachings from which it came. He began to ask around to see who could give such profound instructions. After much searching, he heard that those teachings came from a teacher called Dromtönpa Gyalway Jungnay,[7] who was in residence near Lhasa. But when Chekawa arrived there, he was told that Dromtönpa had recently passed away. Undeterred, he sought out and found another Kadampa lineage holder who had those instructions and from him received these practices.

After receiving extensive instructions and devoting himself to practice, as we can see in Chekawa's own words at the conclusion of the root text, he says, "Now, I can die, and I'll regret nothing."

In terms of the specific lineage of this transmission I have imparted here, mind training has been prolific within the Nyingma tradition. The great Nyingma master Longchenpa[8] received extensive mind trainings. They influenced his presentation of teachings and style of practice in a series of teachings he composed called *The Trilogy of Finding Comfort and Ease.*[9] In the initial homage by the author in this trilogy, Longchenpa gives some of the history of the source mind-training texts upon which his teaching was based. This was then passed on to Jamyang Khyentse Wangpo,[10] and from him to Kongtrul Yonten Gyamtso,[11] as I mentioned in the introduction. Kongtrul Yonten Gyamtso's compilation of teachings titled The Treasury of Oral Instructions are received by most Nyingma practitioners in Tibet. It is this lineage of transmission that I have shared in these teachings and which has now been passed on to you.

APPENDIX 2

THE ROOT TEXT OF THE
SEVEN KEY POINTS OF MIND TRAINING

This quintessential elixir of heart advice, which transforms the five kinds of rampant degeneration into the path of enlightenment, is a transmission from Serlingpa. The awakening of the karmic energy of previous training aroused intense interest in me. Therefore, I ignored suffering and criticism and sought instruction for subduing self-clinging. Now, I can die, and I'll regret nothing.

APPENDIX 3

THE SIX CLASSES OF BEINGS

THE THREE LESS FORTUNATE STATES: NARAKA, PRETA, AND ANIMAL REALMS

The hellish states of existence, called *naraka* in Sanskrit, consist of the worst kind of suffering beings can create for themselves and are defined by the suffering of intense cold or heat. In this realm of karmic appearances, one might perceive any number of intensely painful and unpleasant experiences, just like being frozen or burned in a nightmare.

The hungry-ghost realms, or *pretas* in Sanskrit, are defined by the suffering of hunger, thirst, and discomfort. This too is the product of karma. In this state, beings may be tormented by starvation day and night. Despite their efforts to pursue food and drink, they continuously encounter obstacles. They are not able to find food, or where they do find it, they are unable to ingest it. Food may turn into burning embers when they touch it, or the water they see on the horizon may dry up by the time they reach it, or turn out to be nothing but a mirage, just a piece of dried wood or a rock.

The animal realm is defined by the suffering of mental dullness, a lack of intelligence, and bewilderment. Animals do not have the mental capacity to determine which actions to adopt in order to produce happiness and which actions to discard in order to prevent future suffering. All animals, whether they live in the ocean, on land, or in the sky, have this in common. We can see it if we watch the Animal Planet. There are so many different painful experiences animals endure. They prey upon and eat each other, or they have other animals living on or inside their bodies, such as when numberless little creatures have burrowed into the body of a larger fish, either nesting there or slowly eating its flesh.

The naraka, preta, and animal realms are called the less fortunate states of existence because they are the product of an immense gathering of negative actions accumulated to greater, medium, or lesser degrees, respectively. All such actions are motivated out of disturbing emotions such as anger, avarice, and ignorance. The less fortunate states are a direct reflection of those disturbing emotions and the actions they lead to.

THE THREE MORE FORTUNATE STATES: THE HUMAN, DEMIGOD, AND GOD REALMS

The human, demigod, and god realms—what we call the higher or more fortunate states—do not transcend suffering either. When compared with the less fortunate states, they seem better, but beings in these realms still have a great amount of suffering. So, for example, when we consider being human, we all have the common sufferings of birth, aging, sickness, and death. We also suffer from not getting what we want and from getting what we don't want, and we have the additional challenges of turmoil on the earth, compounded by enormous amounts of distress within ourselves.

The demigods, also known as half gods, have a godlike experience in terms of wealth and abundance, but they are tortured by jealousy and competitiveness. They can see the enjoyments of the full gods and, overcome with intense envy, they wage war with them. As good as the demigods' material circumstances may be, they are unable to be content with what they have.

Beings in the god realms enjoy material, physical, and mental well-being for the duration of their lives, the result of positive karma. But once that karma is exhausted, their lives of pleasure and joy comes to an end, and they then experience intense suffering. Beings in the god realms can see when their death is near. They can also see where they will be reborn next; in other words, where their karma will propel them. They are tormented by this knowledge and the unbearable loss of all of their pleasures. Their suffering is that of change, the fact that all that they enjoyed was impermanent.

In this way, all happiness and pleasure found in the more fortunate realms are temporary and do not last. These passing pleasant experiences are not ultimate happiness. They are impermanent by nature and will result in suffering when they end. That is why happiness is entwined with suffering, why it's fraught with it. From this perspective, the defining characteristic of samsara is suffering.

APPENDIX 4
TONGLEN MEDITATION

Extracted from Practice Instructions
Given by Jamyang Khyentse Wangpo

Meditate that you completely take on all of the suffering and the causes of suffering—negative actions and disturbing emotions—of all sentient beings, the objects of compassion.

Then, meditate on giving all of your happiness in its entirety, including the positive actions that are the causes of that happiness, to each and every being.

This is done using the breath as follows: Visualize that the negativity, obscurations, and suffering of all living beings are gathered together in the form of black light. With each inhalation, breathe in through the nose imagining that light dissolves into your heart. Think, "Through this they are now free of all negativity and suffering forever."

Meditate on all of your happiness and its causes—whatever positive actions you have accumulated—appearing as white light that shimmers like the moon's rays. With the exhalation of the breath, imagine that this light flows out and dissolves into all beings. Think, "Through this they now have temporary and ultimate happiness."

This practice is done in gradual stages.

1. Start by bringing to mind one person who has been very kind to you, such as your mother or father, and imagine that he or she is in front of you. Use this person as the object of tonglen, giving and receiving.
2. Focus on other loved ones, friends and family, as the objects of tonglen.
3. Focus on those whose suffering is unbearable, such as beings in the three lower and less fortunate realms of existence, and use them as the object of tonglen.
4. Focus on those humans who are destitute and suffer more than most, and those who we know engage in harmful and negative actions, as the object of tonglen.
5. Focus on your adversaries—people, ghosts, and spirits who harm you and your loved ones—as the object of tonglen.
6. Finally, embrace all sentient beings as the focus of your tonglen practice.

After practicing this mind training as much as you can, recite the following advice:

When the entire universe and all living beings are filled with negativity, bring all adverse circumstances onto the path of enlightenment. Drive all blame into one and meditate on the kindness of all.

APPENDIX 5

DEDICATION AND
ASPIRATION PRAYERS

The following dedication and aspiration prayers have been recited and cherished by great masters and practitioners of many Buddhist lineages from the time of the Buddha Shakyamuni and the bodhisattva Shantideva respectively, until the present day. Now, following in their footsteps, we too continue this tradition by using these same words to dedicate the merit of our practice and to make aspirations. Recordings of Khentrul Lodrö T'hayé Rinpoche chanting these prayers can be found at www .shambhala.com/powerofmind.

Dedication Prayer extracted from the
Kagyur, *the translated words of the Buddha*

> **sö nam di yi tam chay zik pa nyi**
> **tob nay nyey pai dra nam pam jay nay**
> **kyé ga na chi ba lap truk pa yi**
> **si pai tso lay dro wa drol war shok**
> By this merit, may all beings attain the state of omniscience,
> and by defeating all faults and hindrances,
> may they be liberated from the ocean of conditioned existence,
> which is disturbed by the waves of birth, old age, sickness, and death.

Aspiration Prayer extracted from
The Way of a Bodhisattva *by Shantideva*

jang chhub sem chhok rin po ché
ma kyey pa nam kyey gyur chik
kyey pa nyam pa mey pa dang
gong nay gong du pel war shok
Where precious mind of awakening
has not yet arisen, may it arise;
where it has arisen may it not decline;
and may it continue to increase ever more.

Aspiration Prayer extracted from the
Kagyur, *the translated words of the Buddha*

sem chan tam chay dé wa dang dé wai gyu dang den par gyur chik
duk ngal dang duk ngal gyi gyu dang dral war gyur chik
duk ngal mey pai dé wa dam pa dang mi dral war gyur chik
nyé ring chak dang dang dral wai tang nyom tsay mey pa la yun
ring nay par gyur chik
May all beings, equal to space, have happiness and the causes of happiness;
May they be free from suffering and the causes of suffering;
May they never be separate from supreme happiness that has no suffering;
May their minds abide continuously in the immeasurable equalness
free from the bias of attachment and aversion.

GLOSSARY

All phenomena: This means everything—both the objects of perception and the mind that perceives them.

Avalokiteshvara: Also known as Chenrezig in Tibetan and Quanyin in Chinese. A bodhisattva who embodies the compassion of all buddhas. In different cultures, depicted as male or female.

Bardo: An in-between, intermediate state. Most common usage refers to the intermediate state after one dies and before one takes rebirth.

Beginningless time: This term is used to indicate that we cannot ascribe a specific date or time to when cyclic existence began, so cycling is from time immemorial until now.

Bodhichitta: A Sanskrit term for "awakened mind." In this text it is divided into relative and ultimate bodhichitta. Relative bodhichitta is the aspiration to attain buddhahood for the benefit of all beings. Ultimate bodhichitta is the wisdom that realizes the absolute nature of all things.

Bodhisattva: A Sanskrit term for one who has realized the natural state and operates selflessly, out of complete concern for others. Bodhisattvas have not yet attained buddhahood, but have attained a high level of realization. The closest English equivalent is a saint, but since the term is not identical, the usage of the Sanskrit word has become prevalent in most translations. This term can also refer to those on the path of loving-kindness and compassion who have received the bodhisattva vows.

Buddha: A Sanskrit term for someone who has attained enlightenment, the state of awakening. In Tibetan the term is *sang-gyay*, which means someone who has cleared (*sang-*) away all flaws and completely expanded all qualities and realization (*-gyay*).

Buddha nature: This is the true nature of mind for all sentient beings. It is because of this nature that every being has the potential for buddhahood.

Calm abiding: Called *shamatha* in Sanskrit. This meditation is a one-pointed concentration whereby stillness and clarity emerge by focusing the mind. When the mind is still, clear, and peaceful, it is called calm abiding. This meditation stabilizes the mind and becomes the foundation for all other kinds of meditation practice.

Clear luminosity: This term, *ösel* in Tibetan, is also commonly translated as "clear light," "utter lucidity," and "luminosity." It is used to describe our buddha nature, the nature of mind.

Conditioned existence: Another way of describing all of existence. A synonym for *samsara*. This indicates that all things are conditioned, meaning the product of causes and conditions.

Conduct: Often refers to correct conduct, which can be defined as engaging in actions that produce happiness, such as positive actions, while not engaging in actions that produce suffering, such as harmful actions. It is "correct" because it aligns with our wish to be happy and not to suffer. To have correct conduct, we have to engage in the actions that produce happiness and not engage in the actions that produce suffering.

Cyclic existence: Called *samsara* in Sanskrit, cyclic existence refers to the uninterrupted cycling through one experience after another. It describes the entire universe and all experiences.

Dharma: This is a Sanskrit word that refers to the teachings of the Buddha. It includes the entire path of practice and realization that the Buddha taught. It is defined as the methods that remove the flaws that cause suffering and that enable us to realize our true nature and all positive qualities, the source of happiness.

Dharmakaya: The absolute nature. A synonym for *emptiness*. In the context of describing our ultimate nature, it refers to the emptiness aspect.

Disturbing emotion: In Sanskrit, *klesha*, also translated as "mental affliction." A way of thinking that afflicts or disturbs the mind. The three root afflictions being anger, desire, and ignorance. These are the main sources of suffering and also the causes for engaging in actions that produce future suffering.

Dualistic: When something is experienced in terms of perceiver and perceived, in other words, dualistically. Sometimes referred to in terms of dualistic experiences or dualistic appearances.

Dualistic mind: The mind that operates as a perceiver that experiences being separate from the objects that it perceives.

Emptiness: Free from existing according to any extremes, sometimes described as a freedom from elaborations. It means empty of being existent, nonexistent, both, or neither.

Enlightenment: Derives from the Sanskrit term *bodhi*, which can be literally translated as "total purification" and "realization." It is the point when one has been completely purified of all suffering and the causes of suffering, and when one has complete realization of one's true nature and the positive qualities inherent to true nature. At that point, there is no longer suffering, and true happiness is attained. Other translations include "awakened," "total realization," and the "state of ultimate happiness," or buddhahood.

Five forces: The propelling force, the force of familiarization, the force of planting positive seeds, the force of regret, and the force of aspirations.

Five poisons: Anger, desire, ignorance, jealousy, and pride. These can be subsumed into the three poisons.

Four immeasurables: Immeasurable loving-kindness, immeasurable compassion, immeasurable rejoicing, and immeasurable equalness.

Four kayas: These are *dharmakaya, nirmanakaya, sambhogakaya,* and *svabhavikakaya.*

Four powers: A specific system that allows us to free ourselves from negative karma. They are the power of regret, the power of resolve, the power of the support, and the power of the remedy.

Four thoughts: Precious human birth; impermanence; karma, cause, and result; the suffering of existence. Also called the four thoughts that change the mind.

Habitual imprints: This means a habit that is imprinted in our mind when we think, speak, or act. These habits eventually result in future experiences and are the mechanism for karma, cause, and result.

Interdependent origination: Also translated as dependent origination. All things occur interdependently, that is, a cause is dependent upon its specific causes and conditions, and nothing has independent existence because everything is dependently occurring; for example, the terms *right* and *left* are mutually defining.

Kadampa: A school of Tibetan Buddhism that follows the teachings of Atisha. It focuses on compassion, study, and discipline in the practice of mind training.

Karma: Literally, "actions." This idea means that actions are considered causes that produce results. The term can be used both for the action that is a cause for future experiences and likewise the experience that is a result of prior actions.

Kaya: A Sanskrit term describing ultimate nature. It can be translated as "form" or "body."

Lama: A lama is a respectful title referring to an experienced practitioner, monk, or nun, who has likely done some form of longer meditation retreat, or it can serve as a title for someone who is qualified to teach the dharma.

Lojong: The Tibetan word for mind training.

Mahayana: In English, the "great vehicle." This is the path of bodhisattvas whose goal is to attain complete awakening, the state of perfect buddhahood, for the benefit of all beings. It is based on the great compassion of bodhichitta and the profound wisdom of the view that realizes true nature.

Mantra: A Sanskrit term that has multiple meanings depending on context. It is most commonly known as Sanskrit syllables that are repeated in association with a deity or something of profound nature unable to be translated directly from the original script.

Mantrayana: The path of secret mantra, also known as Vajrayana. A profound and swift approach to practice that contains the most direct level of teachings on the nature of mind. Some methods involve ritual arts including visualizations, mantras, mudras, and sacred substances. There are necessary transmissions for embarking on these practices that include empowerments, an oral reading of the text called a *lung* in Tibetan, and oral instructions.

Merit: This term is a synonym for positive or virtuous actions. It means the accumulated positive actions that will produce positive future results. In the Buddhist tradition there are frequent references to the two accumulations, which are those of merit and wisdom.

Middle Way: Sanskrit *Madhyamika*. The philosophical school that establishes through logical reasoning that all phenomena are nothing but emptiness. It is called the "middle" way because it does not posit any extremes, such as existence or nonexistence, to be ultimately true. Thus, its philosophical stance remains in the middle and never takes a side. See *emptiness*.

Mindfulness: To remember in any situation the methods for training the mind and meditation. Defined in Tibetan Budhist philosophy as "to remember what is virtuous, or positive, in relation to the path."

Mudra: A Sanskrit term for a symbolic ritual gesture done with the hands, fingers, or the whole body.

Ngondro: Preliminary practices of the Mantrayana consisting of nine or ten sequences of training that are usually completed prior to receiving more profound instructions.

Nirmanakaya: A buddha emanation into the impure, ordinary states of existence that is perceived by ordinary beings. In the context of describing our ultimate nature, it refers to the uninterrupted potential for appearances to arise.

Nyingma lineage: The Nyingma lineage, or school, is the oldest of the four major schools of Tibetan Buddhism. Founded by the Vajrayana master Padmasambhava, it is based on the first translations of Buddhist scriptures from Sanskrit into Tibetan beginning in the eighth century.

Obscurations: That which obscures or prevents us from seeing our true nature. This includes ignorance, disturbing emotions, and other mental states.

Parinirvana: A Sanskrit term used to refer to nirvana after death for those who attained it while alive.

Post-meditation: The time of day when we are not in formal meditation. It is seen as a time to do informal practice while eating, walking, talking, working, and so forth.

Pratimoksha precepts: The vows based on the ethical discipline to do no harm. These are the first of the three vows. They include different categories of vows for lay practitioners and for ordained monks and nuns.

Profound insight: Or *vipashyana* in Sanskrit. It means to see the true nature of phenomena, the wisdom that knows emptiness.

Refuge: Considered the doorway to the Buddhist path, one initially goes for refuge in the three jewels—the buddha, dharma, and sangha—in a formal ceremony.

Relative bodhichitta: The aspiration to attain buddhahood for the benefit of all beings. This intention has two goals: the compassionate wish to benefit others and the wisdom that sees the state of total perfection as the means to do so.

Root guru: The primary spiritual teacher a practitioner relies on to guide them through the path. They must be qualified (see qualifications on page 210), and the student must feel a connection, trust, and devotion to them. Typically this relationship begins after both the teacher and the student have observed each other for some time, after which the student formally requests the guru to be their teacher. Once this relationship has been established, it is the teacher's responsibility to provide the necessary teachings and to advise the student what practices to do, and it is the student's responsibility to make time to receive the necessary instructions and to do the practice.

Samadhi: A Sanskrit term for meditative absorption, the one-pointed concentration in meditation.

Samaya: A Sanskrit term that means "commitment" or "vow"; *samayas* are made to uphold the practice of mind training and likewise the precepts of the Mantrayana or Vajrayana path.

Sambhogakaya: A buddha emanation in the pure realms that is perceived by realized bodhisattvas. In the context of describing our ultimate nature, it is the unity of emptiness and appearance.

Samsara: See cyclic existence.

Sangha: A Sanskrit term that means "those intent upon virtue." In the context of refuge, it refers to the sangha of realized bodhisattvas, such as the buddha, dharma, and sangha that we take refuge in. In the sutras, it often refers to the assembly of fully ordained monks and nuns present at the time of the Buddha. In modern usage, sangha commonly refers to the immediate community of people who practice the dharma, a.k.a. practitioners.

Sentient beings: Those "having a mind or being conscious." The term *sentient being* communicates two things: First, that each and every living being has a mind and is conscious and aware. This then implies that they have the sensations of pleasure and pain. Second, it differentiates beings from what is not sentient—what does not have a mind—such as all that is inanimate, as well as the natural outer living world of plants.

Six classes of beings: Classifications for all states of existence based on the experiences of beings within those realms. These are *naraka*, *preta*, animal, and the human, demigod, and god realms.

Six Perfections: Translation of the Sanskrit term the Six Paramitas: generosity, patience, ethical discipline, diligence, meditative concentration, and profound wisdom.

Stupa: A physical representation of enlightened mind.

Sutra: A Sanskrit term for the actual words or discourses of the Buddha.

Svabhavikakaya: The fourth of the four kayas, which demonstrates that the other three kayas are of the same nature, indivisible.

Tantra: A Sanskrit synonym for Vajrayana and Mantrayana. Also used to refer to a class of actual texts in Vajrayana called the tantras. See Mantrayana.

Tara: A female deity, or buddha, often referred to as the mother of all buddhas.

Three excellences: The three stages of any meditation practice. The excellent beginning is the aspiration of bodhichitta; the excellent middle is the key points of the main practice; and the excellent conclusion is the dedication of merit to benefit all beings.

Three poisons: Desire, anger, and perceptible ignorance. Also translated as attachment, aversion, and ignorance. These can be expanded upon in greater detail as the five poisons of the mind.

Three spheres: Subject, object, and action.

Three vows: The *pratimoksha* precepts, bodhisattva vows, and Vajrayana samayas.

Tonglen: The practice of love and compassion through giving and receiving.

Ultimate bodhichitta: The wisdom that realizes the true nature of all phenomena.

Vajrayana: See Mantrayana.

View: Seeing the empty nature of phenomena, the ultimate nature of reality.

Vigilant guard: To be aware of the state of one's body, speech, or mind in any given moment, and seeing if mindfulness is present or not.

Wisdom: Or *prajna* in Sanskrit; the realization of the true nature of phenomena. Sometimes translated as "sublime knowing," "supreme wisdom," or "transcendent knowledge."

Yoga: The Sanskrit term for practice in this context. The ultimate yoga is to immerse the mind in the direct experience of true nature, sometimes translated as immersion in genuine being. Relative yogas are the immersion of the mind with any positive quality being cultivated on the path.

Yogi: A Sanskrit term for a practitioner. Can also refer to a practitioner of a high level of realization who is continuously immersed in the direct experience of true nature. This latter usage is how it is used in this book.

NOTES

INTRODUCTION

1. The historical Buddha. He lived in India and was the founder of Buddhism. He is also referred to as Gautama Buddha and Siddhartha, and lived from 563 to 483 B.C.E.
2. One of the four main lineages of Tibetan Buddhism. The other three are Kagyu, Gelug, and Sakya.

CHAPTER 1: THIS PRECIOUS HUMAN LIFE

1. This is the root text. The entire root text, which is bolded and italicized throughout this book and which provides the framework for these teachings, can be found in appendix 2. For more information on following the presentation style of this teaching, see the Translator's Guide for How to Read This Book on page xiii.
2. That term, *ngey-jung* in Tibetan, "the determination to find freedom," is usually translated into English as "renunciation." Note that the Buddhist concept of renunciation is not the same as the English concept, which usually implies the giving up or rejection of something. In Buddhist philosophy, renunciation is developed from an awareness of the suffering and problems of existence, but it has a positive connotation because it focuses on the problem's solution, which is to find freedom.
3. This is from the Buddhist perspective of past and future lives referred to as reincarnation. This is discussed in more depth in chapter 3.
4. In Buddhist philosophy, the states of existence are classified into six classes of beings, each characterized by the universally shared experiences of beings there. The

hungry-ghost realms, for instance, are characterized by hunger, thirst, and a universal lack of comforts. The animal realms are characterized by mental dullness and an inability to grasp complex or abstract concepts.

5. *Cause* means the direct and unshared cause for something. For example, a rice seed is the cause for a rice plant and nothing else. *Conditions* mean the other factors that are necessary for the plant to grow, such as water, heat, and nutrients. The conditions may not be the direct cause, but they are still essential and also determine, to a certain extent, the size and scope of the result. In terms of karma, there is the specific action that will produce a later result, but how big or small the result is also depends on the immediate conditions, which are the choices and actions that an individual makes in the moment. These provide the conditions for the cause to ripen as an individual's experience. The conditions play as much of a role as the causes do in this case.

6. *Obscurations* are different levels in which we cannot clearly see things according to both their relative and ultimate nature. *Flaws* refer to all of our thoughts and actions that result in suffering. To purify obscurations and flaws is to rid ourselves of both, often by applying a direct remedy.

7. For chair meditation, it is important not to lean back in the chair, unless you are physically unable to sit up by yourself. You will want to keep all of the seven key points of posture that you can, with the obvious exception of sitting cross-legged. If you look at an image of Maitreya, his back is perfectly aligned and his feet are flat on the floor. This may mean you need to place a flat cushion under your feet so that they are squared up and your knees are at a ninety-degree angle. Likewise, you will probably need a cushion to prop up your sitting bones so that your spinal cord can align and be held up without slouching into the chair. A straight back will have the most impact on your meditative experience.

8. The technical term, which you may come across in other teachings, is "the non-referential main part."

CHAPTER 2: IMPERMANENCE

1. Contemplative meditation is a type of formal meditation practice in which one contemplates by reflecting on the meaning of something in relation to their experience or by investigating using logic to arrive at clear certainty as to the nature of something. It is worth noting that meditation practice in this sense is very different from simply sitting in non-thought, which is a common misunderstanding of meditation.

CHAPTER 3: KARMA, CAUSE, AND RESULT

1. The Tibetan term *dray-bu* can be translated as "result" or "effect." Regardless of which translation is used, the Buddhist concept refers to the future karmic result and not the immediate effects on your current experience.

2. True nature from the perspective of wisdom, i.e., the nature of all things, is the

absolute nature of all phenomena that transcends all conceptual ways of perceiving. It is explained in depth later in chapter 5, "Ultimate Bodhichitta," in the second key point of mind training.

3. *Positive intention* is the key term here. This is because someone who engages in a seemingly positive action for self-gain or with a negative motivation is actually acquiring negative karma.

CHAPTER 4: SUFFERING

1. *Transmigration* means to move from one state of existence to another, for example, to death and rebirth. Rather than migration, which is one place within a realm, this could mean from one realm to another realm.

2. *Composite* means anything that is the product of causes and conditions, is composed of multiple parts, and perceived in terms of a past, present, and future.

3. Appearance refers to both appearances and perceptions, the full range of whatever arises within our experience.

CHAPTER 5: ULTIMATE BODHICHITTA

1. There are many key terms in this and future sections, so we have created a glossary to help introduce new terms to readers. Whenever you are unsure what a term means, we encourage you to use the glossary for the correct definitions according to Buddhist philosophy and the context presented in this book.

2. Usually the phrase *all phenomena* refers to both mind and appearances, but in this text it teaches them separately, and so here it only refers to all appearances that are other than mind.

3. This is a concise discussion of emptiness, which is elaborated upon more in chapter 8, "Using Ultimate Reality for Transformation" (page 132). But emptiness should also be studied in greater detail with a qualified spiritual teacher.

4. The *Heart Sutra* is one of the most well-known sutras in the category of wisdom, or emptiness teachings, in Mahayana Buddhism.

5. *Maha* means "great," and *yana* means "vehicle." It is a vehicle because it conveys us where we want to go, the state that transcends suffering. It is the great vehicle because both the motivation of bodhichitta and the view of wisdom that define it are the greatest in extent and profundity. Also see *Mahayana* in the glossary.

6. Correct view, meditation, and conduct, have different philosophical definitions depending upon the context and the vehicle, or approach, they are defining. However, a very general description is as follows: correct view is the view that correctly ascertains the nature of relative or ultimate reality—i.e., on a relative level seeing everything as impermanent, or that actions (karma) are causes that produce results; or on an ultimate level, ascertaining that everything is empty. Correct meditation means a meditation that incorporates a correct view with the proper meditation techniques, resulting in a decrease of disturbing emotions and an increase of positive qualities and wisdom. Correct conduct is how we conduct our-

selves based on those, such as refraining from harmful actions and engaging in positive actions.

7. This term, translated here as "clarity" (*selwa* in Tibetan), is also commonly translated as "lucid," "lucidity," "luminous," "luminosity," "conscious," "consciousness," and more. In this context, it is a synonym for the term *clear luminosity* used above and defined in the glossary.

8. *Mantra* has no English equivalent. This *yana*, or vehicle, is the most esoteric approach among the Buddhist vehicles. It is commonly referred to as secret for two reasons: it is traditionally kept secret from those not yet ready to practice it, and it is also "self-secret," because if an individual does not have the capacity for it, even if they receive instructions and study or practice it, they will be unable to understand it. This approach is based on the scriptures called tantras and included within the Mahayana. Also see Mantrayana in glossary.

9. Transmissions are given to a student by a qualified spiritual teacher before embarking on Mantrayana practices. They include empowerment called a *wang* in Tibetan, an oral reading of the text called a *lung*, and oral instructions.

10. A qualified teacher is described in the seventh statement in chapter 14 about adopting the three principal requisites for practice. You can find this on page 209.

11. Notice that the definition of mindfulness in Buddhism is different from the mainstream, modern understanding of mindfulness. Modern mindfulness is actually vigilant guard. In the majority of Buddhist texts, whenever the term *mindfulness* is used, it means to remember the practice and to remember what is positive and virtuous. The self-awareness that precedes that mindfulness is vigilant guard.

CHAPTER 6: RELATIVE BODHICHITTA

1. This is one of the most well-known texts in the Mahayana tradition on bodhichitta and on training in bodhisattva conduct. It is often referred to in other teachings.

2. Obscurations, when termed in the context of "that which is to be purified," are all the factors that obscure us from seeing our own true nature, which is naturally present right now. These include, but are not limited to, all disturbing emotions, ordinary and dualistic thought processes, and karma.

3. Self-clinging, *dag-dzin*, is also translated as "ego-clinging," "grasping to a self," and the "belief in self." It comes the moment after nonrecognition of true nature, in which the mind conceives of a self and then reifies it. From that comes self-cherishing in which the grasping turns into selfishness.

4. This is a traditional Buddhist viewpoint that ties into the understanding of karma and past and future lives. The basic idea is that if we have had numberless lifetimes, in each we have had a mother and every being has been that to us at some point or another.

5. This is often translated as "immeasurable joy," but joy is not the focus of the meditation. For this practice, we are meditating on seeing positive things that others

have and being happy for them, which is called rejoicing. The side effect of rejoicing is that the practitioner then feels joy, but that feeling isn't the object of meditation—it's just what happens naturally.

6. A great Indian master and Buddhist scholar at Nalanda, the largest university in India's history. Author of *The Way of a Bodhisattva*, he lived ca. 685–763.

7. A Tibetan master renowned for his practice and pith instructions on mind training; he lived ca. 1297–1371.

8. Throughout this commentary "self-centered" does not necessarily carry the connotation of being overly selfish as it usually does in the English language. Instead, it means operating out of a belief in self so that all of our thought processes are centered around, or are related to, that self.

9. This is when self-clinging, as explained in note 3 above, has led to such a strong attachment to our identity of self that we continuously operate out of self-centered concern.

CHAPTER 7: USING RELATIVE REALITY FOR TRANSFORMATION

1. This is a traditional burial practice in Tibet. Most cemeteries, called charnel grounds, are places where corpses are either cremated or offered to vultures. The actual term for sky burial in Tibetan means "scattering for the birds," but the words *sky burial* have been popularly adopted in English as the most common way to describe it. One aspect of this kind of burial is practical since many areas in Tibet were too rocky or hard to bury a corpse. Another aspect is that it is an act of generosity, a way to feed to others what we can no longer use. There are also other purposes explained within the Vajrayana approach, which are outside the scope of this book.

CHAPTER 8: USING ULTIMATE REALITY FOR TRANSFORMATION

1. Ultimate nature, i.e., emptiness, is not taught extensively in the root text or this commentary because the focus of this text is on generating relative bodhichitta. As relative bodhichitta grows, wisdom or ultimate bodhichitta will naturally manifest. To deepen our understanding of ultimate bodhichitta further, it is important to study with a qualified spiritual teacher. The qualifications of a spiritual teacher will be discussed in the seventh key point.

2. The four kayas is a way of describing the single, ultimate nature of emptiness, but from the perspective of its specific attributes, as will be explained. Likewise, for anyone familiar with the three kayas, the four kayas is just a more detailed classification of the three kayas.

3. In addition to the practices of lojong, some practitioners may use techniques found within the profound and esoteric approach of the Mantrayana. Practitioners familiar with these trainings can use a deity practice to transform adversity: Tara,

Guru Rinpoche, or Avalokiteshvara. For example, when a negative emotion such as anger arises, a practitioner of Tara will immediately recollect Tara's face and then allow the mind to rest and be immersed in her enlightened qualities. If the disturbing emotions resolve with this practice, that is sufficient. This pure recollection can be applied to all situations. Someone with sufficient knowledge of these methods can resolve adversity very successfully. Although the Mantrayana is not taught in this book, it is another example of the multitude of practices that can be applied to any situation, thought, or emotion. The key is to develop our capacity to use these tools so we have the ability to transform adversity. If we apply the practices well, we may find ourselves actually benefiting from adverse circumstances.

CHAPTER 9: USING CREATIVE METHODS FOR TRANSFORMATION

1. Called gathering the two accumulations in Buddhist philosophy. These are the accumulation of merit and the accumulation of wisdom.
2. Shrine offerings are traditionally substances placed on a shrine, which represent sensory pleasures, including water, food, candles (called butter lamps), flowers, incense, and anything else beautiful and lovely to behold. Prostrations and circumambulations are traditional Buddhist practices in which a practitioner either bows in front of or walks clockwise around a representation such as a statue or stupa, a temple, or sacred place.
3. A famous Indian master known for his commentaries on the Prajnaparamita, or wisdom scriptures, and teachings on Madhyamaka, or the Middle Way. He lived ca. 150–250.
4. Other kinds of practice might involve visualization and mantra recitation. The remedy we use depends upon the training we've received.
5. There is no identical concept in English of these Tibetan terms. These terms are often used to describe external influences such as energy or nonhuman beings who either help or harm. Gods personify what's positive, and demons personify what's negative. In other contexts, the word *demon* can be used for an afflictive emotion.
6. Tormas are food offerings given in certain practices. Typically they are made of *tsampa* (ground roasted barley flour), one of the staple foods of Tibet.
7. The three jewels refer to the buddha, dharma, and sangha. See glossary for definitions of each term.

CHAPTER 10: HOW TO TRAIN DURING THIS LIFE

1. This term is often translated as "discipline," but within the context of the Six Perfections, it is specifically the ethical discipline of refraining from harm or of engaging in actions that benefit others.
2. Also known as Longchenpa, ca. 1308–1364.

3. He lived ca. 1730–1798.

4. Either ca. 1040–1123 or ca. 1052–1135.

5. A renowned saint of Tibet and the author of *Words of My Perfect Teacher*, ca. 1808–1887.

6. Mind training is meant to be made your own. Being creative is encouraged! For example, the traditional statements and aspirations may use the Sanskrit terms such as *relative* and *ultimate bodhichitta*, and if those terms inspire you, use them. But if you are more inspired by thinking *love, compassion*, and *wisdom*, use the English. The options provided here are just for ideas.

CHAPTER 12: FOUR WAYS TO MEASURE YOUR GROWTH

1. Author of *Thirty-Seven Practices of a Bodhisattva*, see chapter 6, note 7.

CHAPTER 13: SIXTEEN ACTIONS TO AVOID THAT CONTRADICT MIND TRAINING

1. Throughout this section, the term *commitments* refers to all sixteen commitments, or samayas, of mind training. The term *vow* refers to the traditional vows taken on the path that begin with refuge onward. The set of the three vows that will be explained in the book are: the vows of ethical discipline to do no harm (pratimoksha precepts), the vow to benefit beings (bodhisattva vows), and the vows that are called samayas in the Vajrayana tradition. To uphold all the commitments in this section as well as any of the three vows a practitioner has taken is the first universal principle.

2. In the Mantrayana practices, the student is first initiated into the practice by a qualified spiritual teacher through an empowerment. This matures the mind, enabling the student to engage in that practice effectively. Empowerments may include an introduction to visualizations or mantras that may be used in the practice.

3. Crazy wisdom is a potentially controversial topic in modern times, primarily because it is often misunderstood. Basically, at a high level of realization, cultural norms and conceptual constructs no longer mean anything, since they have been transcended. Such masters may at times act in "abnormal" ways to the ordinary perceiver, such as many of the *siddhas* in India, or Milarepa in Tibet. Such masters not only exhibit the qualities of realization but they can also perform miracles, have obvious qualities of the clairvoyance and extrasensory capacities, and so on. So their minds are no longer bound to society's expectations or cultural norms. To behave in this way without exhibiting the capacity for miracles and all the other signs of realization would be a grave mistake and a trick of the ego.

4. There is no equivalent in English for the names of these two kinds of Tibetan livestock, so "oxen" and "cow" are used to demonstrate the different levels of physical strength of species familiar to us in order for the example to make sense.

5. When a realized being sees that peaceful means will not benefit a being but wrath-

ful ones will, they may act wrathfully out of compassion, similar to the expression "tough love."

CHAPTER 14: TWENTY-ONE ACTIONS TO ADOPT THAT SUPPORT MIND TRAINING

1. The word *yoga* can mean many different things in different contexts. In some cases, it is the physical practice that we commonly know as a yoga class, while in others it is referring entirely to immersing one's mind in something. On the highest levels it means immersion in genuine being or resting in the true nature of mind. In some contexts, it can mean "union." In this context, it is synonymous with the term *practice*, when practice is defined as blending a positive quality within the mind and making it one's personal experience.

2. The "commitments" refers to all the mind-training commitments, or samayas, that compose the sixth key point of mind training. And the "vows" refers to the three vows we take on the path (also explained in the sixth key point)—the pratimoksha precepts of ethical discipline, the bodhisattva vows to benefit beings, and the samayas of the Vajrayana.

CHAPTER 15: THE EXCELLENT CONCLUSION

1. In Sanskrit, Serlingpa's name is Dharmakirti, and he was known as a tenth-century master.

2. He lived ca. 1101–1175.

APPENDIX 1: ATISHA'S LIFE STORY AND THE LINEAGE OF MIND TRAINING

1. A traditional way of making offerings when requesting Buddhist teachings, *mandala* can simply be understood as making an offering. It may also indicate the specific kind of offering that was made. For example, the offering could have been an image or a specific number and kind of substances that symbolized offering the entire universe in that culture and time. It could also mean that when he made an offering for the teachings, he recited a specific prayer or did a mudra that symbolized offering the entire universe. In other texts, such as Vajrayana, mandala can mean many different things depending on subject matter and must be learned within context.

2. It is important to distinguish realization from the final state of buddhahood. At the point of buddhahood, there is total omniscience, and so it is called the path of no more learning. Until that point, there is always more to learn because there are still obscurations. But the more realized one is, the quicker they realize whatever is taught. So in this case, whatever Serlingpa taught, Atisha was able to fully assimilate and simultaneously realize. Atisha's example is a teaching for all of us practitioners. We can see how much hardship he endured to receive more teachings

after he was already a very realized master. It is a reminder that we must continuously seek out the dharma and further our study of authentic scriptures. We aren't done with learning until we are a fully awakened buddha.

3. When a practitioner synthesizes all of the key points of practice, they practice what was taught in the text combined with all of the other key points of practice learned from other texts, such as incorporating the determination to be free (renunciation), pure motivation (bodhichitta), one-pointed focus (*shamatha*), the view of emptiness (*vipashyana*), and dedication and aspiration prayers. Each text usually has one aspect of practice that it focuses on teaching in detail. For example, one text may teach extensively on the meaning of emptiness and another will focus on how to cultivate calm-abiding meditation. But no single text could teach on every component in detail. That's why there is such an extensive number of texts comprising the Buddha's teachings. It is also why Atisha called the translator "rotten," because there was an error in the translator's approach. If the translator were to only practice what is taught in one text, he would miss out on essential aspects of practice.

4. Another name for Tibet.

5. Also known as Padmasambhava, he brought Buddhism from India to Tibet. Considered a buddha of our time.

6. A Buddhist scholar of the new translation schools called Sarma in Tibetan.

7. He lived ca. 1004/5–1064.

8. Also known as Longchen Rabjam. A great Tibetan master and one of the main teachers of the Nyingma school of Tibetan Buddhism, ca. 1308–1364.

9. This work by Longchenpa has been published in English as the Trilogy of Rest series.

10. He lived ca. 1829–1870.

11. Most commonly known as Jamgon Kongtrul Lodrö Thaye (no relation to the author of this work), ca. 1813–1899.

INDEX

ABOUT THE AUTHOR

Khentrul Lodrö T'hayé Rinpoche is a Tibetan monk and the director of the United States–based nonprofit Katog Choling, a Tibetan cultural center. Khentrul Rinpoche oversees more than twenty meditation groups across North America and in China, Australia, and South Africa, as well as a large retreat center in the mountains of northwest Arkansas. He is also the abbot of a monastery in Tibet, where he established a Buddhist university, a three-year retreat center, a primary school, and other community outreach programs.

Khentrul Rinpoche was born in Tibet in 1965, toward the end of the great famine, in the middle of the Cultural Revolution. At that time, the practice of Buddhism was not allowed, so practitioners in the generation directly preceding his were denied a traditional Buddhist education. Even so, when Khentrul Rinpoche was a toddler, he was recognized as a reincarnate master, or *tulku*. Because of the religious restrictions, this recognition was kept secret. When he was seven, he privately took the traditional vows of ordination. Slowly, policies relaxed, and by the time Rinpoche was a teenager, dharma teachings had recommenced. He was allowed to wear robes and took the opportunity to study with the last generation of great masters, those who received training prior to the Cultural Revolution. These masters, his teachers, have shown through their examples how to tame the mind and transform adversity in the face of enormous hardship. Khentrul Rinpoche's beloved principal root guru is His Holiness Jigmé Phuntsok Rinpoche. Other primary teachers who have cared for him with great kindness include His Holiness Katog Moksa Tulku and His Holiness Drubwang Padma Norbu Rinpoche.

Khentrul Rinpoche is one of the only people in the world to hold three *khenpo* degrees—the equivalent of three PhDs—in Buddhist philosophy. Two of his degrees were awarded by the "Ivy League" of Nyingma Buddhist universities Larung Gar in Tibet and Namdrol Ling in India. His third khenpo degree came from Katog Monastery, the mother monastery of the Katog lineage. During the course of Khentrul Rinpoche's extensive Buddhist education, he took full ordination as a monk, spent several years in solitary retreat, and became one of the principal abbots of his family monastery.

In 2002, Khentrul Rinpoche was invited to the United States to start a *shedra*, a course for studying the traditional texts on Buddhist philosophy. This has continued every year since, and has become his annual fall teaching. Although Rinpoche's extensive knowledge enables him to teach on any philosophical treatise—up to the most advanced subject matter—he chooses to focus largely on mind training, finding these techniques most relevant and effective today. This has earned him the nickname "the Mind Training Khenpo." And these are the practices Khentrul Rinpoche passes on to us like a lifeline in these turbulent and disturbing times.